Criminal Proceedings

Criminal Proceedings

The Contemporary American Crime Novel

Edited by
Peter Messent

Pluto Press

LONDON • CHICAGO, IL.

First published 1997 by Pluto Press
345 Archway Road, London N6 5AA
and 1436 West Randolph,
Chicago, Illinois 60607, USA

British Library Cataloguing in Publication Data
A catalogue record for this book is available from the British Library

ISBN 0 7453 1017 6 hbk

Library of Congress Cataloging in Publication Data
Criminal proceedings: the contemporary American crime novel/edited
by Peter Messent.
    p. cm.
  Includes bibliographical references.
  ISBN 0–7453–1017–6 (hardcover)
  1. Detective and mystery stories. American—History and criticism.
  2. American fiction—20th century—History and criticism.
  I. Messent, Peter B.
  PS374.D4C75   1997
  813'.087209—dc21   96–47828
                                                          CIP

Designed and produced for Pluto Press by
Chase Production Services, Chadlington, OX7 3LN
Typeset from disk by Stanford DTP Services, Milton Keynes
Printed in Great Britain

Contents

Notes on Contributors

Josh Cohen is Lecturer in English at Goldsmiths College, University of London, where he teaches American Literature and Critical Theory. His essay is a revised section of his D. Phil. thesis, entitled *Postmodern American Fiction and the Politics of Seeing.*

Christopher Gair is Lecturer in English at the College of St. Mark and St. John, Plymouth. He is the author of *Complicity and Resistance in Jack London's Novels: From Nature to Naturalism* (Edwin Mellen, forthcoming). He is an editor of *Over Here: Reviews in American Studies* and founding co-editor of *Symbiosis*. At present he is working on a study of white identity in Progressive Era America.

John Harvey is author of the Nottingham-based Charlie Resnick crime novels, which he has adapted for radio and television. He is also a poet and publisher of Slow Dancer Press.

Nick Heffernan is Senior Lecturer in American Studies at Nene College, Northampton.

Brian Jarvis is a Lecturer in American Literature in the Department of English and Drama at Loughborough University. His research interests include contemporary American fiction and film, and critical theory. He has contributed review essays and articles to various American Studies and Women's Studies journals and is currently completing a project examining understandings of space in contemporary American culture.

Liam Kennedy teaches American literary and cultural studies at the University of Birmingham. He is the author of *Susan*

vii

Sontag: Mind as Passion (Manchester University Press, 1995). He is currently researching and writing on representations of urban space and identity.

Peter Messent is Reader in Modern American Literature at the University of Nottingham. He is the author of *New Readings of the American Novel: Narrative Theory and its Application* (1990), *Ernest Hemingway* (1992), and *Mark Twain* (1997), all published by Macmillan. He has also written widely on the American novel from the 1880s onward.

David Murray teaches in the American and Canadian Studies Department at the University of Nottingham. He is the author of *Forked Tongues: Speech, Writing and Representation in North American Indian Texts*, and editor of *Poetry and Literary Theory* and *American Cultural Critics*. He is now working on a book on early Indian–white cultural and economic exchanges.

Paulina Palmer lectures in English Literature and Women's Studies at the University of Warwick. Her publications include *Contemporary Women's Fiction: Narrative Practice and Feminist Theory* (Harvester Wheatsheaf, 1989) and *Contemporary Lesbian Writing: Dreams, Desire, Difference* (Open University Press, 1993). Her recently completed book on lesbian genre fiction, focusing on fictions of history and Gothic narratives, will be published shortly by Harvester Wheatsheaf.

Barry Taylor is Senior Lecturer in Literary and Cultural Studies at Staffordshire University. In addition to essays on Chandler and Orwell, Martin Cruz Smith, and serial murder, he is the author of *Vagrant Writing: Social and Semiotic Disorders in the English Renaissance* (Harvester Wheatsheaf, 1991).

Sabine Vanacker is a Lecturer in the Department of Dutch Studies at the University of Hull. She has co-written, with Marion Shaw, *Reflecting on Miss Marple* (Routledge, 1991). Her Ph.D. dissertation was on Modernist Autobiography by

Dorothy Richardson, Gertrude Stein and H. D. Her research interests are the detective fiction of Dorothy L. Sayers, the Anglo-Dutch crime writers Robert van Gulik and Janwillem van de Wetering, literary modernism and gender.

Introduction: From Private Eye to Police Procedural – The Logic of Contemporary Crime Fiction

Peter Messent

This volume is both a response to the variety of contemporary crime fiction in America and an illustration of the flexibility of its generic boundaries. Hard-boiled fiction usually deals with criminal activity in a modern urban environment, a world of disconnected signs and anonymous strangers. Crime acts as a connective tissue within this world, and it is the detective's job to trace the hidden relationships crime both indicates yet conceals, to bring them to the surface, and show the way the city works.[1] This helps to account for the common association made between crime fiction and the mainstream of American twentieth-century realism,[2] for in its engagement with the urban social ground and the problems to be found there, crime fiction tackles head-on territory which other literary forms seem often to evade.

Hard-boiled fiction in America has conventionally been filtered through a 'white, heterosexual, male' perspective.[3] Thus, for instance, Marty Roth writes that 'in detective fiction gender is genre and genre is male' with women only figuring to 'flesh out male desire and shadow male sexual fear'.[4] One of the most interesting developments in contemporary crime fiction is the way such limits have been challenged as 'racial and gendered minorities have found voice and visibility',[5] and have used the genre for their own particular ideological ends. A significant number of the chapters in this volume address this issue.

Other chapters suggest some of the different forms that contemporary crime fiction takes. Thus John Harvey, the

1

British crime writer, moves beyond the environment of the city to discuss James Crumley's Western detective novels, while Barry Taylor explores the unsettling landscape of Elmore Leonard's crime fictions and the different (criminal, legal, and paralegal) 'modes of power and practice' they dramatise. Rather than charting the contents of this collection, however, I start by outlining one of the most noticeable changes in crime fiction over recent years: the move from private-eye novel to police procedural. I discuss the implications of the term, private eye, and what it says about the detective's agency and role. Thus one of the strands of my chapter focuses on the sense of authoritative subjectivity within the genre, and the questions that it raises. For recent criticism recognises that the romantic individualism commonly associated with the private eye, and the related sense of alienation from her or his surrounding environment, is a falsification of the actual nature of her or his social role and position. I suggest that, despite the continuing production and popularity of the private-eye story, the generic shift to police procedural has been prompted by a recognition that the marginal position and limited perspective of the PI hero or heroine makes for an ineffectual, and even irrelevant, figure as far as the representation of criminal activity and its containment goes. At this stage, I should say that Barry Taylor's chapter, which follows mine, contains material pointing to a sharp counter-argument, and interrogates the clear sense of generic development (and its relation to issues of social authority and panopticism) which I delineate. The critical dialogues which take place in this collection are intended not to give final answers to the way the genre works, but both to indicate some of the different ways in which its current practitioners are using, and pushing against, its formal constraints, and to suggest the importance and ongoing vitality of the debate about authority and individual agency, centrality and marginality, the law and its limits, and social system and individual criminal act, which it has inspired. All the chapters in this collection, in one way or another, engage this debate.

In the later part of my own chapter I discuss in some detail one novel closely related to the police procedural, Patricia Cornwell's *Postmortem* (1990). I choose this particular text to discuss, not only because it illustrates key features of this sub-genre, but also for its illustration of another tendency increasingly evident in a number of recent American crime novels. There has traditionally been an ambiguity at the heart of the private-eye form that renders it (in the majority of cases) inevitably conservative, in the genre's endorsement of the social status quo whatever the failures in the fabric of American economic and political life it reveals. However, I see in such fictions as Cornwell's an even more conservative turn: for they both endorse the status quo and, in addition, consign crime to the realm of the morally 'monstrous'. The popularity of her Scarpetta novels, and the more general prevalence of such a tactic, may be symptomatic of a deep-rooted need for social reassurance on the part of the contemporary audience for which such texts are written. I end my chapter by briefly suggesting how, in the fiction of James Ellroy, the police procedural can take a very different shape than this.

The two acknowledged father figures of hard-boiled American crime fiction are Dashiell Hammett and Raymond Chandler. Both Sam Spade and Philip Marlowe, their most famous protagonists, are private investigators, PIs, private eyes – the three terms linked in connective chain to one another. Hard-boiled private-eye fiction is certainly still alive and well in America. Robert B. Parker's *Perchance to Dream* (1991) is a sequel and a homage to Chandler's *The Big Sleep* (1939), and indicates the latter writer's powerful influence on his successor. Little sign of the anxiety of influence is apparent here as Parker recreates the sardonic voice and sentimental undertone of his predecessor, and manages similarly to combine 'the epigrammatic flourish of Oscar Wilde with the moral environment of "The Killers"'.[6]

Sara Paretsky's detective heroine, V.I. Warshawski, makes the kind of intertextual reference so common within the genre, when she self-consciously distances herself from Chandler's protagonist. Warshawski does this both in terms of her unwillingness to resort to violence and the nature of her emotional sensibility: 'I'm no Philip Marlowe forever pulling guns out of armpits or glove compartments. Marlowe probably never fainted, either, from the sight of a dead woman's splintered skull.'[7] Nonetheless, as Evelyne Keitel indicates, in her heroine's 'downwardly mobile' quality, her knowledge of the 'mean streets' of (in this case) Chicago, and in her social marginality marked by financial and emotional independence and an unprofitable sense of moral integrity in a corrupt public world, Paretsky also clearly follows in Chandler's footsteps.[8]

Parker, Paretsky, and Sue Grafton too, use – like Chandler – the first-person voice: a device which signals a certain sense of authority on the part of the narrating subject in her or his negotiations with the surrounding world. The use of the wisecrack and the one-liner, distinctive features of hard-boiled language, reinforce such an impression. 'A stylized demonstration of knowledge' expressing 'an irreverence toward ... institutional power', the wisecrack signals 'an assertion of autonomy, a defiant refusal to be brow-beaten', and introduces 'an unsettling element in the interplay of discourses so the chances of the truth gradually unfolding become greater'.[9] Contemporary private-eye fiction takes up where Hammett and Chandler leave off in its reliance on this particular stylistic tactic. Thus Spenser responds to a police fist in the stomach in Robert B. Parker's *Paper Doll* (1993) with the retort:

> 'Who's your trainer?' I said. 'Mary Baker Eddy?'
> He didn't know who Mary Baker Eddy was, but he tried not to let it show.[10]

While V.I. Warshawski, in *Tunnel Vision* (1993), physically barred from entering Jasper Heccomb's office by his assistant, Tish, reacts by saying:

> 'What's he doing in there?' I asked mildly. 'Holding an orgy?'
> Her face flooded with color. 'How can you say things like that?'[11]

Similarly, wittily ironic descriptive language works for Marlowe's successors as it did for him, as a sign both of alienation from the environment through which they move, and of a verbal control over it.[12] Kinsey Millhone describes the young girl with 'a ruby drilled into the side of her nose' in charge of a high school library reference desk in *F is for Fugitive* (1989):

> She had apparently been seized by a fit of self-puncturing because both ears had been pierced repeatedly from the lobe to the helix. In lieu of earrings, she was sporting the sort of items you'd find in my junk drawer at home: paper clips, screws, safety pins, shoelaces, wing nuts. She was perched on a stool with a copy of *Rolling Stone* open on her lap. Mick Jagger was on the cover, looking sixty if a day.[13]

As this quotation suggests, perceptual and verbal control run together in such American crime fictions to assert both individualism and autonomy. The critic Rosemary Jackson relates the idea of the stable self to the seeing eye. Implicit in the ability to see clearly, and the sense of command that comes with the dominance of the eye over a perceptual field, is that sense of authority and comprehension associated with the sovereign subject. From such a perspective, '"I see" … [is] synonymous with "I understand". Knowledge, comprehension, reason, are established through the power of the *look*, through the "*eye*" and the "*I*" of the human subject.' Accordingly, so Jackson suggests, a loss of the sense of visual control introduces a deep uncertainty concerning identity, the authority of the self, and the relation between self and world.[14]

Private-eye fiction is generally marked by exactly this former stress on the power of the eye/I. Walter Benjamin saw 'the figure of the detective … prefigured in that of the flaneur',[15] the walker of the streets and appreciative watcher of the varieties of urban life. The detective genre, in such a reading, becomes 'symptomatic of the experience of modernity'. For the detective operates as a transformed version of the flaneur – the idler now become the searcher, 'dig[ging] into the "discontinuous structure of the [city] world"' (one of arbitrary connections and of temporal and spatial fragmentation) to find the clues which allow a way 'behind the facade and beneath the veils of the metropolitan exterior'.[16]

The detective, then, sifts and sorts, using her or his reasoning powers to penetrate below the surface of things, entering the labyrinth or underworld of the city to do so. She or he rebuilds 'synchronic ... [and] diachronic continuity', both filling in a spatial and temporal gap in a narrative (who was where and when) and restoring the sense of coherence to a community or family history ruptured by a crime.[17] The power of the I/eye enables this process. So detective fiction stresses over and over again the authority that comes from close, continual, and apparently detached observation (the magnifying glass has become an icon of the genre, or at least one branch of it).

Sequences which show the authoritative seeing eye of the detective at work are a repeated and primary feature of the private-eye novel. Kinsey Millhone stares at photos of the dead body of Lorna Kepler in *K is for Killer* (1994) as, somewhat late in the day as far as the committing of this particular crime is concerned, she uses the only means at hand to mimic 'the spiral method of a crime scene search':

> I was frustrated by the flat, two-dimensional images. I wanted to crawl into the frame, examine all the items on the tabletops ... I found myself squinting, moving pictures closer to my face and then back again, as if the subject matter might suddenly leap into sharper focus. I would stare at the body, scanning the background, taking in items through my peripheral vision.[18]

Spenser's initial search to find Pam Shephard in *Promised Land* (1976) is more immediately successful and again depends on the power of the detective's eye:

> What to do now? ... I could stake [the house] out and see what happened ... The safest thing was to stand around and watch. I liked to know as much as I could before I went in where I hadn't been before. ... At four-fifteen Pam Shephard came out of the shabby house with another woman ... and I swung along behind. Pam Shephard and her friend went into a supermarket and I ... watched them through the plate-glass window ... I followed them back to the house on Centre Street and watched them disappear inside. Well, at least I knew where she was.[19]

This process of seeing is paradigmatic to the genre, where the detective acts (so it would appear) as knowledgeable and autonomous subject, restoring order to society through his clear-sightedness at the narrative end. The image of Sherlock Holmes, the model of the classic British detective, as 'the great *doctor* of Victorian society' whose 'spectacular' diagnosis causes social disease to be cured,[20] suggests something of this authoritative role.

But things are never quite this simple in the hard-boiled crime novel. The American private-eye hero differs considerably from Holmes, most particularly in the personal vulnerability that comes from an immersion within the violent world being investigated, in the recognition that corruption is not just confined to this criminal underclass but pervades the entire social fabric, and in the (romantic) sense of alienation and isolation from the social body that accompanies that recognition.

The hard-boiled genre is commonly associated with realism in its use of a terse, tough, and coolly descriptive style.[21] The apparent clear-sightedness of the detective (with the reader's view commonly filtered through her or his perception) seems to exist at one remove from any 'official' version of events. But the private eye by no means provides an unproblematic representation of the way things 'really' are. What the detective sees cannot exist in an ideological vacuum. Though the hard-boiled hero usually appears an ironically detached and objective figure who exists on the *margins* of society (thus again differing from the classic British detective), Bethany Ogdon argues that his values – for it is the male protagonist on whom she focuses – mirror dominant social prejudices, emerging directly as a result of the 'hyper-masculine identity' he would project,[22] and metaphorising women, homosexual or weak male figures, and non-white males, all (variously) in terms of the polluting Other.

Ogdon's argument is one-sided, her description of homophobia, racism and misogyny implying a type of ideological unity and consistency to the genre which this volume would contradict. But her challenge to the apparent transparency and independence of the hard-boiled detective's view, his representation as a solitary individual able to stand free of the normal social bonds and restraints, is to the point.

For the clarity of perception which the focused eye of the private investigator seems to bring with it is misleading. It conceals a peculiarly ambivalent relationship to the dominant social codes and values, and accordingly raises questions about the range and nature of the detective's agency itself. For the detective may generally present her or himself as a liminal figure but, in the last analysis, she or he serves the interests of the dominant social order, however repressive and unjust that order might be. Her or his way of seeing reality (and the apparent detachment and autonomy it appears to suggest) cannot, in other words, finally be separated out from that of the official custodians of the state (the police, the FBI, etc.). Dennis Porter writes that 'in a detective story ... the law itself is never put on trial' and points to the 'generic "conservatism"' of a form that defends the established social system even as it reveals widespread corruption both in leading citizens and in public officialdom.[23] Franco Moretti puts this in a different, but connected, way when he discusses the act of theft, as it is normally represented in detective fictions, in terms of the criminal's 'individualistic ethic' rather than of the larger economic order where it originally (from his political perspective) belongs:

> What, indeed, is theft, if not the redistribution of social wealth? ... But theft is crucial for yet another reason. Money is always the motive of crime in detective fiction, yet the genre is wholly silent about *production*: that unequal exchange between labour-power and wages which is the true source of social wealth. Like popular economics, detective fiction incites people to seek the profit in the sphere of circulation, where it cannot be found – but in compensation, one finds thefts, con-jobs, false pretences, and so on. The indignation against what is rotten and immoral in the economy must concentrate on these phenomena. As for the factory – it is innocent, and thus free to carry on.

Moretti's comments here, and his statement that 'the detective is the figure of the state in the guise of "night watchman", who limits himself to assuring respect for laws',[24] are primarily directed toward classic English detective fiction. Yet they have considerable implication for American hard-boiled fiction too. For the paradox to which Dennis Porter points – that the detective reveals corruption at all levels of the social system but, in doing so, helps to preserve the status quo (her or his authoritative eye and agency subject to its requirements) – is central to the genre. In *Tunnel Vision*, Sara Paretsky, in a typical narrative tactic, uses an act of individual violence, and (again typically) the murder of a woman – Deirdre Messenger – to engage larger issues both of economic injustice (the cut-rate employment of illegal Romanian workers in the American construction industry) and political and financial corruption (resulting from the violation of a grain embargo against Iraq and the consequent laundering of money back in America). The result, however, of all Warshawski's investigations and discoveries, and her solving of the original crime, is 'one giant motherfucking cover-up' (p. 477) in the public sphere, with her only real success coming in the domestic one: the final removal of Emily Messenger from the home of her sexually abusive father. An individual crime is solved, but nothing changes in the larger social scheme of things. As Ralph Willett puts it:

> The challenge offered to the corporate rich – to big medicine, big business, big shipping, etc. – sustains the populism found in much hard-boiled fiction and also its contradictions. The social criticisms of the Warshawski novels are constrained by the nature of the genre. As Paretsky conceded, V. I. is only capable of doing 'some very small things' for individuals.[25]

Paretsky's protagonist directly interrogates the existing social order but cannot finally affect it. Warshawski, like the majority of hard-boiled private-eye protagonists, is caught finally in a kind of in-between world: seeing corruption in, and disliking many aspects of, the environment through which she moves, but serving the interests of the law and the status quo in solving the individual crime and repairing the rent in the social fabric that has occurred. Indeed the very form of the detective novel re-enacts this process. Preserving 'the lost authority of narrative in a chaotic modernist culture', the detective (like the psychoanalyst) 'must produce continuous narrative from a lost narrative as a means of promoting [community] health'.[26] The genre is 'radically anti-novelistic' in the way it operates to restore the social status quo, for 'detective fiction's object is to *return to the beginning* ... [to] reinstate a previous situation' as it was (or almost as it was) before 'disturbing forces broke loose'.[27]

The private eye, then, may appear to see and act from an individualistic and autonomous perspective, but the detective's agency is in fact subordinated to larger forms of social monitoring and control, and her or his vision is limited by the 'private' basis on which she or he operates. In terms of the power and authority of the *Public Eye*, the PI's position might be seen as both marginal and (even) self-deluding. Dashiel Hammett's 'Continental Op' novels (of which *Red Harvest*, published in 1929, is perhaps the best known) start to hint at another route that hard-boiled crime novels can take in their representation of the relationship between the individual detective, criminality, and the larger social system. For the Continental Detective Agency which employs the Op is loosely modelled on the Pinkerton National Detective Agency, for which Hammett himself worked. Founded in 1850, the Pinkertons came to be identified with the icon of the wide-open eye and the motto, 'We Never Sleep'. The Agency was associated with forms of hegemonic authority at the time of the American Civil War, when it acted as a Union spy service, and in its later interventions on behalf of well-regulated American capitalist development, most conspicuously in the late 1870s (The Molly Maguires) and 1892 (the Homestead Strike).

The all-seeing eye of the Pinkertons can be taken to stand, then, as a metonymic representation of a larger and increasingly invasive monitoring on behalf of the state of anything threatening to upset the established social order. Dennis Porter talks of the role of bureaucracy and technology in such a process in terms of the image of the 'unseen seer, who stands at the centre of the social Panopticon and employs his "science" to make all things visible' – or at least who attempts to do so – 'on behalf of the forces of order'.[28] The detective operative working for the Pinkertons was more directly linked with such forces than the conventional private eye. And the police procedural is in many ways the logical end-point to which the Pinkerton detective stories (the fictionalised versions of Agency cases published from 1874 onward) point. The real meaning of detection and its relation to the larger social order can be seen more clearly when the links between the detective and the hegemonic order (and the powers of investigation conferred by that order) are revealed without any of the mystification which the private-eye novel introduces.[29]

Though the latter form still flourishes, the growing turn on the part of practitioners of the detective genre to the police procedural might be seen to constitute a recognition of the social meanings of detection previously rendered opaque. Its popularity, though, can be seen more simply, and perhaps more accurately, as an acknowledgement of the fact that, in a contemporary world where the making visible of crime has come to depend more and more on sophisticated scientific techniques and the ability to collate information quickly and on a large-scale and official basis, the private eye is increasingly irrelevant to, and necessarily blinkered in, this process. James Ellroy captures something of this feeling when, speaking of his own fiction, he says:

> I consciously abandoned the private-eye tradition that formally jazzed me. Evan Hunter wrote, 'the last time a private eye investigated a homicide was never'. The private eye is an iconic totem spawned by pure fiction, romantic moonshine. ... The American cop was the real goods from the gate.[30]

Joyce Carol Oates, in her analysis of the shift from the private-eye novel to the police procedural, also focuses on the element of fantasy in the former (she is writing specifically about Chandler here but her comments can be taken as paradigmatic):

> Private investigator, private 'eye': the fantasy figure of Chandler's detective is not unlike that of an 'invisible' man or a supernatural being with fairy-like powers of observation, intuition, mobility, survival. Philip Marlowe is repeatedly

'sapped' on the head with blackjacks or gun barrels, shot at, beaten, kicked, choked, drugged, trussed up and left for dead, yet he invariably recovers, and sometimes within the space of a few minutes takes his 'dispassionate' revenge on one or another of the caricatured thugs and bit players who populate, like vermin, the Los Angeles/'Bay City' sets of [his] novels.

She, too, points to the irrelevance of the figure of the PI in contemporary criminal investigations: 'private detectives are rarely involved in authentic crime cases, and would have no access, in contemporary times, to the findings of forensics experts'.[31]

The police procedural, then, seems to be supplanting the private-eye novel as 'realistic' crime fiction.[32] While the latter relies on a model of rule-bending individualism, the former puts its emphasis precisely on procedure and *collective* agency. A fantasy of extra-systemic freedom and authenticity gives way to a more problematic vision of individual detectives operating through systemic procedures.[33] If police detectives, like their unofficial counterpart, tend both to reveal widespread social corruption and to preserve the status quo, here the possibility of romantic alienation is held far more firmly in check, for the relationship between the detective's role and the agency of the state is necessarily foregrounded.[34] However, there are (as suggested above, and as one would expect) clear crossovers between these two generic variants, and the police procedural, *despite* the bureaucratic machinery it engages, is not necessarily any more sceptical about individual agency and the power of the I/eye of the detective. In Patricia Cornwell's fiction, for instance, this is far from being the case.

Cornwell's *Postmortem* belongs to one branch of the police procedural category. Her protagonist, Kay Scarpetta, is in fact a forensic pathologist and Virginia's chief medical examiner, but she works to solve crimes with, and uses the resources of, both the local police force and the FBI (though her relationships with both groups are not always comfortable). Oates says that: 'The clue-crammed mystery [of the Ellery Queen type] is currently enjoying a spectacular resuscitation ... as a consequence of recent discoveries in forensic science, including

DNA tracing.' Cornwell's novels rely on such 'scientific detection',[35] the type of detective work which depends on her heroine having the ready access to local and national information and surveillance services that her official status brings.

Scarpetta's investigation of *Postmortem*'s serial murders depends on the technological resources at hand. Thus the initial suspect for the most recent of these crimes (the one with which the novel begins) is identified by fingerprints on the victim's skin, revealed by laser wand. Scarpetta's knowledge and skill with the high-tech tools of her trade give her authority, and allow her finally to see through to the crime's solution. She becomes, like Poe's Dupin, the one with the superior understanding necessary to solve the puzzles challenging her, though, in her case, this comes predominantly from her forensic abilities.

This account of the novel is somewhat reductive, for, like most successful practitioners of the hard-boiled genre, Cornwell takes her reader into a more complicated world than this, where the autonomy and self-confidence of her heroine is threatened, and where the line between a criminal underclass and public officialdom is not as firm as might initially be supposed. For Scarpetta is both a detective rationally investigating a case and also a woman haunted by subconscious fears. The book starts with her dreaming of the 'formless and inhuman ... white face'[36] of the unknown murderer outside her bedroom window, and she refers later to the 'dark areas where I did not want to go' (p. 58). Her very sense of autonomy and selfhood is threatened by the invasive sexual threat that this figure constitutes. Scarpetta identifies with the female victims she examines. They are all young professional women, and Lori Petersen, whose death is the main focus of the narrative, is a doctor: in the words of Scarpetta's niece, Lucy, 'just like you' (p. 37). The investigator in fact ends up as fear-wracked victim, screaming with terror (p. 313) as the murderer finally enters her bedroom – only for the threat to be dispelled as he is shot dead by Marino, the cop who (unknown to Scarpetta) has recognised her danger and is keeping her under surveillance.

If the detective's sense of herself as authoritative and objective subject is challenged in the text, so too are boundaries blurred between criminal exceptionality and apparent social normality and respectability (within the official world in which Scarpetta works). The criminal works with cops, even if he is not one of them: a communications officer hired by the city, he has chosen his victims when hearing their voices on the emergency calls he has processed. When Marino appears in the climactic scene, wearing the same kind of black police jump suit as the murderer, Scarpetta, 'for a paralysing second ... didn't know who was the killer and who was the cop' (p. 317).

This suggestion of collapsed polarities takes more overt form as the sexual aggression the murderer shows his female victims is mirrored by Bill Boltz, the Commonwealth's attorney for Richmond. Scarpetta's relationship with the latter stalls as a result of the 'sudden aggression ... raw brute force' (p. 220) of his sexual hunger. Boltz, it is discovered, has previously sexually assaulted the journalist, Abby Turnbull, after spiking her drink, and both this, and his general attitude toward her, carry echoes of McCorkle's (the murderer's) responses to his victims. The extent of Boltz's responsibility for his wife's suicide, using his gun soon after they have made love, is also subject to Scarpetta's speculation (pp. 196–7).

Boltz, then, is an unconvicted rapist and perhaps, indirectly, a type of murderer. And Commissioner Amburgey tampers with criminal evidence because of his 'hatred' (p. 325) for Scarpetta, who has, through no fault of her own, publicly humiliated him during an earlier case (p. 127). Amburgey, it is indicated, will resign his job as a result of the pressure Abby can bring to bear on him as a journalist, but Boltz remains untouchable. Criminality extends beyond the boundaries of the underworld and remains, in part, finally publicly unrevealed and unpunished.

But this is rendered, if not irrelevant, then secondary to the main business of the text: Scarpetta's solving of the serial murders. Her eventual success here is ensured, even before the criminal's last move against her, by her scientific skill and deductive abilities (together with an unexpected connection which comes about as a result of the thoroughness of her investigative work).[37] For her forensic activities and use of information technology are major elements in her discovery and proof of McCorkle's criminality. DNA coding, access to the resources of the FBI computer to trace related crimes, reliance on the laser to identify the traces of a glittery substance (the borax in soap powder) left by the murderer on his victims' bodies, and the medical knowledge to identify the enzyme defect which affects him – all these help her literally and metaphorically (to refer back to Moretti) to doctor the social disease she encounters. With the withdrawal of the threat to her psychic security on McCorkle's death, and the defeat of Amburgey, her scientific objectivity and personal authority and autonomy is pretty much restored at the novel's end.

Despite the anomolous position of Boltz, then, it is the return to the status quo, both in terms of Scarpetta's sense of her own identity and of the established social order, which is the dominant factor as the novel ends. This restoration is eased and aided by the existence of a strong thematic strand that runs throughout the text and which evasively counters both that blurring of the borders between criminality and normality on which I have previously commented and the possibility of significant social analysis which the novel starts, on occasion, to imply. For the investigation into serial killing seems to lead in just such a latter direction. In Scarpetta's America, the reader is told, 'there were more stranger killings as opposed to crimes of passion' (p. 82). That this is so signals the loss of affect which is so noted a feature of the recent social landscape: the collapse of that web of domestic and community relationships that have conventionally located the subject and which have, in past times, aided the detective in her or his reconstruction of narrative legibility (the rebuilding of a clearly evident causal chain of relationships). Here the logical and direct connections between the criminal and his victim have evaporated almost to the point of complete invisibility.[38] Scarpetta's search for a connection in the chain of victims finally takes her to the 911 calls as the faint and only link between the victims and their killer.

Any discussion of the social causes of crime is, however, largely stifled here by its consignation to the category of the monstrous moral exception to the general rule. This categorisation cuts against other aspects of the relationship between criminality and legality in the text; against the more disturbing aspects of Cornwell's representation of the nature of the social body, and of the stability and authority of the female subject within it. Images of pollution, disease and infection are recurrent in hard-boiled fiction, but that of monstrosity has become especially prevalent in the recent period. Thus, in James Patterson's *Kiss the Girls* (1995), for example, the terms 'monster' and 'bogeyman' are used to describe the two serial killers that homicide detective and psychologist, Alex Cross, attempts to hunt down.[39] To consign crime to the realm of pure evil and individual moral monstrosity is a way of isolating it from all social, political or economic causes, and 'explaining' it as a freakish and psychopathic exception to all that we know to be normal. This is exactly what Cornwell does throughout *Postmortem*. The serial killer is 'the monster' (p. 23). Scarpetta explains to Lucy that he is one of those 'people who are evil ... Like dogs ... Some dogs bite people for no reason. There's something wrong with them. They're bad and will always be bad', and when Lucy replies 'Like Hitler' (p. 39), the simile is allowed to stand unchallenged. This kind of discourse runs throughout the text ('He isn't *sick* ... He's antisocial, he's evil ... ' p. 92) and returns the reader to a black-and-white world where evil stands as pure 'other', finally abolished with the return to social 'normality' brought about by the (mostly) rational, analytic, and commanding figure of the female detective.

Scarpetta's restoration of the status quo, the heroic qualities with which she is associated, and the identification between criminality and moral monstrosity, suggest we can find in this version of the police procedural much of the same 'conservative' tactics (to recall Dennis Porter's earlier comments) to be found in the private-eye novel: indeed, if anything, in exaggerated form. Even the criminal acts committed by members of the ruling Richmond establishment are seen as individual blemishes – sexual passion, a personal grudge – rather than symptoms of systemic corruption. The eventual restoration of Scarpetta's individual authority as scientific investigator (necessary of course for Cornwell's sequence of novels to continue) thus goes together, despite some earlier signs to the contrary, with a continuing confidence in the 'goodness' and efficacy of the law, and a complete acceptance of the social order which it defends.

I am not attempting to lay down absolute rules for the detective novel with the patterns I have identified in this chapter, but to suggest one line of development, and the prominence of a certain set of relationships, within the hard-boiled tradition. The genre is one which, especially in recent years, has been developed in many different directions, and the representation of the relationship between the individual detective and the existing social order *can* be used (as both lesbian detective fiction, and that by members of ethnic and racial minority groups, illustrate) to challenge dominant values and stereotypes. The more effective the nature of that challenge, I would suggest, though, the further the writer must depart from the basic generic model.

That the detective novel, both private-eye and police procedural, is able to contain widely divergent social and political visions can be suggested by brief reference to James Ellroy's work within the latter sub-genre. Ellroy's fictions offer a far more disturbing conception both of the subject and her or his relation to the larger social system than that found in Cornwell. The disorienting narrative tactics he uses (as compared to the majority of detective fictions) challenge standard generic expectations. For the confusing landscape of his novels – the moves between different locations, events, and narrative perspectives, the rapid-fire movement of his elliptic prose, and the sheer number of his characters – works at a textual level to suggest the problematic nature of any authoritative negotiation of the complex and labyrinthine city world he depicts. And, in the thoroughgoing nature of his destabilising of the agency and identity of his detective subjects, he radically challenges the sense of individual autonomy, objectivity and authority on which the detective genre has tended traditionally to rely.[40] Ellroy's fictional refigurations of the history and geography of Los Angeles of the late 1940s and 1950s serve as entry points to a fictional world of collapsing boundaries, uncanny doublings and identity slippage, where political, economic and media interests powerfully combine in the suppression of any version of the 'truth', and where the law (and the investigative actions of his cop protagonists) are always subordinate to such interests. In his later chapter in this collection, Josh Cohen suggests how:

> Ellroy's shift of narrative perspective from the Chandlerian private eye to the waged cop constitutes a critique of the romanticised and historically inaccurate figuration of crime as existential conflict between alienated individual and urban modernity, and consequently marks the progressive cooption of *flaneurie* by the state.

The logic of my own chapter is, then, in many ways continued in his. Ellroy's is a grim and one-sided picture but it is one that cuts through the romantic and existentialist elements of the private-eye genre. And, if his vision of the deep-seated corruption of the public world (and the collapse of the boundaries between criminality and legality) is standard hard-boiled fare, and if his narratives (as one might also expect) conclude with the continuation and restoration of the social status quo, they provide, nonetheless, an effective counter-balance to the less provocative and more conformist fictions of some of his hard-boiled peers. The detective novel, as my final comments suggest, is a generic house with many different rooms. The intent, in the chapters which follow, is critically to unlock and explore at least some of these rooms.[41]

Notes

1. See Marty Roth, *Foul & Fair Play: Reading Genre in Classic Detective Fiction* (Athens: University of Georgia Press, 1995), pp. 158, 176, 185 et al.
2. See Dennis Porter, *The Pursuit of Crime: Art and Ideology in Detective Fiction* (New Haven: Yale University Press, 1981), p. 41. The start of my second paragraph begins to imply, however, the problematic nature of 'realism' as a term.
3. Bethany Ogdon, 'Hard-boiled Ideology', *Critical Quarterly*, vol. 34, no. 1 (Spring, 1992), p. 84.
4. Roth, *Foul & Fair Play*, pp. xiv, 113.
5. Ralph Willett, *Hard-Boiled Detective Fiction, BAAS Pamphlets in American Studies 23* (Halifax: Ryburn, 1992), p. 5.
6. See Porter, *The Pursuit of Crime*, p. 68.

7. Sara Paretsky, *Tunnel Vision* (London: QPD, 1994 [1993]), p. 103.
8. Evelyne Keitel, 'The Woman's Private Eye View', *Amerikastudien: Eine Vierteljahresschrift*, vol. 39 (1994), pp. 170–1. See too Keitel's comments on Sue Grafton's Kinsey Millhone.
9. Willett, *Hard-Boiled Detective Fiction*, pp. 8–9.
10. Robert B. Parker, *Paper Doll* (New York: Berkley, 1994 [1993]), p. 130.
11. Paretsky, *Tunnel Vision*, p. 182.
12. Such control is often in fact illusory, the province merely of the verbal.
13. Sue Grafton, *F is for Fugitive* (New York: Bantam, 1990 [1989]), p. 47.
14. Rosemary Jackson, *Fantasy: The Literature of Subversion* (London: Methuen, 1981), pp. 45, 44–6. James Ellroy's fictions continually metaphorically insist on the loss of such visual control. See, for instance, the play on the idea of Danny Upshaw as 'Man Camera' in *The Big Nowhere* (London: Arrow, 1994 [1989]), pp. 5, 94, 134, 166–7 et al.
15. Quoted in David Frisby's incisive essay, 'Walter Benjamin and Detection', *German Politics and Society*, issue 32 (Summer, 1994), p. 95.
16. See Frisby, 'Walter Benjamin and Detection', pp. 94, 93, 97. For discussion of the difference between 'evidence' and 'clue', and of the concept of 'relatedness', see Roth, *Foul & Fair Play*, pp. 186–92. Roth's comments on the way the detective sifts through '*dirt* or *garbage*' (p. 199) connects with Benjamin's flaneur/detective, searching 'among the refuse ... for secrets among the confusion of things' (Frisby, p. 95).
17. See Roth, *Foul & Fair Play*, p. 164.
18. Sue Grafton, *K is for Killer* (London: Macmillan, 1994), p. 141.
19. Robert B. Parker, *Promised Land* (Harmondsworth, Middlesex: Penguin, 1978 [1976]), pp. 41–2.
20. See Franco Moretti's essay 'Clues', in his *Signs Taken for Wonders: Essays in the Sociology of Literary Forms*, trans. Susan Fischer, David Forgacs, David Miller (London: Verso, 1983). This is one of the most useful and stimulating

essays on detective fiction, though it mainly focuses on the classical rather than the hard-boiled model.

21. See Ogdon, 'Hard-boiled Ideology', pp. 74–5.
22. Ibid., p. 76.
23. Porter, *The Pursuit of Crime*, pp. 122, 125.
24. Moretti, *Signs Taken for Wonders*, pp. 139, 154–5. David Murray repeats the former quote in his chapter on Tony Hillerman. This suggests its importance to any discussion of the detective genre and its social implications.
25. Willett, *Hard-Boiled Detective Fiction*, p. 54. See, too, the section on Paretsky in the same author's *The Naked City: Urban Crime Fiction in the USA* (Manchester: Manchester University Press, 1996), pp. 110–15.
26. Roth, *Foul & Fair Play*, pp. 61, 170.
27. Moretti, *Signs Taken for Wonders*, p. 137.
28. Porter, *The Pursuit of Crime*, p. 125.
29. Though, again, see Barry Taylor's chapter for a counter-argument.
30. James Ellroy, *The American Cop, Without Walls*, Channel 4 (British) TV programme, 29 November, 1994.
31. Joyce Carol Oates, 'The Simple Art of Murder', *The New York Review of Books*, vol. 42, no. 20 (21 December 1995), pp. 34–5.
32. Oates, 'The Simple Art of Murder', p. 34.
33. One place the individualist fantasy has migrated is into the right-wing populism of the *Dirty Harry* and vigilante sub-genres, with their vision of procedure as liberal evasion and obfuscation. This is suggestive of some of the political ambivalences behind the Chandler model itself. I am indebted to Barry Taylor's comments on the draft version of my chapter for my argument here. My thanks to him, and to Dave Murray, for their very helpful advice at this stage.
34. This is not to say that such a sense of alienation and apartness does not exist in such fiction: see, for instance, James Lee Burke's fictional detective, Dave Robicheaux.
35. Oates, 'The Simple Art of Murder', p. 34.
36. Patricia Cornwell, *Postmortem* (New York: Avon, 1991 [1990]), p. 1. Henceforth, page references to follow quotes.

37. Intuition also plays its part here. Later chapters in this collection return to the question of the relationship betweeen reason and intuition.

38. I acknowledge my debt here to a paper given by Barry Taylor on Thomas Harris' *The Silence of the Lambs* (1988) at the British Association for American Studies conference in April 1991. See also his 'The Violence of the Event: Hannibal Lecter in the Lyotardian Sublime', in Steven Earnshaw (ed.), *Postmodern Surroundings* (Amsterdam and Atlanta, Georgia: Editions Rodopi, 1994), pp. 215–30.

39. See James Patterson, *Kiss the Girls* (London: HarperCollins, 1995), pp. 161, 237, 332 et al.

40. Ever since Hammett, the matter of the identity and role of the hard-boiled detective has been far from unproblematic. See, for instance, John Whitley, 'Stirring Things Up: Dashiell Hammett's Continental Op', *Journal of American Studies*, vol. 14, no. 3 (December, 1980), pp. 443–556. In Ellroy, though, this concern is taken to its furthest limits.

41. I dedicate this chapter to the memory of Tony Sycamore. His enthusiasm for detective fiction was contagious.

1

Criminal Suits: Style and Surveillance, Strategy and Tactics in Elmore Leonard

Barry Taylor

> Guys at the top, Tommy said, you didn't have any trouble
> with. You could always deal with guys at the top. But little
> guys with wild hairs up their ass, there was no book on guys
> like that.
>
> Elmore Leonard, *Glitz*

> Cross-cuts, fragments, cracks and lucky hits in the framework
> of a system ... are the practical equivalents of wit.
>
> Michel de Certeau, *The Practice of Everyday Life*

Suits

One thing that distinguishes Elmore Leonard's most extreme
villains is their cheerful self-exposure, their sheer visibility:

> Elvin said to his big brother, Dale Senior, 'How do I look?'
> ... Elvin had looked at his reflection in the bedroom mirror
> and had to grin at himself, man, in that bright blue suit from
> Taiwan China and a bright yellow shirt with the collar
> spread open ... [1]

In the case of *Gold Coast*'s Roland Crowe, too, indifference to
the common codes of fashion and personal style is one of the
identifying signs of the sociopath:

> 'Where'd you get that suit?', Vivian said.
> Roland grinned. 'You like it?'
> 'It's the worst looking suit I ever saw.' [2]

22

In Leonard's novels, dress sense is one of the key indicators by which the reader is invited to form judgements of character, and the narcissistic indifference to contemporary styles of this particular type of villain is countered by the positive judgement solicited for the more restrained, 'classic' style of the Leonard hero. Here journalist Angela Nolan is reporting the opening stages of a trial:

> Under *Witness* she had crossed out the line of notes and written in *Lt. Bryan Hurd*, as he spelled it for the court reporter. Now she underscored it and added *NIFTY* again in capital letters. She liked the way he sat straight but relaxed in his slim-cut dark navy suit and did not become indignant. She liked his hair and his bandit mustache, his hair long but not too long, not styled, and the way his mustache curved down and made him seem a little sad.[3]

There is something a little unsettling in such a clear invitation to make judgements about fashion sense a significant part of our readerly distinctions between heroes and villains. In the crime novel in particular it seems reasonable to expect ethical distinctions to be less entangled with questions of personal grooming. The fact that in a case like Bryan Hurd's the style we are invited to admire consists of a carefully contrived indifference to style (the restrained suit, but 'slim-cut', the hair 'long, but not too long', cut but 'not styled') suggests that the reader in Leonard's work is involved in making semiotic assessments of a far more nuanced and fine-tuned nature than any parcelling out of good and bad guys around the absolute reference point of the law: which is precisely what Leonard's protagonists must do too if they are to survive and thrive.

The skills of alert decoding, of context-sensitive reading, are as essential in this criminal milieu as those of gunplay:

> 'Hi, I'm Robbie Daniels.'
> Bryan thought of a television commercial. 'Hi, I'm Joseph Cotten.' He didn't smile. He gave the handshake enough but not all he had. He liked the guy's sport coat. He didn't like his maize and blue Michigan tie, the way it was tied in a careless knot, the label side of the narrow end showing, *All*

Silk. He had met millionaires before, when he drove for the
mayor and wore black tie with the black mayor and stayed
close to him at functions ... He liked the mayor – enjoyed
hearing him shift as smooth as a smile from street talk to
official pronouncement – but had been indifferent to the
indifferent millionaires he'd met ... He resented this one, the
uncombed hair, the careless tie ... [4]

This is Hurd's first encounter with a man the reader knows
already to be a killer with a mission to kill again. The detective's
assessment of him focuses – once again – on an indifference
to style; the carelessly knotted tie, the uncombed hair. The
reader is involved immediately in distinguishing this kind of
indifference from the positively valued 'classic' indifference
of Hurd himself, and then between Daniels' dressing down
from a style appropriate to his status (in Hurd's eyes, bad) and
the ease with which the mayor adapts his style on the move
'upward' from 'street talk to official pronouncement' (good).
Such complex judgements are at once essential – they are the
means by which Leonard's social actors assess each other and
the nature of the game they are engaged in at any particular
moment – and contingent upon an acquired sensitivity to the
signifying force of tie-knots and other 'trivia'.

Hurd's appreciation of the mayor's ability to play between
styles suggests that, as opposed to what Hurd judges to be
Daniels' narcissistic immersion in the role he has created,
authenticity in this social world is a question of being able to
act as the game of power, status and distinction requires,
while being able to disengage from these performances:

Maguire showered and had another rum and lemon while
he put on his good clothes. Pale beige slacks, dark-blue
sportshirt and a skimpy dacron sportcoat, faded light blue
... He loved the sportcoat because, for some reason, it made
him think of Old Florida and made him feel like a native.
(A Maguire dictum: wherever you are, fit in, look like you
belong. In Colorado wear a sheepskin coat and lace-
up boots). [5]

This artful manipulation of fashion codes is the obverse of the ability to decode and read the surfaces of social life which is required in Leonard's semiotically hot milieu. While decoding supplies the flickers of information which allow a highly provisional, always precarious picture of other characters to be constructed – their likely dispositions and intentions, their strengths and weaknesses, their probable moves – playing the codes allows for a necessary provisionality and flexibility in the protagonist's purchase upon situations, relationships and his own tactical stance.

Plotting and Contingency

While the signifying surfaces of fashion and personal style serve as the *medium* through which contests for power, status and wealth are played out in Leonard's fiction, it is also the case that they have their own autonomous power to motivate desire and aggression in ways which then introduce a viral strain of often unarticulated, contingent motivations into the conscious strategies adopted in those primary contests.

The plot of *City Primeval*, for example, starts with a detour from the villain's main business. Clement Mansell is working a scam with his girlfriend Sandy on Albanian Skender Lulgjaraj and is trying to tail them back to Skender's apartment one night when he is held up by a slow-moving Lincoln Mark VI limousine:

> Realizing the guy in the Mark was a jig with a white girl didn't bother him either, too much. He decided the guy was in numbers or dope and if that's what the girl wanted, some spade with a little fag mustache, fine ... The jig was driving his big car with his white lady; he didn't care who was behind him or if anybody might be in a hurry. That's what got to Clement, the jig's attitude. Also, the jig's hair ... The guy's hair ... looked like a black plastic wig, the twenty-nine dollar tango-model ducktail. Fucking spook. [6]

So Clement drops Sandy and the Albanian, pursues the black guy – who is in fact, and contrary to Clement's 'numbers or dope' reading, Detroit Judge Alvin Guy – and kills him and his companion. In the last quotation, all Clement knows is what he sees by head-lit glimpses through his windscreen: Mark VI, black guy, white girl, 'little fag mustache', the hair. The passage brilliantly suggests how these visual details become tiny anchoring points for a whole set of disavowed or unacknowledged hostilities to do with race, sexual competition (the 'little fag mustache' a means of disavowing the mythology of black male sexual potency even as it is raised by the sight of the black man and white woman) and economic rivalry. The guy's hair becomes the focus for this complex hostility, and the precision with which Clement reads it ('the twenty-nine dollar tango-model ducktail') reveals reading itself to be a powerful mode of aggression, a form of displaced violence which here pins down (and therefore puts down) the black who has got above himself. Reading works to produce a position of analytical superiority which Guy – in every other way that matters to Clement – threatens. The fact that Clement deduces that Guy is a gangster serves to emphasise the precariousness of such reflex decodings, and specifically the way in which unconscious preconceptions and stereotypical assumptions inflect interpretation. It also makes clear – as the implications of inadvertently murdering a judge become clear to Clement – that this is an environment where misreading has consequences.

The narrative of *City Primeval*, then, is set in motion along two divergent, but increasingly entwined pathways: the planned, linear development of the scam (the Albanian plot), and the unforeseen trajectory that follows from the contingent, unconsciously motivated murder of Guy. This double process, with its escalating interplay between the determined and the random, plots and disruptive contingencies, is the characteristic Leonard narrative structure; one, however, which precisely submits structure to the distorting force of what happens to happen.

There are two principal sources of contingency in Leonard's plots, and in those of his protagonists. The first is the quite unpredictable reactions and motivations of the Clement Mansell-style sociopath (*Glitz*'s Teddy Magyck, *Gold Coast*'s Roland Crowe, *Maximum Bob*'s Elvin Crowe). The second is through the figure of the *criminal team*; the group of conspirators or gang who gradually fall apart (along with the plot in its linear, consciously determined sense). This falling apart occurs under the pressure of counter- and sub-plotting, of sexual, racial or status rivalry, of realignments of loyalty, affection and aggression, of divergent responses to the pressure of the criminal event, and the misreadings of character and situation which all these factors both feed and are fed by (here we would need to include at least *Stick*, *Swag*, *The Switch*, *52 Pick-Up*, and *Rum Punch*).

Leonard's fondness for plots constructed around – and therefore derailed by – these individual and collective engines of contingency means that policing in the novels is shifted away from 'classical' models of detection and prevention, and toward open and uncertain practices of crime-management. The cop in Leonard is not someone who is equipped to see through the surface of events to the singular, hidden criminal intention which is their secret organising principle, but one who attempts to track the unpredictable exfoliations of criminality as they develop, trying to foresee the shapes that action and intention, reaction and adjustment will trace in a perpetually unfolding present. Rather than unearthing the truth, cops piece together stories that are in process and driven by continuously shifting imperatives, in the hope that their story is accurate enough to allow a prediction of what the next – and maybe crucial – narrative move will be. Here, for example, are the detectives at the scene of Judge Guy's murder in *City Primeval*:

'If it's robbery, why'd the judge pull in here?'
'To take a leak,' Bryl said. 'How do I know why he pulled in. But he was robbed and that's all we got so far.'
'It was a hit,' Hunter said. 'Two guys. They set him up – see him at the track, arrange a meet. Maybe sell him some dope. One of 'em gets in the car with the judge, like he's gonna make the deal, the other guy – he's not gonna shoot through the window, his partner's in the line of fire. So he hits him through the windshield. With a .45.'
'Now you have the weapon,' Bryl said. 'Where'd you get the .45?'
'Same place you got the piss he had to take,' Hunter said.[7]

Policing, by such means of tentative interpretation and hypothetical storytelling, is not a question of revealing the secret of a crime that has been done and bringing the criminal under the law. It is rather a process of second-guessing a development of events whose aleatory logic is always somewhere out of view, and trying to insinuate a narrative move of one's own which will either stop the criminal process – make an arrest – or disrupt it in ways which may be to the advantage of the law. In either case, law enforcement involves the insecure art of predicting narrative outcomes from the flickers of meaning thrown up by the unfolding criminal 'text'. Law operates through an embroilment with the unsecured processes of the semiotic, rather than stamping its impress upon them from a position of ideal exteriority, as in the Holmesian model of detection.

A symbol of this style of policing is offered by the secondary criminal player, the Bear, in *Get Shorty*, when he talks about his previous role in the movie business:

> 'I've done desk reads in this business,' the Bear said, looking over, 'where somebody wants to know, say, what this executive is up to. Like if he's about to leave with a property he hasn't told the studio about. They want to know if he might be negotiating someplace. I look at the man's telephone notes, play his recorder, see who's on his Rolodex, get to know him. This guy C. Palmer has got nothing that puts him with anybody or tells what he might be doing ... The only thing he had written down on his note pad was "Raji's, Hollywood Blvd. near Vine."'
> Catlett frowned. '*Raji's*? Man, that's a hard rock joint. You can tell looking at Chili Palmer he ain't into that metal shit. I might have to look into that one.' [8]

This is a tactic of legitimate business, recounted by someone who is now deploying it to criminal ends. It is also, as I have suggested, the way Leonard's cops work, as just one among many groups of players using their reading skills to try to stay one step ahead of the game (and in this example again, what counts is semiotic responsiveness, in this case to the clash between an individual's style and a particular music's image).

And for the cops, as for the others, there is no guarantee that the interpretation that results from a desk read, or any other kind, is the correct one. This is only one way in which Leonard's fiction starts from assumptions which put paid to the fantasies of a total, panoptical policing which crime fiction has sometimes been accused of promoting.

Undercover

There is a great deal of surveillance work in Leonard's novels, whether in the form of stake-outs, or undercover operations. The notable point about both forms of surveillance in these novels is that, almost without exception, they don't work. In the case of the undercover operation the problem it faces is the semiotic sensitivity of Leonard's protagonists on both sides of the legal divide. Surrounded by acute readers of clothes, hairstyles, posture and physical moves, the undercover cop is always likely to reveal himself by working too hard at the look of 'criminality' or 'ordinariness':

> Seated now in the Delta terminal ... Catlett had on his dove-gray double-breasted Armani with a nice long roll-lapel. He had on a light-blue shirt with a pearl-grey necktie and pearl cuff links ... Resting on [his] attaché case was a Delta ticket envelope, boarding pass showing – for anyone who might think he was sitting here with some other purpose in mind ... Like that casual young dude wearing the plaid wool shirt over his white T-shirt, with the jeans and black Nikes ... The young dude in the jeans and the wool shirt hanging out, he'd given that outfit some thought.[9]

From the beginnings of detective fiction in the figure of Balzac's police spy Vautrin, the detective as undercover agent has figured as the image of an invisible panoptical look trained secretly upon the citizen. In theory, power moves undercover in order to secure its own gaze in a (non-)place where it, alone and therefore supreme among looks, cannot itself be seen. In theory, the stress is on the *under* in 'undercover'; the disciplinary look scanning out to read and control the surfaces of the social order without itself appearing at the surface.

Here in Leonard, however, the secret look of surveillance is doubled, and so disabled:

> When Raymond came back in the room, Mr Sweety was sitting at one end of the couch with his legs crossed, smoking a cigarette. He said, 'I didn't think you was the dope squad. They come in, you should see the outfits, shirts open down to here, earrings, some of 'em ...'[10]

When power goes undercover in Leonard's novels, it enters a social arena where it is assumed already that the surfaces of clothing, accessories, cars, dwellings, hairstyles, and so on, are the medium through which power displays itself, where status is claimed and challenged, where personal and group identities are asserted and renegotiated, and where theoretically hidden agendas are available to be read. By entering this semiotically charged milieu, the power of the state submits itself to an already feverish activity of reading which makes its cover only one more surface to be decoded. As the two preceding quotations suggest, this also means that the covers adopted by the state become subject to the laws of style and idiom, rhetoric and performance which organise and differentiate the semiotic field of social power. In doing so, they also enter a play of nuance, inflection and insider judgement where the inept, dated or overstated selection of elements in the cover's construction is instantly spotted. In Leonard, then, when power goes undercover, the cover remains in view, semiotically activated, available to be read. The gaze of power is caught up in a logic of representation which it cannot master.

Overlooking

Surveillance is 'over-looking', and this English translation carries on its surface the two key weaknesses of any panoptical mode of power. The first is the inevitability of failing to see, the actual impossibility of any totalising domination of the visual field. Witness the inquest on the failed surveillance operation in the archetypally secure space of the shopping mall in *Rum Punch*:

The girl with the shoulder bag ... said 'That Unitel body mike isn't worth shit in a mall. I couldn't hear anything but Muzak' ... They had a hole in their surveillance.[11]

Alongside the hole in the surveillance, Muzak here can be taken as a figure for all those forms of aural, visual and behavioural *interference* which randomly interrupt and divert the direct gaze of power. As the climax of a criminal plot which is being blown apart by internal conflicts and competition even as it comes to fruition, the *Rum Punch* stake-out is a virtuoso staging of contingency, inadvertence and complexity as they frustrate the goals of surveillance.

The second weakness signalled by 'over-looking' is that of looking *too hard*. I mean by this the blindness of a gaze which is too inflexibly directed by the divisions and classifications of the visual field which must precede and determine any look if things are to become visible at all. We should remember that in crime fiction the look of the amateur detective which actually sees has always been a *supplement* to the 'bureaucratic' gaze of authority: a mode of vision to one side of, or disdained by the agents of the state, and one which highlights the blindspots of the official gaze even as it realises the latter's disciplinary function. This supplementary logic is often overlooked itself in critical accounts of the genre which incline towards seeing it as a fantasy of achieved panoptical power.

In Leonard's novels, survival or the ability to keep ahead of the criminal game (either as a participant or a detective) often depends upon a relaxation of the look and the preconceptions which structure it:

'You think you have insights, is that it?'
'Maybe, if that's the word. I don't expect to see something and then look and say, uh-huh, there it is. I try to look without expecting and see what's actually there. Is that insight?'[12]

This openness and flexibility of attention is a common characteristic of Leonard's heroes. It allows them to see the significance of what is there to be seen, but at the peripheries, in the trivial detail and the overlooked corners of the perceptual field:

> He left Karen in her backyard world putting on sunglasses, lighting a cigarette. Maguire walked up S.E. Seventeenth toward the beach, where he'd left the Mercedes. He wondered if she did know something she wasn't telling. He wondered about the photos of her in the locked room. When this was over he'd ask her about them.
>   Was she lighting a cigarette when he left?
>   He wondered when she had started smoking. Maybe he hadn't been paying attention lately, looking but overlooking, missing something.[13]

Here, Maguire initially overlooks the cigarette, and while he sees the photos, he cannot see their relation to the central situation; they are an anomaly to be asked about afterwards. The adjustment of his vision which begins at this point is one which will bring these overlooked facts about Karen into the centre of vision, as key signs of the nature of her complicity with a scenario in which Maguire has assumed she figured simply as a victim.

The opening of *Split Images* (a title which already signals the necessity for a certain complication of looking to its readers, both inside and outside the narrative) dramatises this opposition between a closed and open looking, and characteristically assigns openness to a marginal, less powerful figure. The shooting by multi-millionaire Robby Daniels of a Haitian refugee on his Palm Beach estate triggers a police enquiry which assumes from the start that this is a case of self-defence against an armed intruder. Daniels' account of the incident squares with that assumption and is unchallenged by the investigating detective, Walter Souza. The possibility of something anomalous in Daniels' narrative, of some other story that might be told, occurs only to the squad-car officer first on the scene, who is sent back to directing traffic once the detectives arrive:

> 'Well, for one thing,' the young cop said, 'the Haitian told it different.'

'I bet he did,' the detective said. 'I bet he said he was fucking assaulted. You been out to Belle Glade lately?'

'Sure.'

'You see how they jungle-up out there, how they live, you want to call it that? ... this guy comes all the way from Belle Glade, stops by four-thirty in the morning see if they got any odd jobs ... Comes strolling up to the guy with a machete and the guy shoots him, you think something funny's going on.'

Gary Hammond was patient. He was going to say what was bothering him.

'He said something to me, Mr. Daniels. He said he come in – he realised somebody was there from the way the place was tossed.'

'Yeah?...'

'He used the word *tossed.*'

'So?'

'I don't know, it seemed weird. Like he used the word all the time, Mr Daniels.'[14]

Here Souza's racial prejudice entails a set of prejudgements, about who will be the victims and perpetrators of crime, which structures what he can see – and what he will be blind to – in the situation. What Hammond hears, on the other hand (and it is interesting that this involves a shift into a sensory mode which is traditionally 'lower' in the perceptual hierarchy), is an anomaly which opens a tiny rent in the fabric of the 'usual story'. This is not a question of a new fact or piece of evidence which must be accommodated within the positivistic framework of police procedure It is rather a semiotic dissonance, the sound of disparate speech codes clashing: a 'fact' which obliges a shift in the framework itself, from the scientific-rational model of police procedure to a mode of knowledge which attends to the vibrations of meaning amongst the styles and surfaces of the social order, to the relations between idioms of speech, fashion and behaviour.

The Paralegal

In Balzacian serial fashion, Gary Hammond comes back, several years in the fictional future, as the detective protagonist of

Maximum Bob.[15] This move towards the centre of professional detection is shown to have brought with it an embeddedness in legal protocol and professional caution which entails a partial closing down of the openness of vision he displays in the earlier novel. In *Maximum Bob*, Hammond is pulled in two directions: on one hand towards professionalism and procedure, which are at once necessary and productive of blindness, and on the other towards a flexibility of looking and acting urged upon him by Kathy Baker, the probation officer with whom he becomes romantically involved during the course of the narrative. In contrast to his ability in *Split Images* to pull a significant difference out of the vestigial informational 'noise' surrounding the Daniels shooting, here it is his inability to admit the importance to the investigation of a piece of rubbish – a discarded take-away pizza box – which leads, indirectly, to his death. Kathy, on the other hand, knows that the pizza box means something and, overriding Hammond's professional caution, aims to get hold of it:

> She said, 'If you have trouble seeing yourself walking in the Sheriff's office with a pizza box, let me do it.' ... When he didn't smile she wanted to take it back and was afraid now his tone would be condescending, putting her in her place ... 'Even if you could somehow place him at the house,' Mr. Methodical went on, 'There's no way you can prove criminal intent ...'
> 'He was there,' Kathy said. 'I saw him.'
> 'You maintain you saw *some*thing, or someone.'
> 'Yeah, that's what I do, I maintain.'[16]

The hunch that leads Kathy to connect her reading of Judge Gibbs' relationship with his wife to the glimpse of a face inside Gibbs' house as it is being shot at, to the pizza box, and then to Elvin Crowe's centrality in the developing scenario, is what brings her to a clear sight of the conspiracy to kill the judge. The professional caution of 'Mr Methodical' blinds Hammond to Elvin's role in this central situation, and is a key factor in his unpreparedness when Elvin comes to kill him. Openness is assigned in *Maximum Bob* to a mode of vision which is subordinated both in gender and professional terms (Kathy's paralegal status as probation officer) but which is the source of the narrative's resolution, while the professionalised 'masculine' gaze of Hammond produces a fatal blindness:

> 'What about the shooter? What's he got to do with it?'
> 'I don't know. Ask [the judge].'
> She watched Gary raise his beer and then pause.
> 'There's no way I could question Gibbs about it. A *judge* pulling a stunt like that? I can't see it.'
> Kathy could, but didn't say anything.[17]

In the final pages of the novel, Kathy's semiotic attentiveness to the significance of the discarded detail – an ability to bring divergent kinds of information into unexpected, meaningful relationship – is aligned with the paranormal vision of the judge's wife, Leanne, mediated through her slave-girl spirit guide, who 'sees' Hammond's death happening at a moment when the reader knows her to be right. This is an unexpected validation of Leanne's visions, their authenticity having been scrupulously left undecided before this, always recuperable by psychological or sociological explanation. Their entanglement at the climax of the plot with the life-and-death question of whether Kathy has seen what she believes she has seen and what significance it should be given, suggests that the paranormal (associated with the discounted voices of the nineteenth-century slave girl and the ridiculed poor white Leanne) is functioning here as a metaphor for a semiotically attuned 'women's looking' which is able to open up the blindspots of the male professional gaze.[18]

The limitations of the gaze of authority are also built into *Maximum Bob* through its treatment of the surveillance on Elvin Crowe and, later on, the house of Dr Vasco, Elvin's criminal employer. From the moment the surveillance unit is put on Elvin, the doubling of the look I spoke of earlier, and the humour it always generates, begins:

> And here was Gary Hammond in his navy-blue suit giving Elvin a friendly hello, 'How you doing?' Introducing himself,

showing the shield pinned to his belt. 'I wonder if we could go inside, have a talk.'
   'I like it here,' Elvin said. 'I get to watch your buddies in the Thunderbird up the street there. They got everybody around here ready to flush their product down the toilet.'[19]

From this point, the TAC surveillance unit is always shadowing the action, but oblivious to the developing conspiracy against Judge Gibbs which is being plotted from Dr Vasco's house. In a studied irony, Vasco is electronically tagged as a condition of his probation following an earlier offence. It is despite the presence of this most technologically advanced and oppressive form of surveillance (and the unmarked cars outside) that his house becomes the centre for a volatile ménage (Vasco, his lover Hector, Elvin, the prostitute Earlene) which generates a whole array of criminal plotting (the conspiracy against Gibbs, Elvin's murder of Hector and planned extortion of Vasco, Vasco's use of Earlene as a supplier of crack, Elvin killing Hammond). The stake-out and the electronic tag are the signs of a power which aims to govern this perverse parody of family domesticity, but the action is happening beyond the reach of surveillance, in the unpredictable antagonisms, renegotiated alliances and loyalties, clashing motivations and personal agendas of the criminal 'family'. The closed doors of the domestic space are at once the most concentrated focus of official disciplinary power, and its chief blindspot.
   Narrative resolution in *Maximum Bob* begins precisely with the freelance action of the paralegal Kathy, when she leaves the TAC man redundant in his unmarked car outside Dr Vasco's and 'makes a house-call' (p. 280). It is Kathy's unofficial freedom to go in, beyond the limits of surveillance, which matters: it is through her ability to read the relationships within the 'family' and then to manipulate its rivalries and antagonisms that the exposure and destruction of Elvin is precipitated. Law is eventually enforced, in other words, through the operation of modes of seeing, knowledge and action which are either disallowed or denigrated by the codes and institutional procedures of legality. It is only by this detour or deviation into a zone of tactical engagement with

the contingent and the uncodifiable – a zone of paralegality – that power realises itself through its effects, but by becoming something other than its legitimation dictates it must claim to be.

In a more general sense, law enforcement in Leonard's novels can be seen as a field of paralegality which is in a supplementary relation to the rule of law and proper procedure: both outside that rule and necessary to its operation. Law properly constitutes itself by its exteriority to the field which it regulates, but in Leonard – as Duncan Webster has suggested in a discussion which links Leonard in this regard to George V. Higgins and K.C. Constantine[20] – the law must engage tactically with the field of illegality, through a range of practices from courtroom deals and negotiations, through undercover work and the use of informers, to entrapment, in order for crime to be contained and managed. Paralegality is the law's inescapable supplement.

Strategy and Tactics

'Lieutenant, what was the purpose of the STRESS operation?'
'To interdict street crime in high incident areas.'
'Sounds like you're reading it,' Mr Randall said. 'So you mingle with the civilians, pretend to be one of us?'
'That's right,' Brian said.
'Which suggests to me,' Mr Randall said, 'an omni-present, omniscient police force indistinguishable from the citizenry, ready to stop crime in progress or prevent its occurrence. Was that the lofty aim?'
Bryan said, 'Or hold crime to acceptable limits.'
'Now you sound like General Haig. That what the book says?'
'There is no book,' Bryan said.[21]

There is no book, because in Leonard law enforcement is precisely where power is not able to operate by the book, where the 'lofty aim[s]' and totalising intent of panoptical *strategy* give way to the deals, compromises and subterfuges of paralegal *tactics*. I allude, in making this opposition between strategy and tactics, to two central terms in Michel de Certeau's model for thinking through the 'practice of everyday life', a model which in a number of ways seems well-adapted to Leonard's fictional environment.

In discussing the ways in which power operates in modern Western societies, and in distancing himself from some of the totalitarian implications of Foucault's account of the Panopticon, de Certeau puts stress on the modalities of a 'weak' power by which subjects create pathways of evasion and flight within the official 'map' of the system. For de Certeau, these would include the 'legerdemain' of subaltern modes of action, the weaving of 'illegitimate' itineraries, plots and projects within and despite the strategic frameworks of power and propriety ('the guileful ruses of *different* interests and desires'),[22] the tactical wit of the operator, the deal-maker, the survivor as an alternative mode of knowledge to strategic oversight. In offering a way of theorising the flights of the deviant, the prodigal and the contingent across the terrain of the everyday, de Certeau undoubtedly opens up enlightening approaches to the vernacular specificity and fertility of Leonard's world, its unpredictable modes of subjectivity and social interaction, intelligence and wit, its basis in the (anti-) principle of plotting as risk, uncertainty and contingency.

On the other hand, Leonard's dramatisation of law enforcement is a mode of narrative 'knowing' which allows us to see a key blindspot in de Certeau's theory. In de Certeau's terms, law enforcement, as one of the most conspicuous expressions of state power, and one which is founded upon a panoptical ambition, would seem to be exemplary of a *strategic* practice, one which:

> postulates a *place* that can be delimited as its *own* and serve as the basis from which relations with an *exteriority* composed of targets or threats ... can be managed.
> ... The division of space makes possible a *panoptic practice* proceeding fróm a place whence the eye can transform foreign forces into objects that can be observed and measured, and thus control and 'include' them within its scope of vision.[23]

Conversely, the 'guileful ruses' of Leonard's criminals and other low-lifes would seem to fit quite precisely de Certeau's description of the tactical:

> It operates in isolated actions, blow by blow. It takes advantage of 'opportunities' and depends on them, being without any base where it could stockpile its winnings, build up its own position, and plan raids ... It must vigilantly make use of the cracks that particular conjunctions open in the surveillance of the proprietary powers. It poaches in them. It creates surprises in them ... In short, a tactic is an art of the weak.[24]

Two different modes of power and practice, then, are placed in stark opposition: 'a tactic is determined by the *absence of power* just as a strategy is organised by the postulation of power'.[25] Where Leonard's narratives complicate and undermine this formulation is in their dramatisation of the constitutive blindness (not merely the conjunctural 'cracks') of any panoptical 'surveillance of the proprietary powers', and, closely linked to it, their sense of the paralegality of law enforcement. In other words, in Leonard's work law enforcement is shown to be a key strategic practice which can only realise itself *as* practice by becoming tactical through and through:

> There were tales of heroics and tales of tricky non-procedural moves, old-pro stunts, told in the Athens Bar on Monroe in Greektown, two short blocks from 1300 Beaubien [Detroit Police HQ]. Raymond wondered if ... the tricky movers ever looked ahead and saw replays, recountings: a twenty-year pro, an insider, telling appreciative someday pros that it wasn't to go beyond this table: 'So he cons the guy into handing over the gun, has ballistics fire it to make sure it's the murder weapon, then – here's the part – he puts it *back* in the guy's basement ... He's got to make the shooter with the gun or he doesn't make him. He's got to set him up ...'[26]

Here to be in the strategic place of the law enforcer ('an insider'), to be a 'pro', is to inherit the unofficial patrimony of 'tricky non-procedural moves', to take up one's place in the oral relay of a narrative wisdom, precisely of the kind which de Certeau sees as a verbal enactment and memorialising of *tactical* knowledge:

> One can then understand the alternations and complicities ... that link the 'arts of speaking' to the 'arts of operating': the same practices appear now in a verbal field, now in a field of non-linguistic actions ... from the workday to the evening, from cooking to legends and gossip, from the devices of lived history to those of history retold.[27]

From the investigator's tentative art of decoding, to the detective's floating of hypothetical narratives and second-guessing of plausible narrative moves, to this characterisation of professional knowledge as the oral transmission of 'guileful ruses', policing in Leonard's fiction is situated on the uncertain ground of simulation, narrative invention and tactical sleight-of-hand. Contrary to de Certeau's still Foucauldian assertion of the panoptical reach of power, Leonard's narratives suggest that the state itself can provide no inviolable place of strategic withdrawal from, and mastery over, 'a world bewitched by the invisible powers of the Other'[28] – the place of power is constituted precisely by the Other's tactical displacements and dispersals.

Notes

1. Elmore Leonard, *Maximum Bob* (Harmondsworth, Middlesex: Penguin Books, 1992 [1991]), p. 171.
2. Elmore Leonard, *Gold Coast* (London: Star Books, 1983 [1980]), p. 49.
3. Elmore Leonard, *Split Images* (London: Star Books, 1984 [1981]), p. 38.
4. Ibid., p. 61.
5. Leonard, *Gold Coast*, p. 59.
6. Elmore Leonard, *City Primeval* (London: Star Books, 1982 [1980]), p. 3.
7. Ibid., pp. 26–7.

8. Elmore Leonard, *Get Shorty* (Harmondsworth, Middlesex: Penguin Books, 1991 [1990]), p. 190.
9. Elmore Leonard, *Rum Punch* (Harmondsworth: Penguin Books, 1993 [1992]), pp. 101–2.
10. Leonard, *Gold Coast*, p. 162.
11. Leonard, *Rum Punch*, pp. 269–70.
12. Leonard, *City Primeval*, pp. 244–5.
13. Leonard, *Gold Coast*, p. 203.
14. Leonard, *Split Images*, pp. 16–17.
15. Duncan Webster comments on Leonard's use of this device more generally in *Looka Yonder!: The Imaginary America of Populist Culture*, (London and New York: Routledge, 1988), p. 151.
16. Leonard, *Maximum Bob*, p. 217.
17. Ibid., p. 142.
18. There is an analogous play-off between different modes of enquiry in the novels of Thomas Harris, in the relationship between high-tech detection and the empathic, intuitive mode identified with Will Graham (in *Red Dragon*) and Clarice Starling in (*The Silence of the Lambs*). In both cases, the individual investigator occupies a supplementary relation to official procedures: at once central to the investigation's success, but also professionally marginalised or subordinate, psychologically entangled with the central killer, and through him with the *unheimlich*.
19. Leonard, *Maximum Bob*, p. 155.
20. Webster, *Looka Yonder!*, pp. 145–8.
21. Leonard, *Split Images*, pp. 36–7.
22. Michel de Certeau, *The Practice of Everyday Life*, trans. Steven Rendall (Berkeley: University of California Press, 1984), p. 34.
23. Ibid., p. 36.
24. Ibid., p. 37.
25. Ibid., p. 38.
26. Leonard, *City Primeval*, p. 228.
27. de Certeau, *The Practice of Everyday Life*, p. 78.
28. Ibid., p. 36.

2

Black *Noir*: Race and Urban Space in Walter Mosley's Detective Fiction

Liam Kennedy

> The streets were dark with something more than night
> Raymond Chandler[1]

Why is hard-boiled detective fiction a white genre? With this question I do not mean to suggest that only white writers have worked in the genre, but rather that hard-boiled fiction's most distinctive narrative codes, conventions, and characterisations have traditionally been structured around the consciousness of a white subject. Drawing attention to 'whiteness' in narrative representation has become a common interest in literary, film and cultural studies in recent years; Richard Dyer, bell hooks, Toni Morrison and Eric Lott are only a few of the influential critics who have argued the need to think critically about the concept.[2] Crucial to this critical project is the insistence that whiteness neither exists outside of culture nor transcends race but functions as the invisible norm of dominant cultural values and assumptions while concealing its dependency upon 'racial' others. In her *Playing in the Dark: Whiteness and the Literary Imagination*, Toni Morrison wonders 'whether the major and championed characteristics of our national literature – individualism, masculinity, social engagement versus historical isolation; acute and ambiguous moral problematics; the thematics of innocence coupled with an obsession with figurations of death and hell – are not in fact responses to a dark, abiding, signing Africanist presence'.[3] In this chapter I want to comment on some general features of whiteness in hard-boiled detective fiction to argue that the genre has traditionally

42

responded to 'a dark ... Africanist presence' by adopting a
parasitic relationship to blackness. These comments will act
as a preliminary to my more detailed study of the distinctively
black *noir* which characterises the fiction of the African-
American writer Walter Mosley.

Hard-boiled Detective Fiction and Race

The racialised constitution of hard-boiled fiction owes a great
deal to the historical period of its emergence and its generic
links with Western and adventure genres in the United States.
The literary origins of hard-boiled fiction are diverse, and any
extensive study of them would have to plot the emergence and
reinvention of key elements across nineteenth-century popular
literatures. One significant line of development is centred on
the myth of democratic heroism, a structural and ideological
feature of the frontier romance which is redeployed in later
nineteenth-century adventure stories of crime and detection
– most notably in the writings of Alan Pinkerton and the 'red-
blooded' dime novels of the last quarter of that century – and
re-emerges in the 'pulp' fiction of the early twentieth century.
Richard Slotkin has argued that the dime novels of the late
nineteenth-century constructed a formula fiction which fused
the figures of the outlaw and the detective to produce heroic
detectives who defend 'the progressive social order, but do so
in the style of the outlaw, always criticising the costs of
progress'.[4] In the post-frontier, rapidly modernising America
of the early twentieth century, this hybrid figure takes on a
more complex ideological cast in the role of the hard-boiled
detective who is 'both an agent of law and an outlaw who acts
outside the structures of legal authority for the sake of a
personal definition of justice' and who has no clear class
position.[5] This hard-boiled hero is invariably represented as
a bastard offspring of modernity and democratic individualism.
He is at once a liminal, rootless figure – modernist thematics
of alienation, homelessness and melancholia recur in the
writings – and a democratic anti-hero, a classless and self-
reliant man able to traverse disparate areas of American society.
This anti-hero reflected many of the social tensions of the
1920s, serving as a populist critic of capitalist powers but also

voicing prejudices and fears about racial 'others' at a time of heightened nativism. *Black Mask* magazine, which was central to the development of hard-boiled detective fiction as a discrete genre in the 1920s, published a 'Ku Klux Klan Number' in 1923, and throughout the decade published stories in which the presence of African Americans (and selected immigrant groups) connotes pathological violence, sexual licence, lack of civilisation, and absence of morality.[6]

The racialisation of hard-boiled detective fiction is not confined to stereotyping, though, for the presence of race often has a more subtle function in defining the liminal whiteness of the detective hero. It is often noted that, as a proto-modernist form, hard-boiled fiction renders universal principles of truth and justice subjective and presages moral inquiry as the detective's singular response to the atomised urban scenes of modernity. It is less often noted that the formulation of moral space in hard-boiled fiction privileges a white subject as autonomous agent while devaluing black subjectivity as extrinsic to rights-assertion and agency. This devaluation often takes the form of stereotyping, with race ordering conceptions of self and other, and categorically rationalising the 'natural' characteristics of black people. But this devaluation is also important as a sign of the white detective's dependency upon racial others. Race functions as a source of psychological and social fantasy for many hard-boiled writers, with 'blackness' often signifying an otherness within the white subject which requires control and mastery. Sin, lack of reason, and absence of discipline not only confront the white detective but are internalised using race as a topos around which images and discourses are organised. In its most simplified form this appears as a juxtaposition of primitive urge and civilising consciousness, but racial signs are everywhere present. Dashiell Hammett and Raymond Chandler, the writers most frequently identified with the 'classic' mode of urban hard-boiled, provide famous examples. In Hammett's *The Maltese Falcon* (1930) Sam Spade is described as a 'blond Satan' to indicate an inner darkness due to his associations with criminality. In Chandler's *The Big Sleep* (1939) Philip Marlowe is represented as a 'knight' who has fallen from purity and become less than white. In both instances the white detective introjects or internalises the 'difference' of the racial other.[7]

What I am suggesting here is that the white detective appropriates signs of blackness to signify his liminal isolation and difference. This appropriation is particularly striking in the urban imaginary of what is variously termed the 'dark street' or 'mean streets' down which the lone detective walks. Chandler's 'dark street' is a romantic image, a fantasy sphere in which ideas of justice, morality and heroism can be tested out while the psychological focus remains securely on the liminal white subject. The city streets are the site of degeneracy, disorder, lawlessness, and moral corruption, a universalised and fantastical urbanism which elides questions of racial identity. This elision facilitates the white subject's colonisation of social spaces traditionally associated with 'blackness' in American culture, and these degenerate and anarchic spaces expressively heighten the white detective's transgressions, providing voyeuristic pleasures for white readers. In *The Dain Curse* (1929) Hammett's Continental Op follows his investigations to 'a Negro neighborhood, which made the getting of reasonably accurate information twice as unlikely as it always was', and Hammett represents this neighborhood as a 'darktown' of easy criminality and degraded passions.[8] Chandler's *Farewell, My Lovely* (1940) opens with Philip Marlowe's observation 'It was one of the mixed blocks over on Central Avenue, the blocks that are not yet all Negro.' This observation prefaces Marlowe and Moose Malloy's entry into a black club where Moose assaults the bouncer and kills the club manager.[9] In both instances the white detective transgresses race boundaries into what is depicted as alien and degraded urban spaces, to discover an excessive (passionate, violent) difference in blackness. These transgressions stimulate a white imaginary, for these spaces, though geographically specific, are symbolic repositories of white fears and fantasies.

In this chapter I am particularly concerned with narrative representation of urban space, for space is a modality through which relations of racial domination and subordination are naturalised. In racialised urban spaces we find metaphorical and material manifestations of the power structures which regulate and constrain the formations of racial identity and knowledge. Terms such as 'urban jungle', 'ghetto', 'inner city', and 'underclass' have distinctive racial connotations and in public discourse they function to name and naturalise spheres of racial poverty and immiseration. Universal norms of justice and rights are qualified and delimited in these terms, setting boundaries on recognition of those who are and are not active participants of the civic *polis*. As David Goldberg notes: 'Citizens and strangers are controlled through the spatial confines of divided place. These geometries – the spatial categories through and in which the lived world is largely mapped, experienced, and disciplined – impose a set of interiorities and exteriorities.'[10] Spatial categories have a significant presence in hard-boiled fiction where relations between inside and outside, and between depth and surface, interact with the primary dialectic of truth and deception. In classic hard-boiled writings these relations are structured to privilege the perspective of the white subject as a private eye in public space. In the hard-boiled writings of Walter Mosley, as we shall see, these relations undergo connotative defamiliarisation and inversion as he plots the urban scene around the perspective of a black subject.

Easy Rawlins, Race, and Urban Space

To understand the significance of the relationship between race and urban space in Mosley's fiction we need to consider the geographical and historical setting of his texts. The hard-boiled detective novels he has written to date are set in the Watts area of Los Angeles in the postwar years, and Mosley has very self-consciously appropriated hard-boiled conventions in order to write a *noir* history of black life in the city. Los Angeles is a deeply mythologised city and its mythologisers include detective writers and, more broadly, those writers and film-makers associated with *noir*. The category is often thought of in filmic terms but it has broader cultural resonances, for, as Mike Davis has argued, *noir* is a complex corpus of literary and cinematic production, generally focused on unmasking Los Angeles as a 'bright, guilty place'. By depicting Los Angeles as 'the nightmare at the terminus of American history', Davis observes, *noir* dystopianisation of the city has developed as a powerful anti-myth countering 'the accumulated ideological capital of the region's boosters'.[11] Black writers and film-makers have not figured large in the construction and maintenance of this anti-myth, but there are dystopian representations of the city in black culture.

In the early twentieth century Los Angeles appealed to many African Americans as a locus of opportunity, especially during the boom years of wartime industry, and a place of escape from Jim Crow. The idea of opportunity is apparent in W.E.B. DuBois' confident statement, made in 1913: 'LA is wonderful. Nowhere in the US is the Negro so well and beautifully housed ... Out here in the matchless Southern California there would seem to be no limit to your opportunities, your possibilities.'[12] But for many African Americans Los Angeles did not prove to be the melting pot under the sun, as opportunities and possibilities were eclipsed by a climate of unremitting deprivation, and as the luxury of space (highlighted by DuBois) became an experience of spatial confinement and surveillance. The African-American writer Chester Himes worked in segregated defence plants in Los Angeles during the Second World War and drew on this experience in writing his first novel *If He Hollers Let Him Go* (1945). The novel details the psychological deterioration of Bob Jones, a skilled shipyard worker, under pressures of white racism. Bob Jones has a utopian wish:

> I didn't want to be the biggest Negro who ever lived ... Because deep inside of me, where the white folks couldn't see, it didn't mean a thing. If you couldn't swing down Hollywood Boulevard and know that you belonged; if you couldn't make a polite pass at Lana Turner at Ciro's without having the gendarmes beat the black off you for getting out of your place, ... being a great big 'Mister' Nigger didn't mean a thing ... I'd settle for a leaderman job at Atlas Shipyard – if I could be a man, defined by Webster as a male human being. That's all I'd ever wanted – just to be accepted as a man – without ambition, without distinction, either of race, creed, or colour; just a simple Joe walking down an American street.[13]

This utopian wish is articulated in spatial terms: what he yearns for is the freedom to move through urban spaces with a sense of belonging and without a fear of violent attack. The idea of 'getting out of your place' takes on a double meaning, signifying both geographic location and social prohibition. These meanings converge in the spatial metaphor of 'place'. Himes draws attention to relations between 'knowing one's (racial) place' in the city and the social structures of racial space.[14] These relations inform the tensions and ironies of his narrative; the desire to be 'just a simple Joe walking down an American street' is a desire for an invisibility and ordinariness which is associated with white subjects. Knowing one's place is not only a geographic imperative but a racial(ised) one, and ultimately an issue of survival for the black subject in a racist society.

The double meanings of knowing one's place are everywhere evident in Walter Mosley's black *noir*. The protagonist of his five detective novels is Easy Rawlins, a migrant from Houston, Texas, who arrives in Los Angeles shortly after the Second World War in which he served in the United States army. The novels – *Devil in a Blue Dress* (1990), *A Red Death* (1991), *White Butterfly* (1992), *Black Betty* (1994) and *A Little Yellow Dog* (1996) – follow Easy's life in Los Angeles from 1948 to 1961, and Mosley plans several more novels in the series. The development of the series has a strong historical impetus which Mosley terms 'a migration ... through time'.[15] He begins in 1948 because it was a period of 'absolute possibility' for the Southern blacks who moved to Los Angeles in great numbers: 'they could go get a good job and buy property and live with some measure of equality. So that was the beginning of a period of transition and hope that didn't quite work out. I want to provide a map through the years of how it didn't.'[16] In mapping this failure of promise Mosley blends history and memory to produce a critical perspective on the development of race relations in Los Angeles. His novels look both backwards and forwards from the present tense of narrative time, situating Easy Rawlins in a continuum of black diaspora experiences while distinguishing the particular locale and psychological complexity of his protagonist. In Mosley's words, 'I wanted to talk about [Easy] as this incredible, complex psyche who comes out of the Deep South into LA with all of these hopes and aspirations and what he can and cannot do for both external and internal reasons.'[17] The external and internal registers of possibility and prohibition are socially formed (if not always consciously recognised) and in Mosley's novels it is the shifting relations between and within these registers which impels the psychological drama of Easy's investigations into the meanings of racial difference and identity in Los Angeles.

Although Easy takes on a range of jobs in the novels (gardener, aircraft mechanic, janitor) he finds himself most consistently, if often reluctantly, employed as a private investigator. As he reflects in *White Butterfly*, 'In my time I had done work for the numbers runners, churchgoers, businessmen, and even the police. Somewhere along the line I had slipped into the role of a confidential agent who represented people when the law broke down.'[18] As these comments suggest, Easy is within the tradition of the liminal detective hero who operates on the boundaries of the law, but his slippage into this role is notably facilitated by conventional perceptions of black agency and representation. Mosley has observed of his protagonist:

Easy knows how to pay attention to details. He can read the streets as well as a woodsman can read skat. He is educated in the ways of desperation and crime by a lifetime of poverty. Now when Easy gets around white people they may be afraid of him, but they never suspect that he has the smarts of some kind of agent trying to glean their secrets. Turn the coin over: when Easy comes into a bar or church in the Watts community everybody thinks they know by his color that no white man would trust him with a mission. Easy has become invisible by virtue of his skin.[19]

Mosley makes ready use of the trope of invisibility in his novels to explore the meanings of racial difference and identity. In *Devil in a Blue Dress*, Easy reflects on his first experiences of working as a detective: 'Nobody knew what I was up to and that made me sort of invisible; people thought that they saw me but what they really saw was an illusion of me, something that wasn't real.'[20] The disparities between illusion and reality signified by the trope of invisibility are complexly figured throughout the novels to depict a social world in which racial perceptions are rarely stable and invariably infused with issues of power and control. Easy's manipulation of his identity affords him (and ironically parodies) the autonomy and freedom of movement traditionally associated with the white detective. Yet Easy's movements through Los Angeles are also constrained by white powers. While his role as a detective broadens possibilities for transgressing established racialised and spatial limits, race nonetheless moulds the boundaries of social identity and mobility.

Devil in a Blue Dress

Devil in a Blue Dress details Easy's first experience of working as a private investigator. Set in 1948, it introduces Easy at a point when he has been recently fired by his employer, Champion Aircraft, and is worried about defaulting on the mortgage for his small house in Watts. The investigative narrative is initiated when he is hired by a white gangster to search for a woman named Daphne Monet, a central figure in a local political conspiracy. Easy's search for Daphne takes him on a journey through diverse social spaces in Los Angeles and into conflict with racist police and corrupt politicians. With the help of Mouse, his violent childhood friend, Easy finds Daphne, and the bad guys are either killed or outwitted. More compelling than the plot development is what psychologically underpins it: Easy's journey into a paranoid world of illusion, fear, and desire where secure referents of meaning and value begin to dissolve and race is revealed as the most disturbing site of mystery and transgression.

Devil in a Blue Dress opens with a scene of transgression as a white gangster, DeWitt Albright, enters a black bar in Watts. His entry is observed by Easy:

> I was surprised to see a white man walk into Joppy's bar. It's not just that he was white but he wore an off-white linen suit and shirt with a Panama straw hat and bone shoes over flashing white silk socks. His skin was smooth and pale with just a few freckles. One lick of strawberry-blond hair

escaped the band of his hat. He stopped in the doorway, filling it with his large frame, and surveyed the room with pale eyes; not a color I'd seen in a man's eyes. When he looked at me I felt a thrill of fear, but that went away quickly because I was used to white people by 1948. (p. 9)

Opening the narrative in this way Mosley immediately foregrounds the distinctly black point of view of his first-person narrator and draws attention to whiteness as a category of identity. The passage is ethnographic in detail and the attention to whiteness is notably excessive, associating it with power. Easy is not only 'surprised' due to the incongruity of the white man's presence in a black space, but he also feels fear in response to this excessive whiteness. This fear is founded on his experiences of racism and the hegemony of white power, and, although his experiences in the Second World War have demythologised whiteness ('I killed enough blue-eyed young men to know that they were just as afraid to die as I was,' p. 9), he retains a residual sense of its 'terrorising' potential.[21] By decoding the meanings of whiteness, Mosley interrogates its privileged neutrality at the same time as he establishes the racial identity of his protagonist and his immediate culture. The opening of the novel is a suggestive inversion (and perhaps an intentional critical parody) of the opening of Chandler's *Farewell, My Lovely*. In both novels a white gangster enters a second-storey black bar in Watts in search of a woman, a search then taken up by the detective. Whereas Chandler exoticises blackness in his stereotyping of the bar's inhabitants and assumes the reader's interest in the white character's point of view, Mosley inflates whiteness as a cultural signifier and introduces a black perspective.

Where Chandler treats Watts as alien and exotic territory, Mosley represents it as a living community. In his detailed attention to the black social spaces Easy inhabits – the bars, clubs, churches, barber shops, pool halls, and whore houses – Mosley treats them as the *loci* of black culture as a way of life, a normative system of behaviour and expression, attitudes and values. He is not interested in romanticising the poverty of Watts nor in exoticising the violence which marks the lives of many of Easy's associates.[22] He represents the black 'ghetto' as a discrete if immiserated community which offers some insulation from the white world and has its own distinctive history and patterns of life. Easy is a part of this culture, and shares with many of its inhabitants a Southern background. His use of dialect, his choice of food, his tastes in music, and much more, are influenced by this background. His sense of being a displaced Southerner also sharpens his self-consciousness about racial oppression in a Los Angeles environment. He describes his entry into an illegal nightclub:

> When I opened the door I was slapped in the face by the force of Lips' alto horn. I had been hearing Lips and Willie and Flattop since I was a boy in Houston. All of them and John and half the people in that crowded room had migrated from Houston after the war, and some before that. California was like heaven for the Southern Negro. People told stories of how you could eat fruit right off the trees and get enough work to retire one day. The stories were true for the most part but the truth wasn't like the dream. Life was still hard in L.A. and if you worked every day you still found yourself on the bottom.
>
> But being on the bottom didn't feel so bad if you could come to John's now and then and remember how it felt back home in Texas, dreaming about California. (p. 34)

This bittersweet commentary registers the need for a sustaining cultural life for the migrant community of Southern African Americans, while recognising utopian delusion in the dream (articulated by DuBois above) of opportunity and prosperity.

Easy's strong attachment to, and knowledge of, the culture of the migrant community in Watts distinguishes his role as a detective. He knows where and how to seek information in this culture: 'I wanted to find out the whereabouts of Frank Green but it had to come up in normal conversation. Most barbers know all the important information in the community. That's why I was getting my hair cut' (p. 138). Bars and pool rooms are often concealed from public gaze and entry is not open to all: 'Ricardo's [Pool Room] was just a hole-in-the-wall with no windows and only one door. There was no name out front because either you knew where Ricardo's was or you didn't belong there at all' (p. 129). It is not only this cultural knowledge which distinguishes Easy as a black detective but his sense of responsibility to a community. Mosley has stressed that this sense of responsibility sets his protagonist apart from the detective heroes of classic hard-boiled fiction:

> ... the earlier gumshoes who I like, they are White men of European descent who have no mother, no father, no sister, no brother, no property, no job. So they don't have anything that would make them responsible to the world. Easy isn't like that. Easy has a wife, or, at least an ex-wife, he has children, he has friends, he has property, he has things that make him have to do things in the world ... I think the earlier fiction was necessary, but Easy answers moral questions by being implicated in the world, rather than being perfect.[23]

Mosley embeds Easy in local networks of social and cultural relations which play an important part in determining his values and actions.

However, Easy is not only bound within the social and cultural relations peculiar to the black community, he is also subject to a larger and more oppressive system of relations organised by the dominant white world. Transgression, as I noted above, marks race relations in the novel, and Easy's role as a detective frequently takes him beyond the relative cultural security of Watts into white Los Angeles. Although he can play on white ignorance of his role, he constantly feels vulnerable to racist perspectives: 'It was fifteen blocks to John's speak and I had to keep telling myself to slow down. I knew that a patrol car would arrest any sprinting Negro they encountered' (p. 83). His knowledge of racism and segregation in Los Angeles determines his cognitive map of the city as a racialised landscape of invisible boundaries and prohibitions. When he enters distinctly white social spaces he is frequently perceived as a threatening presence. The opening scene of the novel is turned around when Easy visits Albright to accept his offer of money to search for Daphne Monet. Albright's residence is 'a long drive from Watts' (p. 13) in a white area of the city, and on arrival there Easy is confronted by a white porter who asks:

'Who are you looking for?'

He was a little white man wearing a suit that was also a uniform.

'I'm looking for, um ... ah ...,' I stuttered. I forgot the name. I had to squint so that the room wouldn't start spinning.

It was a habit I developed in Texas when I was a boy. Sometimes, when a white man of authority would catch me off guard, I'd empty my head of everything so I was unable to say anything. 'The less you know, the less trouble you find,' they used to say. I hated myself for it but I also hated white people, and colored people too, for making me that way.

'Can I help you?' the white man asked. He had curly red hair and a pointed nose. When I still couldn't answer he said, 'We only take deliveries between nine and six.' (p. 21)

The confrontation emphasises the sense of dislocation Easy experiences due to the interpellating gaze and questioning of the white man. His 'habit' of stuttering and falling silent is learned through everyday experiences in a racist environment and internalised as a survival mechanism. The association of knowledge with danger is acutely underlined by Easy's transgression into white space for he is – socially as well as geographically – out of place. He reflects: 'That little white man had convinced me that I was in the wrong place. I was ready to go back home' (p. 22). Time and again in the novel Mosley explores how discrete social spaces mediate his protagonist's understanding of relations between knowledge and power, morality and justice, in a world in which he is denied 'rights'.[24]

Easy's desire 'to go back home' is recurrent in the novel, symbolising a need for security, but to the degree that it announces a desire to escape the racist white world it is impossible to fulfil. It is important to recognise that Easy is drawn into conflict with this world in part due to his aspirations. While he is sceptical of the African-American dream of opportunity and prosperity in Los Angeles, he nonetheless has aspirations which are distinctly material and middle-class. This is most clearly articulated in relation to property with his strong desire to own his own house: 'I felt that I was just as good as any white man, but if I didn't even

own my front door then people would look at me like just
another poor beggar, with his hand outstretched' (p. 16). (In
later novels he buys several properties and moves to a black
middle-class neighborhood.) Easy's house materialises the
desire for 'ordinariness' we found also in Chester Himes'
protagonist in *If He Hollers Let Him Go*.[25] But this desire, both
Himes and Mosley indicate, is also an implicit claim to
normative citizenship which is powerfully circumscribed by
white society. Easy recognises that his desire for ownership
creates dangerous new relationships: '... when I got that
mortgage I found that I needed more than just friendship. Mr.
Albright wasn't a friend but he had what I needed' (p. 28).
Needing money, Easy's acceptance of Albright's proposition
moves him more fully into the system of capitalist exchange
and control – to the degree that he may be said to mortgage
his black identity. This is clearly indicated when Albright
refuses Easy's efforts to return his payment: 'Too late for that,
Mr. Rawlins. You take my money and you belong to me ... We
all owe out something, Easy. When you owe out then you're
in debt and when you're in debt then you can't be your own
man. That's capitalism' (pp. 108–9). Capitalism, in these terms,
is a system of dependency, structured around debt and
ownership, and a powerful force in the fashioning of social
freedoms and subjugations. In racial terms, Easy's debt implies
a master–slave relationship: 'Money bought everything ...,' he
reflects, 'I got the idea, somehow, that if I got enough money
then maybe I could buy my own life back' (p. 127).

Easy is caught up in webs of racist social control and coercion
from which he cannot easily extract himself. Mosley's depiction
of this dilemma is subtly handled and reflects his intention
to portray 'both external and internal' factors which mediate
the meanings of autonomy and self-sufficiency for a black
subject. More particularly, he wants to explore what these
may mean for a black *male* subject, for Easy's desire for self-
sufficiency has distinctive gender as well as economic
connotations. When he decides to accept Albright's money he
reasons that he does so not only to pay his mortgage but
also because:

> DeWitt Albright made me a little nervous. He was a big man, and powerful by the look of him. You could tell by the way he held his shoulders that he was full of violence. But I was a big man too ... Whether he knew it or not, DeWitt Albright had me caught by my own pride. The more I was afraid of him, I was that much more certain to take the job he offered. (p. 20)

Easy is drawn into the complex relationship with Albright as much through a sense of male pride as through economic need. In Easy's responses to Albright and other white men, Mosley emphasises the intersection of a 'masculine mystique' with institutional racism and draws attention to 'the racial dialectic of projection and internalisation through which white and black men have shaped their masks of masculinity'.[26] This dialectic is at work in Easy's need for white recognition of his masculinity and demand for 'respect' from white men (p. 73). Mosley's treatment of this dialectic further distinguishes his representation of Easy as a 'tough guy' of the hard-boiled type. Easy's mask of masculinity barely conceals the deep divisions in his subjectivity.[27] In *Devil in a Blue Dress* the instability of his masculine identity is foregrounded in his psychological struggles to come to terms with the violence of his past; throughout the narrative he reflects upon violent experiences and in his dreams is haunted by them as scenes of trauma. His memories of his childhood friend Mouse – 'He could put a knife in a man's stomach and ten minutes later sit down to a plate of spaghetti' (p. 55) – and of action in the war frequently puncture the narrative to illustrate his ambivalence about violent assertions of masculinity. Easy's desire for upward mobility represents an effort to escape the horrors of the past but he remains inexorably 'caught' in legacies of racism and violence which have traumatised black male subjectivity.

The divisions within Easy are mirrored in the instability of his narrative authority and the challenges posed to any secure position of truth or knowledge in the construction of identity. This narrative instability is most potently figured in Easy's search for Daphne Monet, the eponymous 'devil in a blue dress'. Daphne is an excessively enigmatic character whose identity is curiously unstable to Easy's eyes:

> Her face was beautiful. More beautiful than the photograph. Wavy hair so light brown that you might have called it blond from a distance, and eyes that were either green or blue depending on how she held her head. Her cheekbones were high but her face was full enough that it didn't make her seem severe. (p. 96)

Daphne's identity appears to shift and change under Easy's gaze – neither hair colour, nor eye colour, nor facial structure remain constant – and it is with some perturbation that he observes: 'Daphne was like the chameleon lizard. She changed for her man' (p. 187). Mysterious, sexually attractive, and dangerous, Daphne is very much in the *noir* tradition of the 'dark woman' or *femme fatale*, but the variable effect of her identity quite literally defamiliarises the conventional racial encoding of this figure.[28] Daphne, as Easy (and the reader) discovers near the end of the narrative, is a figure of racial masquerade, a mulatto who passes as white; her other identity is that of Ruby Hanks, the half-sister of a black gangster. Easy, who experiences a strong sexual and emotional attraction to Daphne, is shocked at the discovery of her double identity: 'I had only been in an earthquake once but the feeling was the same: The ground under me seemed to shift. I looked at her to see the truth. But it wasn't there. Her nose, cheeks, her skin color – they were white. Daphne was a white woman' (p. 205). The 'shifting ground' to which Easy refers underlines the arbitrariness of social indicators of racial difference and identity, particularly as these privilege the visible as the surest ground of evidence. There is considerable irony of course in Easy's shock at this revelation, for he had begun to pride himself in his own form of masquerade: 'people thought that they saw me but what they really saw was an illusion of me, something that wasn't real'. In the figure of Daphne/Ruby, Mosley gives a further twist to the meanings of the 'interiorities and exteriorities' which structure racial knowledge and identity.

The relationship between Easy and Daphne has significant consequences for the dialectic of truth and deception in the

novel. While the perspective of the black detective is privileged
he discovers the inadequacies of his own racial knowledge as
well as that of the broader social texts. There is no hidden 'truth'
of racial being for Easy to discover or uncover, though there
is much to be learned in his quest about the indeterminacy
of 'race' as a social epistemology and categorical sign of
difference. Mosley questions the existence of an essence of
racial difference as the secure *locus* of identity formation.
Easy's friend Mouse expresses an essentialist position when he
warns Easy:

> You learn stuff and you be thinkin' like white men be
> thinkin'. You be thinkin' that what's right fo' them is right
> fo' you. [Daphne] look like she white and you think like you
> white. But brother you don't know that you both poor
> niggers. And a nigger ain't never gonna be happy 'less he
> accept what he is. (p. 209)

Easy has no answer to this statement but his desires and
actions do not reflect the coherence of racial identification
Mouse articulates. Mosley does not ascribe an essence to his
black subjects; rather, he represents them, and Easy in
particular, as complexly constituted in both interracial and
intraracial relations. He emphasises his protagonist's urge to
self-invention while detailing the powerful racist prohibitions
on this process and the dialectics of power, fear, and desire
which shape it internally.

Walter Mosley's Black *Noir*

Mosley has observed of Easy, 'he does make it here in America.
But how he makes it is flawed and scarred.'[29] This statement
points up the author's efforts to represent and interrogate
utopian and dystopian features of black experiences in Los
Angeles. In doing so he defamiliarises the conventionally
white co-ordinates of *noir*'s counter-mythologising. Mosley's
black *noir* appropriates key elements of classic hard-boiled
fiction – the tough-guy persona, the *femme fatale*, the corrupt
police and politicians, the quest for a hidden truth, the
paranoid imaginary – yet is much more than a critical parody

of earlier white writers. If, as Mike Davis, proposes, 'L.A. understands its past ... through a robust fiction called *noir*', then Mosley has used this conduit of historical memory to produce a critical history of race relations in the city and to illuminate the cultural history of people who have come to be pathologised as an 'underclass'.[30] His postwar Los Angeles is observed through cultural and ideological categories of the present time in which he writes. It is a culturally hybrid world, but not a multicultural melting pot, in which racial transgressions haunt individual and collective identities. In the 1990s, Davis argues, Los Angeles is characterised by a 'paranoid spatiality' which is produced by, and reinforces, social differences and prejudices.[31] Mosley's postwar Los Angeles already shows much evidence of this paranoid spatiality, and, in his revisionist *noir*, race dominates the fantasies, fears and repressions which shadow the divisions of a virtually apartheid city. In this city's dark streets, the black detective's search for freedom, truth and justice is also an investigation into the meanings of racial difference and identity.

Notes

1. Raymond Chandler, 'Introduction', *The Smell of Fear* (London: Hamish Hamilton, 1973), p. 9.
2. See, for example, Richard Dyer, 'White', *Screen*, vol. 29 (Autumn, 1988), pp. 44–64; bell hooks, 'Representations of Whiteness', *Black Looks: Race and Representation* (London: Turnaround, 1992), pp. 165–78; Toni Morrison, *Playing in the Dark: Whiteness and the Literary Imagination* (New York: Random House, 1992); Eric Lott, 'White Like Me: Racial Cross-Dressing and the Construction of American Whiteness' in Amy Kaplan and Donald Pease (eds), *Cultures of United States Imperialism* (Durham: Duke University Press, 1993), pp. 236–60.
3. Morrison, *Playing in the Dark*, p. 17.
4. Richard Slotkin, *Gunfighter Nation: The Myth of the Frontier in Twentieth Century America* (New York: Atheneum, 1992), p. 154.
5. Ibid., p. 219.

6. See Frankie Y. Bailey, *Out of the Woodpile: Black Characters in Crime and Detective Fiction* (Westport, CT: Greenwood Press, 1991), pp. 41–3.
7. For a stimulating analysis of (racial) introjection in 'the construction of American whiteness', see Lott, 'White Like Me'.
8. Dashiell Hammett, *The Dain Curse*, in *Dashiell Hammett: Five Complete Novels* (New York: Avenel, 1980), pp. 152–60.
9. Raymond Chandler, *Farewell, My Lovely* (Harmondsworth Middlesex: Penguin, 1949), pp. 7–18.
10. David Theo Goldberg, *Racist Culture: Philosophy and the Politics of Meaning* (Oxford: Blackwell, 1993), p. 186.
11. Mike Davis, *City of Quartz: Excavating the Future in Los Angeles* (London: Verso, 1990), p. 20.
12. W.E.B. DuBois, quoted in Lynell George, *No Crystal Stair: African-Americans in the City of Angels* (London: Verso, 1991), p. 17.
13. Chester Himes, *If He Hollers Let Him Go* (London: Pluto Press, 1986), p. 153.
14. Goldberg, *Racist Culture*, p. 205.
15. Charles L.P. Silet, 'The Other Side of Those Mean Streets: An Interview With Walter Mosley', *The Armchair Detective*, vol. 26, no. 4 (1993), p. 11.
16. Richard Maidment (ed.), *American Conversations* (London: Hodder and Stoughton, 1995), p. 68.
17. Silet, 'The Other Side', p. 12.
18. Walter Mosley, *White Butterfly* (London: Pan, 1994), p. 17.
19. Walter Mosley, 'The Black Dick', in Philomena Mariani (ed.), *Critical Fictions: The Politics of Imaginative Writing* (Seattle: Bay Press, 1991), pp. 132–3.
20. Walter Mosley, *Devil in a Blue Dress* (London: Pan, 1992), p. 135. Further page references to this novel will appear in the text.
21. See hooks, 'Representations'.
22. Mosley has observed: 'poverty is tattooed on black and brown skins. Ignorance and violence, sex and criminality are deeply etched in Hispanic and African hues. If you're not white it is hard to get out of the slums.' Mosley, 'The Black Dick', p. 132.
23. Maidment, *American Conversations*, p. 71.

24. The issue of rights is made violently explicit when Easy is arrested by two white policemen: '"I've got the right to know why you're taking me" [Easy]. "You got a right to fall down and break your face, nigger. You got a right to die" [policeman], ... Then he hit me in the diaphragm' (p. 75).

25. More than a sign of economic independence, Easy's house is an important site of psychic security. It is a deeply subjective space in the novel where Easy's propensity for self-reflection is often at its most intense. As such, it follows a tradition in African-American literature of representing the house as 'inside space', a semi-autonomous realm of belonging and identity. See Charles Scruggs, *Sweet Home: Invisible Cities in the Afro-American Novel* (Baltimore: Johns Hopkins University Press, 1993).

26. Kobena Mercer and Isaac Julien, 'Race, Sexual Politics and Black Masculinity: A Dossier', in Rowena Chapman and Jonathan Rutherford (eds), *Male Order: Unwrapping Masculinity* (London: Lawrence and Wishart, 1988), p. 99.

27. In the hard-boiled genre the male hero's subjectivity is often split or decentred as a position of narrative authority. See Frank Krutnik, *In A Lonely Street: Film Noir, Genre, Masculinity* (London: Routledge, 1991), pp. 128–9.

28. See Mary Ann Doane, *Femmes Fatales: Feminism, Film Theory, Psychoanalysis* (London: Routledge, 1991).

29. Silet, 'The Other Side', p. 12.

30. Davis, *City of Quartz*, pp. 15–97.

31. Ibid., pp. 221–63.

3

V.I. Warshawski, Kinsey Millhone and Kay Scarpetta: Creating a Feminist Detective Hero

Sabine Vanacker

Introduction

The popular genre of crime fiction has shown a surprising vigour and versatility. The classical, Golden Age ratiocinative puzzle, the contemporary hard-boiled adventure, the spy novel, the police procedural, and the psychological crime novel are but a few in a seemingly unending succession of sub-genres. Indeed, Evelyne Keitel points to this re-creative strength of the crime novel as its basic characteristic:

> [D]etective fiction is a genre of variation. Variations are an essential and characteristic feature of the genre, occurring, as they do, on two different levels: within the genre (every novel is a rewriting of the novels that preceded it) and within an author's work (the adventures of the hero or heroine must be constantly varied).[1]

Especially fascinating, however, has been the spectacular rise of the feminist detective novel. Traditionally associated with conservative, occasionally downright sexist gender views and only marginal female characters, the crime novel is now redirected to represent a feminist ideology and reconceived with a woman hero at its centre.[2] Of the three highly successful American crime novelists here discussed, two – Sara Paretsky and Sue Grafton – have chosen to site their feminist detectives within the framework of the hard-boiled detective novel, and, in doing so, act to subvert its frequently misogynist ideology. The third, Patricia D. Cornwell, has inserted her woman detective into the police procedural. All three novelists, in their efforts at redirecting the genre, frequently indicate a certain ambivalence about the figure of the detective hero, as they position their feminist detectives on an axis of opposites. On the one hand, the conventional gender assumptions of the crime genre, like individualism, 'masculine' action and aggression, are felt to be empowering and attractive. At the same time, however, they clearly signal awareness of anti-feminist aspects within the make-up of the traditional detective and seek to undermine these.

The gender assumptions of the traditional detective novel had previously been explicitly critiqued in one of the earliest feminist crime novels, Barbara Wilson's *Murder in the Collective* (1984). Wilson investigates the inherently sexist ideology behind the typical detective's hunt for clues and signs. This novel, and her second, *Sisters of the Road* (1986), constitute a probing interrogation of the crime genre and of the dubious nature of the detective's search for knowledge and truth.[3] Pam Nilsen, her would-be detective, discovers that being a feminist and a detective are incompatible categories. In a hilarious evolution, this liberal detective finds herself 'getting in touch' with her proto-fascist self as she interviews witnesses, questions suspects and checks clues. Eventually, Nilsen must learn that in order to understand how the murder in her printing collective occurred she must show empathy with, and even trust in, others rather than question, analyse and investigate. With such a conclusion, Wilson's novels might well have been both the first and the last feminist crime novels, since she invalidates what is the main thrust of the genre: the investigative analysis of a crime by a ratiocinative male detective.

Similarly, Paretsky, Grafton and Cornwell explore the implications of applying the conventional characteristics of the detective hero to a female protagonist. Thus, certain ambivalent effects are created: they seek to retain those features they see as empowering and liberating for women (like their self-determination and independence), while, at the same time, the furthest limits of autonomous subjectivity (traditionally associated with the figure of the male detective) are explicitly checked and queried. So, in the novels of Paretsky and Grafton, the heroic persistence and bravery of Warshawski and Millhone can be at once admired and questioned. Added to this creation of a new detective hero is the undermining of the genre's traditional basic notion – again linked to the figure of the male hero – of the availability and discovery of a single 'truth'. In fact, these feminine crime novels re-examine the whole business of the gathering of information and the pursuit of knowledge to show the limitations of the male epistemological ideal and to suggest a preferred feminist alternative. It is in their treatment of this subject that the most important redefinition of the detective hero by these writers occurs.

The Detective Hero

V.I. Warshawski is, in Kathleen Gregory Klein's words, 'one of the best developed and most convincing female private eyes in contemporary fiction'.[4] She has a credible blue-collar, immigrant background, and an education at the University of Chicago Law School. Her feminist and progressive credentials are impeccable, with an involvement in the underground abortion movement and the Louisiana freedom marches of the 1960s. Sue Grafton's detective, Kinsey Millhone, also comes from a blue-collar family and an equally idealistic background: a police officer, disenchanted with public 'justice', she then became a private eye.[5]

Typical for the genre, the Warshawski novels are detailed and devoted pictures of the city in which she works (Chicago), and they excel in the nail-biting description of life-threatening adventures, involving an escape from a burning hotel, the bombing of a Great Lakes grain carrier, and, in inevitable escalation, Warshawski's descent into flooded Chicago sewers in *Tunnel Vision*.[6] Millhone's location too is prime hard-boiled territory, the strangely anonymous, modern urban sprawl of 'Santa Teresa, California'.[7] Consistently, Grafton foregrounds another hard-boiled motif, the contrast between the brash, conspicuous wealth of the California rich, marvelled at by blue-collar Kinsey Millhone, and the vulgar poverty and delinquency of the prostitutes, fraudsters and murderers with which it intersects. Both detectives share the standard voice of the hard-boiled private eye: a sparse, cynical tone alternating with flashes of metaphoric description.[8]

Warshawski and Millhone, then, are female heroes to replace the hard-boiled male PI. Like their male counterparts, they present attractive role models for their readers, showing determined, assertive and powerful women whose actions are both incisive and significant. Tough-talking and resolute, Millhone and Warshawski are women who act and are liberating characters for the woman reader in their unified subjectivity, with an ability to be unquestioningly active, and to be blunt and direct rather than exhibiting conventional 'female' qualities of tact, diplomacy, politeness and the like. Above all, they have no need to be liked, and have thus liberated themselves from that quality so subversive to female self-confidence.

However, these female detectives are not quite the 'tough guy' equivalents of their male counterparts and often admit to feeling afraid, bullied, and disaster-bound. In *Toxic Shock*, V.I. is 'well and truly scared' (p. 183), and admits that '[T]o my annoyance my lips were trembling. The image of the rank marsh grasses ... made me shiver uncontrollably' (p. 146).[9] Nonetheless, she refuses to tell all she knows to the police, because it would mean abdicating her 'responsibility for my life' (pp. 183–4). The power and heroic appeal for the reader clearly lie precisely in this determination to accept fear, recognise the dangers, and yet go beyond them. To their readers, Warshawski and Millhone seem able to act as heroic subjects, even despite their fears of attack, rape, or murder.

The more recent novels of Patricia Cornwell belong to the tradition of the police procedural, rather than the hard-boiled novel. Pathologist Kay Scarpetta, a disciplined, clean-living justice official, is a more muted character than Millhone or Warshawski. However, on a fundamental level she too represents an attractive female version of the heroic detective subject. Indeed, as Richmond county's chief coroner, she has radically crossed the limits of her gender role, with her choice of the most unsavoury and 'unfeminine' of professions. The extensive presentation of Scarpetta's postmortems is initially shocking and she reports to the reader in the cool assertive voice of an objective forensic scientist:

Any honest forensic pathologist will admit that autopsy artefacts are ghastly. There is nothing quite like the Y incision in any premortem surgical procedure, for it looks like its name. The scalpel goes from each clavicle to sternum, runs the length of the torso, and ends at the pubis after a small detour around the navel. The incision made from ear to ear at the back of the head before sawing open the skull is not attractive, either.[10]

She then goes on to describe how she wedges a chisel between the child victim's molars to see whether she bit her tongue and was conscious just before her death (p. 132). Indeed, as a pathologist, Scarpetta functions in the reader's emotional field like a Dr Frankenstein in reverse, unpicking what used to be a living body into its component parts. Not only does she assume the unselfquestioning activity of the male detective's unified subject position – her actions are indeed determined, confident and incisive – but she also departs considerably from the traditional constraints and qualities associated with her gender. Rather than being culturally associated (as female) with life and life giving, this woman hero is a dealer in death, who aggressively 'manhandles' the corpses of victims and gruesomely thrives off decaying and decomposing bodies.

The macabre nature of Scarpetta's profession is frequently highlighted. Leaving her office after the postmortem on an executed murderer, she and her staff are abused by anti-death penalty protestors: 'A chant rose with tribal intensity. "Butchers, butchers, butchers ..."'[11] When, on another occasion, a victim's mother manages to get into her office, Scarpetta is acutely embarrassed by the scene of crime photographs, bloodied clothing, and 'an excise stab wound suspended in a small bottle of formalin', dotted around her room.[12] In *Cruel and Unusual*, her autopsy assistant is pregnant, further transgressing gender expectations. The radical reversal of gender positions in the role and actions of Cornwell's hero is again underlined (in *All That Remains*) when detective Marino, impressed with her cooking, refers to this more 'feminine' occupation: 'Maybe you ought to forget cutting up dead bodies and open a restaurant' (*ATR*, p. 167). Here, in a powerful moment of defamiliarisation, the reader receives the discomforting picture of what is a culturally acceptable but in fact equally gruesome occupation – that of the housewife slicing up what is, after all, dead meat to make the family dinner. Cornwell thus uses Scarpetta to subvert traditional gender roles which associate femininity both with the giving of life and preparing of food.

Feminist crime fiction, then, exploits the heroic status of the woman detective to offer a fascinating, dynamic role model and a focus for its readers' escapism and fantasies. However, this is paradoxically combined with a suspicious investigation into the very concept of a 'feminist hero' and an awareness that, while such a representation might be both attractive and empowering, it is one which ultimately cannot be endorsed or sustained. Like Barbara Wilson, Paretsky is aware of sinister, anti-feminist, and even fascist qualities within the make-up of her detective protagonist. Many feminist commentators on Sara Paretsky have referred to Warshawski's violence. In *Toxic Shock*, for instance, Warshawski uncovers the fact that a local chemical plant, Xerxes, has knowingly exposed its employees to chemical toxins. When the company's attempts at a cover-up almost result in the murder of her friend Louisa, the detective's outrage moves her to violence. Paretsky's supposedly liberal feminist detective first shoots the villain, and then proceeds to attack his elderly accomplice:

> Fury was riding me, though, choking the breath from me, covering my eyes with a hazy film. I shot Jurshak in the chest ... Chigwell had stood next to Louisa's stretcher throughout the fracas, his hands flaccidly at his side, his head hunched into his coat. I went over to him and slapped his face. I meant at first just to rouse him from his stupor, but my rage was consuming me so that I found myself pounding him over and over, screaming at him that he was a traitor to his oath, a miserable worm of a man, on and on, over and over. (p. 280)

With a feminist hero performing excessive acts of violence on an elderly man, this scene contains ethical ambiguities for the Paretsky reader. For if she may empathise with the justified rage and aggression of the hero, the feminist context of the novels implicitly condemns and questions such violence, leaving such a reader off-balance and uneasy about identification with the protagonist.

Another feature of Warshawski's heroism – that bravery normally taken as an admirable given by the detective form – is questioned more explicitly in Paretsky's texts.[13] As her doctor friend Lotty Herschel suggests, Warshawski's courage can be in fact interpreted in other ways than the heroic, as motivated by a deep, masochistic and unhealthy obsession with danger:

'I would ask that you not be reckless, Victoria. I would ask it except that you seem to be in love with danger and death. You make life very hard for those who love you.' (*TS*, p. 191)

Indeed, every Warshawski story contains a hospital narrative, a compelling moment of physical weakness after the detective has pushed herself to the limit, when she is forced to consider her own helplessness and death ('cursing my lack of stamina', *TS*, p. 180), or to worry about such possibilities as developing Alzheimer's disease as a result of her fights (*BM*, p. 188). Time and again, Warshawski is made helpless and passive, forced to accept the care of others, being punished, or so it would seem, for her assumption of the male heroic mode. However, she also consistently and heroically relearns to talk and walk, and always leaves hospital both prematurely and on her own terms, pushing her body to the very limit and yet still getting away with it. As this female Lazarus picks up her bed and walks away, the traditional hard-boiled detective's heroism is transferred to the female subject, while, on the other hand, such heroic status is interrogated, undermined by the many sensible voices in the novels who caution Warshawski about her recklessness. Paretsky and her readers are at once attracted to this literary cliché from conventional crime fiction, while also ambiguously critical of it.

Kinsey Millhone's bravery is also explored in terms of her identity as female, and is interestingly related to a pre-feminist past when the detective-to-be was both fearful and timid.[14] In fact it seems to stem from a frightened and vulnerable childhood, and the self-emancipation which then occurred, first into quasi-delinquent adolescence, and then into the tough assertiveness of the female private eye:

> I hadn't liked school. I'd always been overwhelmed by the dangers I sensed ... I was the kind of kid who, for no apparent reason, wept piteously or threw up on myself. On an especially scary day, I sometimes did both ... Between classes, the other kids hardly looked at me, embarrassed on my behalf.[15]

When she is frightened, her grown-up fears remind Millhone of her school days, and this fires up her independence (*G*, pp. 54, 178). In the case of both these female hard-boiled detectives, then, courage and assertiveness go hand-in-hand with vulnerability. The idea of the heroic subject is consequently at least partially undermined, the detective's bravery covering, in the one case, an awareness of the dangers of excess in this area and, in the other, a potentially self-defeating fear that she cannot permit herself to acknowledge.

In the latter respect, it is interesting to note the repeated association of Kinsey with smallness and miniaturisation, as it introduces a fantasy element apparently incongruous with the figure of a hard-boiled detective. Small in body shape, she owns a small car, and a tiny, doll's-house apartment where everything fits into tight hyper-designed corners. Rebuilt after a bombing, her living space looks like a 'ship's interior ... with shelves and cubby-holes on every side' and with 'kitchenette ... pint-size stove and refrigerator ... tiny bathroom [and] ... tiny spiral staircase'. From this womb-like nest Grafton's protagonist can survey the world around her, but in all safety, with elements of childlike fantasy involved: 'I could bathe among the treetops, looking out at the ocean where the clouds were piling up like bubbles' (*G*, pp. 4–5). This characteristic is stressed in several novels,[16] and, combined with the fact that this hard-boiled detective lives in 'a Barbie-doll penthouse in its own carrying case' (*G*, p. 123), serves as a bizarre undermining of Millhone's self-proclaimed toughness.

The macho aspects of Paretsky and Grafton's heroes are further undermined by an explicit interpretation of their psychological composition in terms of gender. Warshawski is portrayed as combining her parents' characteristics: the active engagement with the urban world of her American policeman father with the culture of her Italian mother and her opera-singing past. Warshawski almost becomes, as a result, a latter-day version of Renaissance (wo)man, an all-action hero who hides vital case evidence between her 'Italienischer Liederbuch' and Mozart's Concert Arias; the only private eye with a trained operatic voice. Grafton too combines contrasting gender attributes within her heroic make-up, taught both male and female activities by her eccentric aunt:

> Firing a handgun, she felt, would teach me to appreciate both safety and accuracy. It would also help me develop good hand–eye co-ordination, which she thought was useful. She'd taught me to knit and crochet so that I'd learn patience and an eye for detail. She'd refused to teach me to cook as she felt it was boring and would only make me fat ... (*D*, p. 102)

In fact, Grafton and Paretsky present their feminist detectives as combinations of traditional gender characteristics, ideally conjoining the two genders. Similarly, Warshawski uses household metaphors to describe her methods of detection. In *Killing Orders*, she reports that her methods are similar to Julia Child's description of her cooking: 'Grab a lot of ingredients from the shelves, put them in a pot and stir, and see what happens.'[17] When a client wants her to stop the course of an investigation, she again returns to such metaphors, describing herself as 'not a blender' that can be switched off (*TV*, p. 190). Elsewhere, female detecting is compared with unravelling a sweater:

> I used to watch my granny take old sweaters apart so she could use the yarn on something new. She'd start with a shapeless wad, tugging at it here and there until suddenly she'd find the thread that would turn the wad into a long string. I'm hoping Cyrus has the thread. (*TV*, p. 373)

Another distinctive feature of the male detective hero, and one generally depicted as admirable, is his separateness, his self-sufficiency and independence, his status as a genuine private 'I'. It is precisely because he stands alone and needs no help or support that he is a hero, a unified subject on whom incomplete and frustrated others depend. Paretsky, Grafton and Cornwell react to the traditional representations of the whole and separate detective hero. Significantly, they position their feminist detectives on the axis between independence and dependence. Both Millhone and Warshawski have liberated themselves from pre-feminist manipulative marriages. Millhone was in fact married twice, with one past husband who was adulterous, drug-addicted, and emotionally manipulative (*C*, p. 86). Warshawski's lawyer husband expected her to sacrifice her career to his ambition.[18] Importantly, neither PI has children or living parents, though both have alternative elder role models or parental surrogates. This paradoxical situation proves to be empowering, however. The detectives are free from the frustrations and limitations that characterise the traditional patriarchal family, free from the daughter role, but they benefit from the support of a looser, less emotionally binding family. Thus orphaned Kinsey Millhone was raised by an eccentric but self-sufficient and unemotional aunt who instilled the following rule into her:

> Rule Number One, first and foremost, above and beyond all else, was financial independence. A woman should never, never, never be financially dependent on anyone, especially a man, because the minute you were dependent, you could be abused. (*D*, p. 102)

By going to university and becoming an independent woman, V.I., too, fulfilled her dead mother's wishes. Her strong need for independence finds its psychological source in frustration at her mother's helplessness, wasted opportunities and painful death:

> I knew then that it was a terrible mistake to depend on someone else to solve my problems for me. Now I seem to be too terrorised to solve them for myself and I'm thrashing around. But when I ask for help it just drives me wild. (*TS*, p. 221).

Richard Goodkin notes V.I.'s deeply symbolic name, Victoria Iphigenia, which designates her as the woman who will transcend her mother's defeats and become victoriously self-sufficient. However, he stresses that she is also the daughter under a generational burden, sacrificed on the emotional altar of her parents' marriage, and still responding to their demands:[19]

> Often when I feel like quitting I hear my mother's voice in my head, exhorting me. Her fierce energy was tireless – the worst thing I could ever do in her eyes was to give up. Tonight, though, I heard no echoes in my head. (*BM*, p. 227)

If V.I.'s 'quixotic' dead mother is a troublesome role model, her death has liberated the detective from irksome emotional obligations (*TS*, p. 116). In Kinsey's case, the emotional ties with her mother and father have been violently severed, freeing the detective from the obligations of a parent–daughter relationship.

But again there is deep ambivalence concerning the issue of dependence or independence. Interestingly, both Warshawski and Millhone not only have older, mothering women friends,[20] but also surrogate fathers, both retired working men with whom they share a house and who take an interest in their professional and private lives. Warshawski's Mr Contreras and Millhone's Henry Pitts are the image of the benevolent patriarch, the harmless elderly man with whom they can have a caring relationship without the dangerously dependent family strings. They combine the censorship of the patriarch with the absence of any real power over the women. Both men miraculously avoid any illness or infirmity, offering an ideal of an active, alert, sexy old age that holds no demands of practical care for the detectives. Unlike Warshawski, Kinsey Millhone's relationship with Pitts involves a certain sexual attraction, but again it is an undemanding, physically unexpressed form of sexuality, perhaps that which marks the ideal safe and enabling Freudian sexy father (*A*, p. 21). Mr Contreras shows 'critical jealousy' of Warshawski's male friends, but is ultimately powerless, placed outside the field of emotional and sexual exchange: 'If he was twenty years younger, he'd be beating up any guy who came visiting me. It's tiresome, but he's essentially so good-hearted I can't bring myself to punch him down' (*BM*, p. 209). Both men interestingly have taken on female roles, which removes them even further from the traditional, powerful father: Contreras has taken up cooking since the death of his wife (*TS*, p. 33), while Pitts bakes semi-professionally. Sentimental but ultimately safe, fussing around and 'mothering' the woman detective, these are examples of idealised father–daughter relationships.[21] Warshawski and Millhone can have their family cake and eat it.

Since patriarchy and the law of the father are instilled in the family atmosphere, the absence of biological parents frees these detectives from such forms of censure and control. At the same time Paretsky, Cornwell and Grafton embed their female heroic subjects explicitly in a network of emotional relationships, a pointed feminist undercutting of the myth of the separate self. Having freed their detectives from the patriarchal family, the three crime writers underline the importance of a binding feminist solidarity. These personal/political ties influence the actions of the woman detective, prevent her from being a complete and separate unit, and thus help to critique such a (traditional generic) notion.

Accordingly, all three women detectives form part of a network of women, both supportive and demanding, where different generations, family members and friends are linked in relationships of mutual aid. Paretsky's plots especially focus explicitly on the importance of this female network. In *Burn Marks*, V.I. feels compelled to assist her seedy aunt Elena, a completely untrustworthy drunk (*BM*, p. 196) but a family member for whom she feels irrationally responsible. The support for her aunt involves Warshawski in helping others: her aunt's equally suspect female friend and her family.

Toxic Shock is another novel where a network of female solidarity emerges. Again, Warshawski is dragged into an irksome supportive role, here for Caroline, the girl she unwillingly childminded as a teenager:

'You can't. I need you,' she wailed loudly ... It brought back all the times Gabriella had come to the door – saying 'What difference can it make to you, Victoria? Take the child with you' – so forcibly it was all I could do not to slap Caroline's wide trembling mouth. (*TS*, p. 15)

Despite what seems her excessively violent reaction, Warshawski is ultimately unable to reject Caroline's needs because she has known and helped her all her life (*TS*, p. 27).

The female networks Paretsky describes are transgenerational and serve to embrace both private and public spheres. In *Tunnel Vision*, the net of solidarity embraces both a poor battered woman, and Deirdre Messenger, a rich woman on the board of a women's refuge, yet (ironically) herself a battered wife (p. 67). The same theme of wife-beating and domestic violence is thus mirrored in high and low society, a connection Vic makes (p. 91). But Warshawski's involvement also helps Emily Messenger escape from the hands of her sexually abusive father and the memory of a drunken, jealous mother (pp. 52–3). Meanwhile, long-suffering police officer Neely decides to leave the force so that she can help women victims more directly, acknowledging as she does so her own history as an abused child (p. 104). Persistently, V.I. causes a helping line of female solidarity in the course of her investigation (*TV*, p. 305). The feminist detective, then, has the best of both worlds: she is a free agent, in charge of her own actions, yet motivated by female solidarity. But there is a paradox here, for as indicated in *Burn Marks*, this sense of duty constantly counters the representation of the female hero as a 'complete' and unified subject:

> Did I have a duty to Elena that overrode all considerations of myself, my work, my own longing for wholeness?
> I'd held glasses of water for Gabriella when her arms were too weak to lift them herself, emptied wheelchair pots for Tony when he could no longer move from chair to toilet. I've done enough, I kept repeating, I've done enough. But I couldn't quite convince myself. (*BM*, p. 197)

This mesh of relationships prevents Warshawski's belief in an illusion of wholeness and separateness, and highlights her feelings of frustration and incompleteness.

In the novels of Grafton and Cornwell, the network of female solidarity is not thematised to the same extent. However, Millhone is also surrounded by a group of mutually supportive friends. In *A is for Alibi*, her strong friend Nell, 'a creature of high intellect and wry humour', is an empowering influence (p. 137), while her sexually sophisticated and assertive friend from work, Vera, comes to the fore in the later novels (*G*, p. 25). Elsewhere, Millhone finds a Hispanic woman in the police department to be her ally (*I*, p. 25), while in *C is for Corpse*, she confesses more generally: 'I like older women as a rule. I like almost all women, as a matter of fact. I find them open and confiding by nature, amusingly candid when it comes to talk of men' (p. 15).

Equally, many of Millhone's cases range her on the side of women clients and witnesses, and foreground what are explicitly feminist themes and motifs. Like Warshawski in *Burn Marks*, a rebellious Kinsey Millhone, in *G is for Gumshoe*, is roped into looking after an old lady, and a caring role for which she has not bargained:

What really bugged me was the suspicion that nobody would have even suggested that a boy detective do likewise ... Why does everybody assume women are so nurturing? My maternal instincts were extinguished by my Betsy Wetsy doll. Every time she peed in her little flannel didies, I could feel my temper climb (*G*, p. 79).

Despite her protestations, however, she too subscribes to female solidarity, and the novel 'rewards' her for this attitude with a love interest: her bodyguard and colleague Robert Dietz falls in love with Kinsey specifically because she has cared for the old lady (*G*, p. 219).

As with Paretsky, Grafton's plots use a feminist solidarity to promote the emancipation of other female characters from inequalities in the patriarchal, traditional family. Thus, *A is for Alibi* describes the chaos left in the wake of a persistently adulterous husband. Kinsey meets his ex-wife, who introduces herself as 'the dutiful wife': 'She stopped and laughed at the image of herself, pretending to pull a string from her neck. "Hello, I'm Gwen. I'm a good wife"' (*A*, p. 41). In *G is for*

Gumshoe, her client is Mrs Irene Gersh, an asthmatic, traumatised woman. Kinsey is appalled by her emotional and physical dependency, and her intervention causes a liberating catharsis (p. 239). The victim in *I is for Innocent* is a rich, talented woman, with 'no self-esteem to speak of', whose basic insecurity makes her 'a sitting duck for anybody with a kind word' (p. 9).

Scarpetta is the only detective of the three under discussion with a living parent and sibling, although her relationship with an egotistical mother and sister is an uneasy one and she keeps these relatives at a distance (*ATR*, p. 23). However, Scarpetta herself functions as surrogate mother to her niece Lucy, a computer whiz-kid neglected by her mother. With this surrogate daughter Scarpetta mentions having felt an immediate bonding (*ATR*, p. 248), based on a 'secret shame born of abandonment and isolation', and says that '[w]hen I tended to her wounds, I was tending to my own' (*BF*, p. 46). In a certain sense, then, this detective too is positioned on the axis between separateness and dependence.

However, Patricia Cornwell thematises another issue concerning the feminist detective hero's struggle within a patriarchal society. Here, her conclusions concerning the power of female support are bleaker ones. Scarpetta's unit, working alongside a more macho police force, contains a lot of female colleagues, appointed by her. The Cornwell novels, however, recurrently discuss the loneliness and vulnerability of the successful woman in a masculine hierarchy and the ease with which she can be ousted from her professional role. Temporarily without 'her accouterments of authority', like a state car with stretchers (so that she can transport bodies), she realises, in *All That Remains*, that a young police officer is blocking her access to a murder scene because he cannot believe she could be the coroner: 'At a glance, I was a not-so-young yuppie running errands in her dark gray Mercedes, a distracted ash-blonde en route to the nearest shopping mall' (*ATR*, p. 6). In *Postmortem*, she feels the police and state machinery are out to undermine her authority as a woman scientist. The aversion of her closest collaborator, Sergeant Marino, for a female colleague is explicitly linked by Scarpetta to the sexism to which she was subjected in medical school.[22]

All That Remains concerns a powerful woman politician whom Scarpetta admires, the victim's mother. When the FBI feel threatened by her questions, this woman is thrown to the media wolves (*ATR*, p. 15). Scarpetta watches her fate in dismay, but is in such a vulnerable position herself with regard to the secretive intrigues of the male hierarchy which surrounds her that she does not get involved. In this way, she too is a woman outsider, pitched against a patriarchal organisation that has its own unspoken and unshared rules.

Cornwell's novels contain the clearest discussion of the position of the successful but lonely woman in a large male organisation, where female solidarity has as yet no significant oppositional power. Scarpetta is involved with police sections that do not trust each other sufficiently to pass on all the information they know, and are even capable of fabricating evidence. The insecurity of her status is reflected in the fact that in *All That Remains*, *Postmortem* (pp. 344–54), and *Cruel and Unusual* (p. 334), she worries that her computer has been broken into, and that vital case information has been tampered with (*ATR*, p. 129). Her professional status, moreover, is questioned in almost every novel as, for instance, criminals or conspirators manage to infiltrate her administration to plant evidence. Even her lover, FBI agent Mark James, seems to be conspiring and spying against her (*BE*, pp. 114–15; *ATR*, p. 118).

All three detectives are involved in a fight against patriarchy in the shape of large masculine organisations, and are supported in that fight by female lines of solidarity. Most explicit in the case of Warshawski, the oppositional forces are composed from corrupt, dangerous intersections of male politicians, big business, the mob, trade unions and even the police force.[23] Warshawski associates Corn Giant, the company she breaks into in *Tunnel Vision*, with Nazism (pp. 228, 230). The closed male culture of the police force ultimately leads to Michael Fury's downfall, when he cannot distance himself from a macho solidarity with lifelong, but now criminal friends (*BM*, 220). Opposed to these closed, patriarchal worlds, are the progressive forces of detectives, journalists, doctors and activists which effectively constitute a mutually supportive feminist network.

The Search for Knowledge

Ultimately, the strongest attraction of the crime genre for all writers and readers is the detective's possession of knowledge, information, and the 'truth'. All crime stories strain towards narrative closure connected with the acquisition of ultimate knowledge: who committed murder and why. Before this moment, however, the narrative entertains a number of alternative 'readings' of the clues available.

> The detective, whether male or female, is primarily a reader, but a reader more than ordinarily sensitive to nuances of meaning and to implications. The text presented to the detective is a fragmented one, with the detective taking on the task of both reading and writing this text: he/she takes the signs presented (clues) and, eventually, turns them into a coherent narrative, making the text of the crime whole again and the actual text whole and fully legible for the first time.[24]

Indeed, part of the attraction of the crime genre lies in its recognition of possible other readings, highlighting different clues and identifying different suspects with different motives. The frisson of the detective novel resides in the tension between these various potential 'realities' as the genre continuously enacts the search for information. At the end of the story, however, the detective narrows down all such possible 'readings' to one, and establishes narrative closure and final 'truth' at one and the same time; thus acting, in Sally Munt's words, as ultimate 'purveyor of meaning'.[25] It is as the theatre of the search for knowledge that the feminist detective novel, like any detective novel, presents the greatest attraction to its readers and authors. Importantly, however, the author of meaning is now a woman and the interpretation of signs and clues occurs from a feminist perspective. In such novels, knowledge and the detective's attitude toward it, is another aspect of the genre which is being redefined.

Feminist epistemologists have pointed to the gender polarities that deeply mark a phallocentric Western culture, which has tended to associate masculinity with the search for knowledge, and femininity with the object of this search. The mythological hero, Prometheus, is the main paradigm for this association, the tireless and transgressing seeker who discovered the sacred and divine knowledge of fire.[26] The male heroes of the crime novel, indeed, are latter-day incarnations of this epistemological subject, individuals who traverse the mean streets to reach understanding as they 'read' the conspiracy behind the incomplete clues available. Typically, and traditionally, the genre's *femme fatale* has been associated with the mystery, one of the signs to be read. In feminist detective fiction this gender binarity is undone, for it is the woman detective who assumes the role of reading signs and chasing knowledge. The ultimate authoritative reading is now a feminist one, privileging women's voices, offering a woman-centred interpretation rather than masculine readings. Knowledge is power, and the enactment of this epistemological power is at the heart of the feminist crime novel. However, the ideal of powerful knowledge is qualified in feminist detective novels, which – in line with Barbara Wilson's suggestive example (to which I referred earlier) – posit a subjective, involved, empathic type of knowing (different from the objective, distanced knowledge which is the masculine epistemological ideal).

On various levels, Grafton, Paretsky and Cornwell enact this powerful search for knowledge and information. As co-detective, the reader too acts out her own similar needs. To read these novels is to gather enticing information, about California homicide law (*I*, p. 19), or the PI's daily routine of researching insurance fraud or doing personnel checks. Indeed, Paretsky's prefaces outline the research conducted for each novel and acknowledge the specialists consulted. Her research typically involves 'police procedure, handgun use', corporate and technical matters, health issues, the construction of a skyscraper, and, in the final novel, photographs of the inaccessible tunnels under Chicago's business district (*TV*, p. vii).

The reader acquires equally fascinating information in Patricia Cornwell's novels concerning forensic science, the process of decomposition, the interpretation of wounds and animal bites on the body (*ATR*, p. 112), and the practice of autoerotic asphyxiation (*BF*, p. 58). Scarpetta considers physical symptoms like the potassium levels of the victims she examines, their vital brain reaction (*BF*, p. 23), or the 'doughy and dry' skin (that suggests the body was refrigerated after death, *BF*, p. 31). Undoubtedly, these selections of specialist information offered to the reader form an important attraction of the genre.

If the reader's desire for knowledge is hereby satisfied, the fictional detectives themselves eulogise the pleasures of gaining information and knowledge with an explicitness and enthusiasm seldom seen in the male detective novel. Kinsey Millhone is the most voluble on the subject. She is a detective because of her love of independence, and because she is 'curious at heart': 'I like sticking my nose in where it doesn't belong' (*G*, p. 189). When all the pieces of a puzzle fall into place, she is prone to unmitigated joy:

> We were getting close to the answer and I was beginning to fly. I could feel my brain cells doing a little tap dance of delight. I was half-skipping, excitement bubbling out of me as we crossed the street. 'I love information. I love information. Isn't this great? God, it's fun ...' (*G*, p. 277)

So too, when Warshawski discovers an important fact, she feels – using an odd hunting image – 'that primitive adrenaline jolt that lets you know you're getting close to the saber-toothed tiger' (*TS*, p. 201).[27] In *Tunnel Vision*, Warshawski's involvement in the crime plot stems purely from her uncheckable need to know. When a women's collective is unexpectedly successful in their bid for a city housing project (*TV*, p. 86), she feels she has to investigate, even to the point of endangering the bid. In this novel, Warshawski is persistently, and it would seem justifiedly, asked to stop her obsessive search for hidden conspiracy. Even the illegal scheme she does indeed uncover seems secondary to the emphasis on her need to know.

The Western male epistemological ideal is that of unemotional, objective, distanced knowledge. Barbara Wilson's critique of the genre focuses explicitly on the limitations of such an objective search; as her detective manhandles the facts to fit a theory and ignores the subjective, the interactive knowledge which can only be gathered by empathising with her 'suspects' and in the engaging of the detective's emotions. Paretsky and Cornwell go one step further as they remodel the genre, rejecting the concept of a detective who can remain unaffected by her research. The masculine ideal of objectified knowledge is exposed in their novels as a dangerous illusion. Scarpetta, for one, remembers the faces of every victim's parents (*ATR*, p. 23). Her work has influenced her, 'perched darkly over me, like a huge insatiable bird' (*BF*, p. 29). She grows increasingly less sanguine about the murders she reviews:

> [G]radually over the years something perniciously shifted. I began to dread working late at night, and was prone to bad dreams when terrible images from my life popped up in the slot machine of my unconscious (*BF*, p. 2).

As part of a typical police procedural, Scarpetta's detection method consists of detailed pathological examination and systematic documentation and requires professional impartiality. But this is combined, however, with an imaginative and empathic reconstruction of how the victim felt, how the culprit reasoned, of the emotional processes determining how and why the murder occurred. In this way, she empathically realises that the murderer in *All That Remains* was in fact frightened into a panic decision, because his victim suddenly reacted in an unexpected way (*ATR*, p. 252). In the same way, she deduces that the killer imagines himself to be a hunter. Equally, she imagines 'the existentialist terror Emily Steiner must have felt before she died' (*BF*, p. 72). On the basis of this additional knowledge, she typically retraces the murderer's or victim's steps to find previously overlooked clues (*ATR*, p. 363).

Of the three female detectives, Scarpetta's relationship to knowledge is the most intensely thematised and explored. On the one hand, her level of scientific 'knowledge' is extreme, including that of the processes of death and decay. As she mentions in *Body of Evidence*, Scarpetta literally knows every inch of the dead body (*BE*, p. 5).[28] But the level of her information goes further than that, involving her in a virtual dialogue with nature, which (as she represents it) has equally been damaged by the murder.

In *The Body Farm*, Scarpetta retraces the child victim's final walk, seeking out the disruption to the forest that has occurred because of the crime. It is as if the crime scene shares the quality of the living body, needing to cry out against the crime committed. In these novels, all signs of violence can ultimately be discovered in the pathologist's laboratory, for no violent act can occur without leaving a trace:

> I had worked enough violent crimes in my career to have learned one very important truth. A crime scene has a life of its own. It remembers trauma in soil, insects altered by body fluids, and plants trampled by feet. It loses its privacy just as any witness does, for no stone is left undisturbed, and the curious do not stop coming just because there are no further questions to ask. (*BF*, p. 114)

Likewise, under laboratory conditions, Scarpetta 'wondered what microscopic witnesses had been silenced' (*BF*, p. 32). Because of recent advances in the science of pathology, Scarpetta as a detective finds herself in a type of enclosed Holmesian world. Now, the smallest changes in nature or the victims' bodies can be researched to become a clue (*BF*, p. 96).

In this newly closed epistemological world, Cornwell elevates the knowledge-gathering of the detective to an almost mythical level of retribution and the fight against evil. Moreover, Scarpetta's knowledge is extreme, both visual and auditory: opening up the bodies she can see everything, while, moroever, the bodies on the autopsy table scream out to her. Talking about the criminal uses of duct tape, she says:

> I could not count the times I had peeled it from the mouths of people who were not allowed to scream until they were wheeled into my morgue. For it was only there the body could speak freely. It was only there someone cared about every awful thing that had been done. (*BF*, p. 196)

However, Scarpetta is finally far from the traditional Holmesian detective, for it is the *emotional* response to her analytic enquiries that Cornwell constantly foregrounds. Thus in *The Body Farm*, the pathologist becomes not just a detective, but one who has the ability to commune with the dead, and in this way to allow victims to be heard. The eponymous Body Farm is a rural university research centre into the processes of decomposition, where corpses have been left, some open to the elements and some in sheds, with cameras recording the changes after death:

> People like me intended no irreverence when we called it that, for no one respects the dead more than those of us who work with them and hear their silent stories. The purpose is to help the living. (*BF*, p. 316).

The farm is run by a Dr Lyall Shade: 'It was true he communed with the ghosts of people past through their flesh and bones and what they revealed as they lay for months on the ground' (*BF*, p. 317). During autopsies, the odours connected with death and postmortems must not be taken away by perfume, cigars or Vicks: 'Odors were as much a part of the language of the dead as scars and tattoos were' (*BF*, p. 321). When Scarpetta drives away from the Body Farm she looks back across the river and sees a truly mythical sight:

> At a bend in it I could see the top of the Farm's back fence peeking above trees, and I thought of the River Styx. I thought of crossing the water and ending up in that place as the husband and wife from our work had done. I thanked them in my mind, for the dead were silent armies I mustered to save us all. (*BF*, p. 325).

As a professional reader of the signs and traumas left on the victims' bodies, Scarpetta is the essential feminist detective in search of knowledge and information. She performs tasks that fly in the face of nature, opening up what must remain closed, and is in this sense a disrupter of the natural, obsessed by 'anatomical detail' (*ATR*, p. 36). But the representation of her profession in the novels ties in with the empathy which permits a different, more involved, closer, deeper knowledge than that of the male epistemological ideal.

In their detective novels, then, Paretsky, Grafton and Cornwell offer us an altered detective hero, now revised from a feminist perspective which rejects the aggressiveness, the separateness of the masculine hero subject, while revamping the dynamism, freedom and activity of the detective in defence of a feminist solidarity. Moreover, in different ways, and most clearly thematised by Cornwell, the three novelists point to the true attraction of the genre for its writers and readers: establishing a feminist purveyor of meaning, and a new relationship with knowledge.

Notes

1. Evelyne Keitel, 'The Woman's Private Eye View', *Amerikastudien/American Studies*, vol. 39, (1994) pp. 161–82.
2. In *Writing Beyond the Ending*, Rachel Blau DuPlessis discusses the very limited plot-lines open to the traditional novelistic heroine, bound for a story of romance, suffering, marriage or death, and the difficulty for twentieth-century women writers in breaking through these limitations. As a result, I have opted for 'woman hero' rather than the patriarchally tainted word 'heroine'. Rachel Blau DuPlessis, *Writing Beyond the Ending: Narrative Strategies of Twentieth-Century Women Writers* (Bloomington, Ind.: Indiana University Press, 1985).
3. Barbara Wilson, *Murder in the Collective* (London: The Women's Press, 1984), and *Sisters of the Road* (London: The Women's Press, 1987).
4. Kathleen Gregory Klein, *The Woman Detective: Gender and Genre* (Urbana and Chicago: University of Illinois Press, 1988), p. 212.
5. Sue Grafton, *B is for Burglar* (London: Pan Books/ Macmillan, 1990 [1985]), p. 1. Hereafter, quotations will be followed by an abbreviation of the title. In Sue Grafton's case, the alphabet letter of the book in question will be used, so *A*, *B*, *C* etc.
6. Sara Paretsky, *Burn Marks* (London: Virago, 1991 [1990]) p. 181; *Deadlock* (Harmondsworth, Middlesex: Penguin, 1987 [1984]), pp. 157–60; *Tunnel Vision* (Harmondsworth, Middlesex: Penguin, 1995 [1994]), pp. 312–29. Henceforth, *BM*, *D*, *TV* respectively.

7. Sue Grafton, *C is for Corpse* (London: Pan Books/ Macmillan, 1990 [1986]), p. 1.
8. Scott Christianson identifies this style as typical of hard-boiled detective fiction generally in 'Tough Talk and Wisecracks', in Glenwood Irons (ed.), *Gender, Language and Myth: Essays on Popular Narrative* (Toronto, Buffalo, London: University of Toronto Press, 1992), pp. 142–56.
9. Sara Paretsky, *Toxic Shock* (Harmondsworth, Middlesex: Penguin, 1988), pp. 146, 183. Original US title: *Blood Shot.* Henceforth, *TS*.
10 Patricia Cornwell, *The Body Farm* (London: Warner Books, 1995 [1994]), p. 131. Henceforth, *BF*.
11. Patricia Cornwell, *Cruel and Unusual* (London: Warner Books, 1994 [1993]), p. 17.
12. Patricia Cornwell, *All That Remains* (London: Warner Books, 1995 [1992]), p. 107. Henceforth, *ATR*.
13. Generally, both Paretsky and Grafton have their detectives clearly reject a macho stance with regards to unnecessary danger and violence. Millhone gets a bodyguard when she is threatened; Warshawski phones the police to check out her appartment when she feels threatened.
14. In fact, if the blurb of *A is for Alibi* is to be believed, Sue Grafton's Kinsey Millhone seems to have been born as a fantasy figure of power and protection for her author, who started writing feminist crime fiction after the breakdown of her marriage, to deflect her pent-up anger and frustration towards her ex-husband. Sue Grafton, *A is for Alibi* (London: Pan Books/Macmillan, 1990 [1986]).
15. Sue Grafton, *G is for Gumshoe* (New York: Fawcett Crest, 1993 [1990]), pp. 53–4.
16. Sue Grafton, *C is for Corpse*, p. 12; *D is for Deadbeat* (London: Pan Books/Macmillan, 1990 [1987]), p. 20; *I is for Innocent* (London: Pan Books/Macmillan, 1993 [1992]), p. 49.
17. Sara Paretsky, *Killing Orders* (Harmondsworth, Middlesex: Penguin, 1987 [1985]), p. 46. Henceforth, *KO*.
18. Sara Paretsky, *Guardian Angel* (Harmondsworth, Middlesex: Penguin, 1992) p. 17. Henceforth, *GA*.

19. See Richard E. Goodkin, 'Killing Order(s): Iphigenia and the Detection of Tragic Intertextuality', *Yale French Studies*, vol. 76 (1989), pp. 87–93.

20. Warshawski frequently seeks solace from Lotty Herschel, while Millhone has her work friend Vera, as well as Rosie, a Hungarian restaurant owner who even decides what she is going to eat.

21. V.I. is even contrasted with Contreras' daughter Ruthie: 'Every time I look at Ruthie it beats me how Clara and I coulda had a kid like that. When I see you it's like looking at my own flesh and blood' (*TS*, p. 165).

22. Patricia Cornwell, *Postmortem* (London: Warner Books, 1995 [1990]), pp. 84–5. Henceforth, *P*.

23. See Linda S. Wells, 'Popular Literature and Postmodernism: Sara Paretsky's Hard-Boiled Feminist', *Proteus: A Journal of Ideas*, vol. 6, no. 1 (Spring 1989), pp. 51–6, and Klein, *The Woman Detective*.

24. Maureen T. Reddy, *Sisters in Crime: Feminism and the Crime Novel* (New York: Continuum, 1988), p. 10.

25. Sally Munt, 'The Inverstigators: Lesbian Crime Fiction', in Susannah Radstone (ed.), *Sweet Dreams: Sexuality, Gender and Popular Fiction* (London: Lawrence & Wishart, 1988), pp. 91–119.

26. In mythology the female thirst for knowledge is dangerous and unbefitting. One mythological heroine, Pandora, is sent down to earth carrying a box or vase containing all the evils of the world. Unable to suppress her curiosity she opens the box and allows their escape.

27. A frequent motif in this genre is the niggling memory which finally slots into place. Thus, in *Toxic Shock*, Caroline's words 'triggered an elusive memory ... I frowned, trying to drag it to the surface, but I couldn't get hold of it' (p. 226). The obverse of this devotion to information is Warshawski and Millhone's sharing of a certain pride in their ability to cover up information, to lie. See *TS*, p. 52 and *D*, pp. 1, 5, 227; *I*, p. 280.

28. Patricia Cornwell, *Body of Evidence* (London: Warner Books, 1995 [1991]).

4

The Lesbian Thriller: Transgressive Investigations

Paulina Palmer

For Cambridge Lesbian Line

> Something nice about a murder where all women are involved.
>
> Mary Wings, *She Came in a Flash*

Crime Detection – and Contradictions

The development of the lesbian thriller in the past fifteen years is by no means an isolated phenomenon but forms part of the growth of feminist genre fiction in general. The tendency of women writers to reject the kind of narratives which are overtly political, and experiment, instead, with reworking popular genres, such as the thriller and science fiction, is a distinctive feature of the feminist literary scene in the 1980s and 1990s. The texts which they produce, while achieving success with readers, have provoked controversy among critics, especially those working in the academy. Champions of postmodern literary trends, such as Helen Carr, welcome the feminist experimentation with popular genres on the grounds that it encourages writers to mingle high and low forms of culture, thus challenging a hierarchical view of literature.[1] Carr argues, in addition, that a focus on genre foregrounds the significance of the contract between reader and writer, and promotes a recognition of the varied forms which women's writing can take. Other critics, however, such as Patricia Duncker, view the trend negatively. Duncker complains that a preoccupation with genre, as well as promoting commercialism, diminishes the writer's originality by imprisoning her within a set of rigid codes and conventions.[2]

A controversy of a similar kind revolves around the advent of the lesbian thriller. Barbara Wilson, a contributor to the genre whose novels are discussed here, regards it as an acceptable choice for writers who identify as lesbian. Commenting on the way that, throughout history, patriarchal forces have pressured women into assuming the role of silent 'victim or bystander of many nameless and hidden crimes such as battery, rape, sexual abuse',[3] she equates the appropriation of the figure of the sleuth by lesbian feminists with a demand for justice. She comments:

> To take the role of investigator means to open the doors upon silence, to name the crimes, to force the confessions, to call for justice and see justice done. And even, sometimes, to take justice into one's own hands ... For lesbian writers and readers, the appeal of novels of investigation also seems clear. Not only have most of us been silenced as women, but as lesbians another layer of silence surrounds our lives.[4]

Sally Munt and Gillian Whitlock, two critics working in the field of popular fiction, regard the lesbian thriller in a similarly positive light. Discussing the modifications which lesbian feminist perspectives have effected in the genre, they focus attention on the way that, by challenging traditional notions of authority and focusing attention on the interaction between the public and private dimensions of women's lives, writers successfully reformulate existing gender definitions and concepts of sexual politics.[5]

Other critics, however, disagree with their point of view. As well as directing at the thriller writer the predictable accusation of commercialism, they highlight the problematic features of the genre itself. There is, they note, a marked discrepancy between the masculinist values and roles which the classic thriller endorses, and those accepted by women. Marilyn Stasio elaborates this point:

> Women don't fit well into a trench coat and slouch hat ... The hard-boiled private eye is a special figure in American mythology. It's a staple of the myth that he should be a cynical loner, a man at odds with society and its values.

That's not something that women relate to. Women aren't
cynical loners – that's not how they like to work.[6]

This discrepancy of values, as we shall see, plays a significant
part in the construction of the lesbian thriller, constituting
either a stumbling block, or, alternatively, its strength. While
confronting the writer with an obstacle, it simultaneously
represents a challenge to her creative abilities, giving her the
opportunity to demonstrate her skills of parody and
transformation.

One of the few points on which detractors and defenders
of the lesbian thriller agree is that the problematic aspects of
the genre, as far as its use as a vehicle for lesbian themes is
concerned, hinge on the figure of the sleuth. To what degree
is this chauvinistic and arrogant loner, familiar to readers
from the detective fiction of Sir Arthur Conan Doyle and
Agatha Christie and the crime fiction of Raymond Chandler
and Dashiell Hammett, who prides himself on his
independence and exists to impose justice on a disordered
world, capable of transformation? Whether portrayed as the
rational interpreter of clues who, like Sherlock Holmes and
Hercule Poirot, regards the investigation as an intellectual
puzzle, or as the private eye whose interests are, like Marlowe's,
primarily psychological, his characterisation presents the
writer with difficulties. The privileges which his status as a
heterosexual male confers on him, along with his authoritative
position and ruthless behaviour, are at odds with the portrayal
of a lesbian protagonist. The woman who identifies as lesbian
does not enjoy these privileges and is likely to be socially
marginal. She is a member of an oppressed minority, and her
lifestyle, in the respect that it challenges patriarchal values and
conventions, tends to be regarded by the public as transgressive
and eccentric. And, while Christie's Miss Marple furnishes
the writer with an example of a female sleuth, her conservative
approach to sex and class makes her an inappropriate model
for the lesbian investigator.

The majority of writers of lesbian crime fiction, it is
interesting to note, rather than taking as their model the
British detective novel represented by the works of Conan
Doyle, Christie and Dorothy Sayers, base their texts on the

structures of the hard-boiled American crime novel, represented by the works of Chandler and Hammett. This choice of model, in addition to reflecting the American origins of feminist crime fiction, is attributable, as I argue elsewhere,[7] to the fact that the urban location and psychological focus of American crime fiction is more easily adapted to lesbian interests than is the frequently rural setting and emphasis on the 'puzzle' aspect of the crime associated with its British variant. It also reflects the fact that certain features of the sleuth's portrayal in American crime fiction lend themselves particularly well to lesbian reworking. The solitariness and air of defensiveness, displayed by Chandler's Marlowe, can be adapted, in the lesbian thriller, to the feelings of loneliness and sense of alienation which the woman who identifies as lesbian experiences in hetero-patriarchal society. The two figures, though differing in many respects, both see themselves as independent loners and, to a degree, social misfits. Another feature they have in common is a discrepancy between role and identity. Whereas the investigator in the American thriller, as commentators point out,[8] frequently adopts a social mask, concealing attributes of sensitivity and intelligence under a taciturn veneer, the lesbian, in order to negotiate encounters with the general public and avoid stigmatisation, often hides her sexual orientation under a heterosexual persona. The powers of observation displayed by the investigator in the American thriller in reconnoitring the urban scene and studying the behaviour of suspects are also applicable, with a degree of modification, to the figure of the lesbian who, living as she does on the margins of society, is accustomed to playing the role of observer and 'spy'. In the fiction of Mary Wings and Sarah Schulman, her observational skills take on, in addition, a tinge of sexual voyeurism.

However, other characteristics of the investigator in the American crime novel, such as his misogyny, ruthlessness and propensity to violence, are, as critics observe, distinctly unsuited to the portrayal of the lesbian – and writers employ a variety of strategies to modify his macho image. While preserving, to a degree, the aura of loner and individualist which surrounds him, they erase the more brutal attributes of his persona, in this way remodelling his character. To achieve this, they sometimes introduce a note of romance into the narrative and transform the murder investigation into a cooperative enterprise between the sleuth and her partner, as Wilson does in *Murder in the Collective* (1984).[9] They also highlight the contradictions of power/powerlessness, strength/vulnerability which, on account of her gender and sexual orientation, the lesbian investigator displays. The treatment of these contradictions differs from text to text. Emma Victor, the protagonist of Wings' *She Came Too Late* (1986), is, in her investigative role, as her name implies, a quick-witted and confident figure who vanquishes opposition and successfully tracks down the criminal. However, her gender makes her vulnerable to the dangers attendant on city life, such as assault and bouts of loneliness, and Wings goes out of her way to emphasise their debilitating effect. Kate Delafield, the lesbian policewoman assigned the role of sleuth in Katherine V. Forrest's *Murder at the Nightwood Bar* (1987), reveals ambiguities of a different kind. Her professional authority as a member of the Los Angeles police is undermined at times by insecurities and conflicts of loyalty relating to her sexual orientation – as on the occasion when she is required to investigate a murder perpetrated at the local lesbian bar. Being a lesbian cop, she discovers, is, from a political point of view, something of a paradox.

A particularly extreme example of the contraries of power/powerlessness is exemplified by the unnamed sleuth in Schulman's *After Delores* (1988). A waitress in a New York diner who, due to a disappointment in love, feels compelled to 'think about sad things',[10] she exists on the margins of society and suffers from fits of depression. With a gun in her hands, however, she experiences a sudden surge of power. As she comments, aggressively articulating the contradictions of her position:

> Everybody's always pushing me around or walking out, or not showing up or somehow not coming through. And I'm the worthless piece of trash that's hurting like hell because of it.
>
> It was just then that I jammed my hand into my jacket pocket and smashed my knuckles on a cold piece of metal.

> Then I remembered I had a gun in my possession. I could
> use it any time I chose ... I knew I didn't have to worry
> anymore, because the next time somebody went too far, I
> had the power to go further. I had a gun. (pp. 26–7)

Here, the contrast between the protagonist's abject feelings of
impotence and the sense of power which the gun confers, along
with her sudden disturbing swing of mood from self-pity to
elation, give an ambiguous note of menace and pathos to
Schulman's portrayal of the lesbian sleuth.

The complexity of the lesbian sleuth's position – one which,
as indicated above, is marked by conflicts and anomalies – is
accentuated by another device which writers employ to
foreground the problematic aspects of her situation. This is the
breaking-down of the division between the roles of the
investigator and the criminal by emphasising the connections
between the two figures. In utilising this, writers develop a
strategy employed by male writers such as Edgar Allan Poe,
Conan Doyle and John Le Carré, who sometimes portray the
criminal not as the polar opposite of the investigator but as
his alter ego and double.[11] Wings takes a similar course in *She
Came Too Late*. On first encountering Stacy Weldemeer, the
biologist whom she subsequently discovers to have perpetrated
the murder she is investigating, Emma Victor feels a sneaking
sense of affinity with her; she admits 'Our styles were
alarmingly similar.'[12] Kate Delafield, the police investigator in
Forrest's *Murder at the Nightwood Bar*, also reveals points of
resemblance with the female criminal whose identity she
tracks down. Here, both sleuth and criminal, though differing
in age and ideological attitudes, are portrayed as strong and
self-reliant. Both, moreover, though priding themselves on their
sense of morality and respect for law and order, are capable,
as Kate herself perceives, of committing an act of violence when
circumstances pressure them to do so.

The position of the lesbian sleuth is further complicated by
the fact that, rather than always siding with the police and
the legal establishment, the orthodox guardians of public
security, she is frequently depicted as critical of them on
account of the misogyny and racism they manifest. Wilson's
Murder in the Collective explores this issue in some detail,

highlighting the conflicts in which it can involve the investigator. Wilson's novel, as well as exploring the problems which feminists and socialists encounter in attempting to operate collective practices in a capitalist economy, brings together themes of race and gender by examining the oppressive treatment of Filipino immigrants to the US. The sleuth Pam Nilsen, on discovering that the perpetrators of the two crimes she is investigating are, in fact, members of the collectives in which she is involved and regarding their motives as just, refuses to take the conventional course and hand them over to the police. The latter have shown themselves, throughout, as insensitive to the situation of women and blacks. The unorthodox manner in which the investigation terminates is interesting from an ideological perspective, since it foregrounds the conflict between lesbian/feminist values and those of the patriarchal, white establishment.

In the thrillers of Forrest, Wilson and Wings, the perpetrator of the crime is portrayed as female, rather than male – and this has significant consequences. To start with, it enables writers to avoid tritely equating femininity with virtue and masculinity with vice, as is the case in certain less successful examples of the genre, such as as Val McDermid's *Report for Murder* (1987). In addition, as is fitting in the case of a lesbian text, it focuses attention very firmly on relationships and encounters *between women*. As Terry Castle points out, one of the achievements of lesbian fiction, in ideological terms, is to deconstruct 'the "canonical" triangular arrangement of male desire',[13] in which woman functions as an object of exchange or mediator between two men, that, till recently, has dominated Western literature. The lesbian novel, in fact, either substitutes a female-male-female triangle, or, in the case of a number of contemporary texts, erases the male term altogether. Forrest, Wilson and Wings all employ the latter, more radical option. By portraying the three key figures in the investigative scenario – the sleuth, the perpetrator of the crime, and (in the case of Forrest and Wings) the victim – as female, they place both the narrative and psychological interest of the text emphatically 'between women'.[14] In this respect, their texts differ from the design of the classic thriller, represented by the works of Conan Doyle, Chandler and Hammett, and its conventional sexual plotting. In classic crime fiction the investigator and the perpetrator of the crime are generally portrayed as male, with the third term in the triangle represented by a woman – more often than not in the ultra-passive role of corpse!

The portrayal of the lesbian sleuth, far from remaining static, has undergone a number of changes since the advent of the role in the early 1980s. Like characters in other lesbian genres,[15] her representation displays, with increasing frequency, the influence of postmodern perspectives. No longer is she depicted as an exemplary role model, as was the case with early figures such as Wilson's Pam Nilsen, whose political correctness and devotion to duty cause her to resemble a lesbian feminist version of a school prefect. On the contrary, in the fiction of Wings and Schulman she is represented as a 'subject', her identity and way of life a product of the fragmented discourses and sub-cultures of the contemporary urban scene. Differences emerge between the two writers' treatment of postmodern concepts of subjectivity. Wings' sleuth Emma Victor displays a strong degree of agency. Despite the occasional misadventure, which draws attention to her vulnerability and illustrates the precariousness with which she maintains her position of power, Emma successfully exploits the contradictions existing between the patriarchal establishment and minority lesbian/ feminist culture. Schulman, in contrast, treats these contradictions in a more disturbing manner. Her unnamed investigator, though managing to survive the ruthless climate of New York City and achieve a personal form of justice, experiences difficulty in interpreting and decoding the decentred and fractured world of American urban society. Her lack of agency, combined with her frequent emotional outbursts and the errors of judgement, are at odds with the attributes of self-control and perception which we expect from the figure of the sleuth. Other aspects of her situation are similarly unusual. Not only is she, like the majority of lesbian investigators, an amateur at the job, but she becomes involved in the search for the murderer of Marianne Walker (the disco dancer, whom she nicknames Punkette) by accident, rather than design. Her decision to track down her killer is motivated by passion, not reason.

As is typical of Schulman's unorthodox thriller, the discovery of the identity of the murderer, with which it concludes, depends not on skill but chance – and is the reverse of what both sleuth and reader expect. The sleuth discovers, to her surprise, that Charlotte and Beatriz, the two women involved in alternative theatre whom she initially regards as suspects, are innocent, and the murderer is, in fact, male. Having teased the reader into believing that the crime took place 'between women', Schulman unexpectedly reveals, at the last moment, that it did not. Similarly anticlimactic is the fact that the murderer, rather than being a central figure in the narrative, is insignificant and peripheral. This, as well as disappointing our expectations of a psychological struggle between the investigator and perpetrator of the crime, makes the murder and its investigation appear somehow random and pointless.

However, the conclusion which Schulman chooses to impose on her murder mystery, though disappointing in conventional terms, is, from the point of view of the themes which the novel treats, strikingly apt. As well as being convincing from a sociological point of view (the majority of urban crimes of violence are, in fact, committed by men), it accords with one of the novel's key motifs – the transforming power of fantasy. The sleuth's initial failure to identify the murderer as male, and her projection onto Charlotte and Beatriz of the role of killer, act as a metaphor for this. Led astray by her attraction to women and her addiction to sensationalist S/M scenarios, she mentally transforms the murder mystery into a lesbian romance, while ignoring, to her cost, the mundane but brutal facts of male violence which characterise American urban life.

Gender and Sexuality

The changes which have occurred in the portrayal of the sleuth in recent years, discussed above, have been accompanied by significant modifications in other areas of the lesbian thriller. While the social and political focus introduced by writers in the 1980s continues to inform the genre, the thriller has become increasingly an arena for the discussion of another pair of topics of particular interest to women who identify as lesbian or bisexual – gender and sexuality.

The lesbian thriller has, in fact, always been to the fore in the treatment of themes relating to sex. In the early 1980s, fears of promoting male voyeurism, combined with repressive tendencies in the lesbian feminist movement, frequently deterred writers from introducing explicit representations of sex in their novels. Even then, however, thriller writers such as Forrest and Wings, relying on the 'entertainment' dimension of the genre, focused attention on aspects of lesbian relationships, such as butch–femme role-play and power struggles between partners, the representation of which was regarded by some feminists as politically incorrect. Challenging the generally accepted model of lesbian attraction, they depicted 'difference', rather than 'identification', as the mainspring of sexual desire. In the present period a number of factors have helped to accentuate the focus on sex. The emergence of theorists such as Gayle Rubin and Joan Nestle, who champion the right of women to explore a variety of sexual practices in their lives and writing, along with the advent of Queer Politics, with its emphasis on a variety of transgressive sexualities and its problematising of a clearcut division between the categories 'gay' and 'straight', have served to give the topic of sexuality new prominence.[16] The influence of postmodern perspectives, which lesbian writers and theorists themselves have helped to articulate and popularise, have also brought it to the fore. Postmodern motifs which find expression in the lesbian thriller include the representation of the individual as the product of cultural and psychic drives, the portrayal of sexuality and subjectivity as produced through fantasy, and the representation of sexual identity and gender in terms of performance and masquerade. Ideas relating to the performative nature of gender lend themselves particularly well to fictional treatment. Wings, Wilson and Schulman approach them, as we shall see, from notably different perspectives.

The concept of gender as performance is chiefly associated with the theoretical writing of Judith Butler. Gender, Butler argues, rather than reflecting an essence, is constituted through a set of 'discursively constrained acts that produce the body through and within the categories of sex'.[17] A performative approach to gender is, of course, particularly pertinent to the discussion of lesbian and gay roles, and their connection with heterosexual ones. As Butler argues, butch/femme and gay roles do not, as is generally assumed to be the case, mirror original heterosexual identities but, on the contrary, have the effect of exposing and 'bringing into relief the utterly constructed status of the so-called heterosexual original'. They achieve this by introducing an element of excess and parody. Butler's analysis of gender roles leads her to conclude that 'gay is to straight *not* as copy is to original, but, rather, as copy is to copy. The parodic repetition of the "the original" ... reveals the original to be nothing other than a parody of the *idea* of the natural and the original' (p. 31).

Another version of 'gender as performance', one which concentrates on exploring femininity and its construction, is put forward by the French theorist Luce Irigaray. Basing her analysis on the concept of the feminine masquerade associated in psychoanalysis with Joan Rivière, Irigaray describes the masquerade as the acting out by the female subject of a set of male-defined roles and scripts. The masquerade represents, in her words: 'What women do in order to recuperate some element of desire, to participate in man's desire, but at the price of renouncing their own.'[18] Irigaray, however, does not leave the matter there, with woman as the passive victim of male scripting. She recommends a strategy of resistance which women can employ to challenge male-defined roles. This, she terms, 'playing with mimesis' (pp. 76–7). By parodically mimicking conventional images of femininity, and introducing into their performance a note of 'excess', women, Irigaray argues, can expose their inauthenticity, and, at the same time, assume a degree of agency.

A focus on the performative aspect of gender, far from being out of place in the thriller, develops certain themes traditionally associated with the genre. It creates a contemporary variation on the topics of role-play and disguise which are, of course, standard motifs in mainstream crime fiction. Writers of lesbian crime fiction inventively bring together themes of disguise and sexual role-play.

The connection between role-play in the sexual sense, and disguise as a cover for crime investigation, is exemplified in Wings' *She Came Too Late*. The verb 'play' is frequently on

Emma's lips, linking the idea of amusement with role and performance. On being asked by the waiter to taste the wine when dining at a restaurant with the murder victim's flatmate, she humorously remarks, 'I guessed I was playing the butch that night' (p. 53). Sexual roles, and their construction, are, as this quotation indicates, key themes in the novel. In keeping with postmodern approaches, encounters between women, both sexual and social, are described in terms of dominant/ submissive positions, but these positions, rather than being represented in an essentialist light, are described as shifting and interchangeable. The interaction between the two is frequently articulated by reference to dress and costume. Although Emma generally dresses in the androgynous or butch style which has become the accepted image for lesbians in the Western world, she is perfectly capable of playing a feminine role when her investigative activities so require. Clothes which are excessively feminine in style are associated, it is interesting to note, with masquerade and disguise. This is apparent from the episode when Emma irons the elaborate dress (purchased cheaply at a charity shop!) which she intends to use as cover to infiltrate a society party to pursue her investigative activities. Complaining of the difficulty which she experiences in pressing the garment, she comments:

> The dress had seen better days: pressing it flat was like trying to iron an origami bird. And the press didn't set; just as I completed one shoulder, I'd be wrinkling the other. Once I had it on I was afraid to sit down in it. I might as well wear a paper envelope.
>
>   I put on the black stockings, and some stilettos completed the disguise. When I noticed the little black hairs poking through the stockings I peeled them off and sat on the bathtub and shaved my legs. (p. 89)

The word 'disguise', employed in this passage, carries two different meanings. In addition to signifying the assumption of a false persona for purposes of deception (the meaning it generally assumes in crime fiction), it also denotes the feminine masquerade, in the Irigarayan sense, which woman performs in enacting male-defined scripts and roles. In ironing the dress and putting it on, Emma brings together both meanings of the term. She simultaneously assumes a disguise and plays with mimesis. By dressing up in an ultra-feminine manner and parodically mimicking woman's archetypal role as decorative spectacle, she exposes its artifice and inauthenticity. A note of parody and excess is clearly apparent in the passage. It is audible in Wings' allusion to the difficulty which Emma encounters in ironing the dress ('pressing it flat was like trying to iron an origami bird') and in the restrictions which wearing it imposes on her movements ('I was afraid to sit down in it'). It is also reflected in the unglamorous reference to 'the little black hairs poking through the stockings' which, in order to perform the feminine masquerade successfully, Emma feels forced to shave. And, with the aim of reminding the reader that the dress is merely a disguise and alerting her to the inauthenticity of the image it represents, Wings concludes the episode by portraying Emma don an item of clothing which carries butch connotations and acts as a signifier of female power; Emma tells the reader:

> I had no conceivable jacket to complete my ensemble. So I shrugged on my leather flying jacket, the battered brown skin feeling appropriately silly above the flaring skirt. I felt like Joan Crawford wearing a dead cow. (pp. 89–90)

The incongruous appearance of the leather flying jacket subverts Emma's image as decorative icon, transforming her, so she feels, into its opposite: a figure who transgresses the conventional feminine role and is thus typecast as eccentric and weird ('Joan Crawford wearing a dead cow'). The bizarre nature of the image serves to remind the reader of the degrading roles which homophobic society traditionally assigns to the lesbian – freak and monster.

In addition to disguise, other motifs from the classic thriller acquire sexual connotations in Wings' novel. The sleuth's propensity for voyeurism, reflected in the observation of clues and the scrutiny of suspects, assumes erotic significance when Emma, appropriating the male 'look', gazes with desire at her lover Frances. The power-struggles which conventionally take place between murderer and victim, sleuth and suspect, also take on sexual significance. Emma's lovemaking with her girlfriend Frances takes the form of an interplay between dominant/submissive positions, with Wings introducing references to S/M.

In contrast to Wings, who employs reference to the performative aspects of gender to expose the artifice of gender roles and examine power relations between women, Wilson utilises it in *Gaudí Afternoon* (1990) to construct a social comedy of mistaken identities. *Gaudí Afternoon* opens with Cassandra Reilly, translator and private eye, being commissioned by Frankie Stevens to travel to Barcelona and track down the whereabouts of her errant husband Ben. Frankie, however, fails to divulge the unconventional aspects of their sexuality. She herself, in fact, is a male-to-female transsexual while her 'husband' Ben (Bernadette) is a butch lesbian. Having married young and produced a child, they subsequently found fulfilment in less orthodox identities and engineered a change of sex role. Humour arises from the fact that Cassandra, though a fluent translator of Spanish, notably fails to 'translate' and decipher the complexities of her client's situation. On arriving in Barcelona she makes a series of comic errors, mistaking Hamilton, a friend of the couple, for Ben, and Ben for a friend. Though priding herself on her lesbian lifestyle and her sophisticated understanding of sex, she emerges, unlike the investigator in the classic thriller, as a naive figure who, initially, is thoroughly bemused by the sexual permutations and psychological conundrums of the gender-bending scenario in which she finds herself involved. As she comments:

It was as if I was at a masquerade ball and everyone, at the very same moment, lifted their masks, and I saw gender for what it was, something that stood between us and our true selves. Something that one could take off and put on at will. Something that was, strangely, like a game.[19]

One of the most inventive representations of the performative aspects of gender occurs in Schulman's *After Delores*. Here, an emphasis on role-play, in addition to being a means to explore power relations between women, facilitates an investigation into the links between sex and fantasy. The urban environment, which furnishes the novel's setting, is established on the opening page as a surreal milieu characterised by illusion and transformation. In an attempt to escape the ghost of her faithless lover Delores, which she feels is haunting her apartment, the sleuth walks out into the street where, with the snow falling, 'the sky became sheets of clear plastic, ... turning the city into a night of transparent corridors' (p. 1). She enters a basement where a gay party is taking place – and further transformations occur. The 'winter night that had been walls turned into men and women dancing together and by themselves' (p. 1). Many of the characters whom she encounters in her search for Punkette's murderer live out their fantasies, both personal and professional, by adopting false personae. Priscilla, who gives her the gun which she employs to achieve justice, masquerades as Elvis Presley's wife, while Delores' new girlfriend changes her name to Mary Sunshine when she lands herself a prestigious post with Vogue magazine. Delores herself exists for the reader more as an image in the sleuth's head, on which she projects her personal passions and obsessions, than as an actual character, thus foregrounding the connections between love and fantasy. As the sleuth ruefully comments, 'You always fall for someone thinking they're something they're not. Sometimes I think that fashion was made for Delores, because it's so dependent on illusion' (p. 11).

Charlotte and her lover Beatriz, the couple working in alternative theatre whom the sleuth initially regards as suspects, exemplify similar connections for, as Charlotte herself confesses, they are both inveterate liars. Their propensity for lying and pretence, far from alienating the sleuth, serves to bind her more closely to them, since it feeds her craving for emotional scenarios, in this case spiced with an element of S/M. As she smugly comments, congratulating herself on her masochistic attachment to the couple, 'Their lies enabled them to keep a passionate relationship. I was one of them now. I was so evil. I was in love with them' (p. 126).

A pleasurable, though dangerous, aspect of Charlotte's and Beatriz' involvement in the duplicitous world of 'theatre' is that it has the effect of blurring the distinction between fact and fiction. On first seeing Charlotte on stage, the sleuth becomes so engrossed in the scene of lesbian self-humiliation she is acting that she mistakes the performance for real life: 'It was only when she finished that I remembered it wasn't real. I felt like a spy in a private conversation, and when the conversation was over, I had a stake in it' (p. 36).

The image of the spy, introduced in the episode in the theatre cited above, recurs in a subsequent one, where it is transferred to an intimate, domestic setting. Peering through the peephole in the door to the apartment where Charlotte and Beatriz live, the sleuth surreptitiously watches the couple perform a love scene – and this time, it is for real. She describes how: 'The light was out in the hallway, so I stood, like a thief in the night, like a traitor committing espionage. I looked in and they were naked. Charlotte sitting strong and beautiful on a kitchen chair with her arms round Beatriz's tiny waist ...' (p. 126).

Schulman's reference to 'the spy' and 'the traitor committing espionage', as well as relating the novel to the genre of spy fiction, also forges a connection between homosexuality and espionage, one common in fiction and politics. The two are related not only on a literal plane, in the respect that some spies, like the members of the Cambridge Apostles, are either homosexual or typecast as such, but also on a metaphorical one. The position of the closet lesbian or homosexual who conceals her/his sexual orientation under a heterosexual mask is sometimes compared to the duplicitous role played by 'the double agent', a figure who, while pretending to work for one political regime, in fact works for 'the enemy'. In portraying her lesbian protagonist succumbing to voyeuristic desires and guiltily admitting to playing, as she she puts it, the roles of 'spy ' and 'traitor', Schulman constructs her as 'abject'. Julia Kristeva, listing individuals who exemplify the concept of abjection in the respect that they 'disturb identity, system, order' by playing a hypocritical role in political or moral life, includes in her list 'the traitor, the liar, the criminal with a good conscience'.[20] Schulman's emphasis on her protagonist's abject position highlights the perverse nature of her voyeuristic pleasures and is at odds with the heroic role conventionally assigned to the investigator. Instead of portraying her as an agent for the restoration of order, Schulman depicts her, in the episodes treating her relations with Charlotte and Beatriz, as dominated by passion and sexual fantasy.

The City Transformed

In re-creating the conventional characters associated with the thriller and introducing new themes into this popular form of writing, writers of lesbian crime fiction also become involved in transforming the location which furnishes its context – the urban environment, the atmospheric description of which helps to account for the popularity of the genre. The 'mean streets' of the American city which the private eye frequents appear very different when viewed through female eyes instead of male ones,[21] and the gendered vision of the lesbian investigator gives an exceptionally vivid insight into both the pleasures and the dangers with which an urban location confronts women.

The ambiguous nature of the modern city, and the forces it involves, have been amply charted by critics. Contemporary urban experience, Marshall Berman observes, places us in 'an environment that promises us adventure, power, joy, growth, transformation of ourselves and the world – and, at the same time, that threatens to destroy everything we have, everything we know, everything we are'.[22] While uniting people in an enclosed space, the city simultaneously comprises an assortment of fragmented groups and lifestyles, reflecting differences of race, class and sexual orientation. Its unity is, in this sense, illusory and paradoxical for, like the experience of modernity itself, it 'shatters into a multitude of fragments' (p. 17).

The contradictions with which the city presents women, particularly those who identify as lesbian or bisexual, are especially acute. On the one hand, it represents a place of opportunity, both personal and professional. It offers an escape route from the restrictions of the family unit, in which women have traditionally been enclosed, and, in contrast to the village or provincial town, affords the individual the pleasures of self-discovery combined with the protection of anonymity. While opening up avenues for paid employment, it gives scope for a social life based on entertainment centres and the workplace. On the other hand, however, the city is also a place of danger. The individual, if she succeeds in steering clear of assault and sexual harassment, may fall prey to the ills of poverty, poor housing or loneliness. And a lesbian lifestyle, while providing entry to an alternative world of women's groups and clubs, is achieved at the cost of vulnerability. As the critic Elizabeth Wilson, commenting on this aspect of city life, points out:

> Lesbians and gay men created communities or 'ghettos' both for safety and for a sense of identity. Urban life provided a space in which subcultures could flourish and create their own identities, yet the more visible and confident they became, the more vulnerable that made them to surveillance and containment.[23]

The antithetical facets of city life, summarised above, as well as providing the setting for the lesbian thriller, also furnish its themes. A standard episode in works of lesbian crime fiction, one which frequent repetition has made conventional, is the portrayal of the sleuth driving alone along the freeway and, safely cocooned in her car, contemplating the view she sees through the windscreen. Barbara Wilson's *Sisters of the Road*, an example of fiction of debate[24] set in Seattle which discusses the topic of prostitution, opens with just such a scene. Driving along the Pacific Highway South, colloquially known as the 'Sea-Tac Strip', the sleuth Pam Nilsen alerts us to the dangers that the area holds for women: 'The street', she thinks grimly, 'was so often mentioned as "the last place seen". The last place a girl or young woman had been seen before she turned up as a heap of bones and teeth to be identified in some wooded, desolate spot nearby.' [25] The association of the city with violence, with woman predictably assigned the role of victim, is, however, countered in other passages where Pam acknowledges its attractions. In a subsequent episode, where she walks through the red light district in search of clues to the murder of a teenage prostitute, her perspective is considerably more complex. Identifying with the teenage murder victim, she recognises the allure which an urban environment holds for the young, and experiences at first hand the air of 'sexual energy, the danger, the excitement. The way the music was bringing back memories of reckless sexy new kinds of feeling. The way the cold air felt like freedom downtown at night' (p. 53).

In Wings' *She Came Too Late* the sleuth's drive along the highway is positioned at a later point in the narrative, after Emma has discovered the corpse of the murder victim and embarked on the search for her killer. Her train of thought commences on a positive note, with reference to romantic encounters, but becomes increasingly gloomy as she envisages the acts of male violence in which, as a member of the Women's Hotline, she knows such meetings all too often terminate:

> I concentrated on the heavy flow of Friday night traffic. I always wondered what people were doing, where they were going, as I saw the faces briefly illuminated by passing headlights in the streaming freeway. Most people were alone in the cars, which made me think they were going to meet someone. It was not altogether a lonely thought, sharing the road with people on their way to meeting someone. It's just that I knew what the weekend staff at Women's Hotline were dealing with. Weekends were the busiest, ugliest times. (p. 51)

She Came Too Late, in addition to registering the contradictions which an urban lifestyle holds for heterosexual women, gives an illuminating insight into the problems with which it confronts lesbians. As Emma recognises, since the period of the 1960s political and social gains have certainly been achieved. The women's movement has promoted the establishing of various support groups and women's centres, while the commercial scene is also flourishing. The Franca Club, which Emma visits, is frequented, she notes, not only by women who identify as lesbian but by married bisexuals who flock to the place in search of sexual diversion. As a lesbian visitor to the club humorously remarks:

> This place is becoming a real amusement park for the ladies from the suburbs. The male strip joints they show on the

tube are all for gay boys anyway, and the gals are getting
tired of hard on soft anyway. It only leads in one direction.
(p. 39)

However, as Wings takes pains to emphasise, this veneer of
success and frivolity in the lesbian/feminist scene represents
only one side of the coin. The other gives a bleaker picture.
With the economic situation deteriorating, funding for
women's support agencies is in the process of drying up, and,
as a consequence, many are forced to close. And while lesbians
are in demand in the closeted world of the club, little
improvement has occurred in their public or professional
status. Coming out, whether one is a pop star or a lawyer, is
a risky business since it frequently results in scandal or dismissal
from work. And the married bisexual, though happy to enjoy
a one-night stand, is seldom willing to make a commitment
either to a particular woman or to feminist politics.

Schulman's *After Delores*, like *She Came Too Late*, achieves
much of its interest and vitality from its detailed delineation
of women's complex and contradictory position in American
urban life. However, in contrast to Wings, who locates her
narrative in Boston and adopts a chiefly middle-class focus,
Schulman centres on New York and draws her characters from
the underprivileged mass of casual workers and drop-outs
who people the city. Her image of urban life, represented from
the drink-hazed perspective of her unnamed sleuth, highlights
extremes. While convincingly evoking the heady excitement
of the place, it also concentrates attention on its menacing side
– as in the following scary account of a ride on the subway:

> When the guy started screaming on the subway to Penn
> station, I felt for Priscilla's gun in the pocket of my spring
> coat. When the second guy started screaming in the Amtrak
> waiting room, I felt it again. The terminal reeked of urine-
> soaked clothing and roasting frankfurters. It was revolting.
> Danger lurked everywhere. (p. 22)

The murder investigation hinges, in the final chapters, on the
sleuth's first-hand understanding of woman's role as sexual
commodity, and on her ability to decipher the intricate

semiotics of urban life, in contrast to the ignorant and misogynistic attitude of the police. The murder victim Punkette, worked as a dancer in a bar in Newark. When she informed the police that a man had phoned her apartment threatening to kill her, the officer to whom she spoke refused to take her statement seriously. Assuming her to be a call-girl, he rejected her claim that she could identify the man's voice on the grounds that she 'talks to lots of men' (p. 156). The sleuth, however, is certain that Punkette was not a call-girl and knows that the statement she made is the truth. Not only did Punkette identify as lesbian but the fact that she made the effort to work out of town is proof of her decision, as the sleuth puts it, to 'preserve some distinct sense of limit' as regards sex. As the sleuth wryly observes,

> New Jersey is a very sweaty state. The only reason girls truck out there to dance anyway is because they don't have to go topless like they do in the city and for the ones trying hard to maintain some distinct sense of limit, it's worth the commute. (p. 23)

Here, as in other episodes in the novel, the recognition of woman's sexual commodification and the degradation it involves, is accompanied by an emphasis on the acts of resistance, albeit mundane and limited, which individual women perform in an effort to preserve some sense of personal integrity.

The city, as well as providing the context for lesbian crime fiction and furnishing its themes, also assumes, in certain texts, symbolic significance. In Barbara Wilson's novels, reference to architecture and urban development highlights the constructed aspect of culture and, by implication, that of the institutions and roles related to it. In *Gaudí Afternoon* the convoluted design of the cathedral of Sagrada Família becomes, unexpectedly, an image for the grotesque facets of the Christian concept of the family. Contemplating the edifice, Cassandra thinks, 'It was monumentally, phenomenally bizarre, like the Christian notion of family itself, a combination of organic and tortured form' (p. 81).

Representations of the urban scene in lesbian crime fiction appear, on occasion, self-reflexive since they draw attention to the focus on transformation and change which is a feature of the lesbian thriller itself. Chapter 16 of *Sisters of the Road* opens with Pam Nilsen describing the alterations which have taken place in her home town Seattle since her childhood, and envisaging possible future ones. She observes 'whole blocks of two storey buildings boarded up and unoccupied, scheduled for demolition. The gentrification of the Market was creeping up First Avenue, like a pretty disease, remodelling and refurbishing anything and everything ...' (p. 72). The episode serves to remind both her and the reader that the contemporary world we live in is one of change, where everything, including constructs of sexuality and attitudes to gender and sexual orientation, are continually shifting and in a state of perpetual flux.

The lesbian thriller, in addition to representing, as Wilson herself argues, a breaking of the silence and a demand for justice on the part of one particular social group, introduces the reader to a variety of social and psychological issues. Though focusing increasingly on interests of a postmodern kind, it has by no means lost the political vigour which characterised the genre in its early stages but continues, in a manner likely to ensure its survival, to successfully interrelate sexual politics with entertainment.

Notes

1. Helen Carr (ed.), *From My Guy to Sci Fi: Genre and Women's Writing in the Postmodern World* (London: Pandora, 1989), pp. 5–10.
2. Patricia Duncker, *Sisters and Strangers: An Introduction to Contemporary Feminist Fiction* (Oxford: Blackwell, 1992), pp. 90–101, 124–5.
3. Barbara Wilson, 'The Outside Edge: Lesbian Mysteries' in Liz Gibbs (ed.), *Daring to Dissent: Lesbian Culture from Margin to Mainstream* (London: Cassell, 1994), p. 222.
4. Ibid.
5. See Sally Munt, *Murder by the Book: Feminism and the Crime Novel* (London: Routledge, 1994), pp. 170–89; and Gillian

Whitlock, '"Cop it Sweet": Lesbian Crime Fiction', in Diane Hamer and Belinda Budge (eds), *The Good, the Bad and the Gorgeous: Popular Culture's Romance with Lesbianism* (London: Pandora, 1994), pp. 109–11.

6. Marilyn Stasio, 'Lady Gumshoes: boiled less hard', *New York Times Book Review*, 28 April, 1985, p. 1, quoted by Anne Cranny-Francis in *Feminist Fiction: Feminist Uses of Generic Fiction* (Cambridge: Polity Press, 1990), p. 143.

7. See Paulina Palmer, 'The Lesbian Feminist Thriller and Detective Novel' in Elaine Hobby and Chris White (eds), *What Lesbians Do in Books* (London: Women's Press, 1991), p. 12.

8. See Stephen Knight, '"A Hard Cheerfulness": An Introduction to Raymond Chandler' in Brian Docherty (ed.), *American Crime Fiction: Studies in the Genre* (Basingstoke: Macmillan, 1988), pp. 80–2.

9. For detailed reference to this strategy, see Palmer, *Contemporary Lesbian Writing: Dreams, Desire, Difference* (Buckingham: Open University Press, 1993), pp. 70–1.

10. Sarah Schulman, *After Delores* (London: Sheba Feminist Publishers, 1990 [1988]), p. 9. Subsequent references are to this edition and are in the text. Munt's *Murder by the Book* includes an informative critique of the novel.

11. For discussion of this device, see Christopher Rollason, 'The Detective Myth in Edgar Allan Poe's Dupin Trilogy', in Docherty (ed.), *American Crime Fiction*, pp. 7–9.

12. Mary Wings, *She Came Too Late* (London: Women's Press, 1986), p. 109. Subsequent references are to this edition and are in the text.

13. Terry Castle, 'Sylvia Townsend Warner and the Counterplot of Lesbian Fiction' in Joseph Bristow (ed.), *Sexual Sameness: Textual Differences in Lesbian and Gay Writing* (London: Routledge, 1992), p. 132.

14. Castle's analysis of lesbian fiction develops ideas explored by Eve Kosofsky Sedgwick in *Between Men: English Literature and Male Homosocial Desire* (New York: Columbia University Press, 1985).

15. Examples occur in the fiction of Jeanette Winterson and Jane DeLynn.

16. For reference to changing concepts of lesbian sexuality and the influence of Queer Politics, see Cherry Smyth, *Lesbians Talk Queer Notions* (London: Scarlet Press, 1992).

17. Judith Butler, *Gender Trouble: Feminism and the Subversion of Identity* (London: Routledge, 1990), p. x. Subsequent references are to this edition and are in the text.

18. Luce Irigaray, *This Sex Which Is Not One*, trans. Catherine Porter with Carolyn Burke (New York: Cornell University Press, 1985), p. 133. (*Ce Sexe qui n'en est pas un,* Paris: Minuit, 1977) Subsequent references are to the English translation and are in the text.

19. Barbara Wilson, *Gaudí Afternoon* (London: Virago, 1991 [1990]), p. 77. Subsequent references are to this edition and are in the text.

20. Julia Kristeva, *Powers of Horror: An Essay on Abjection*, trans. Leon S. Roudiez (New York, Columbia University Press, 1982), p. 4.

21. Raymond Chandler, 'The Simple Art of Murder' in *Pearls Are a Nuisance* (Harmondsworth, Middlesex: Penguin, 1964), p. 198.

22. Marshall Berman, *All That is Solid Melts into Air: The Experience of Modernity* (London: Verso, 1983 [1982]), p. 15.

23. Elizabeth Wilson, *The Sphinx in the City: Urban Life, the Control of Disorder, and Women* (London: Virago, 1991), p. 120.

24. For clarification of this term see Palmer, 'The Lesbian Thriller: Crimes, Clues and Contradictions' in Gabriele Griffin (ed.), *Outwrite: Lesbianism and Popular Culture* (London: Pluto, 1993), pp. 100–5.

25. Barbara Wilson, *Sisters of the Road* (London: Women's Press, 1986), p. 5. Subsequent references are to this edition and are in the text.

5

Policing the Margins: Barbara Wilson's *Gaudí Afternoon* and *Troubles in Transylvania*

Christopher Gair

When is a crime novel not a crime novel? What kinds of crime provide suitable material for the genre? And what are the limits to acceptable forms of closure in crime fiction? Indeed, does 'closure', in its traditional sense, retain a place in the working vocabulary of the crime writer or critic in a climate where the boundaries between criminal and detective, centre and margin, and right and wrong have been either entirely erased or else become increasingly unclear, and where the possibility of final comprehension of the world seems remote?

These and other questions occurred to me whilst reading Barbara Wilson's novels *Gaudí Afternoon* (1990) and *Troubles in Transylvania* (1993). Given that Wilson already has a proven track record in crime fiction via her Pam Nilsen trilogy,[1] that the books are published in the United Kingdom as part of the Virago Crime series, and that *Gaudí Afternoon* won the Crime Writers' Association Award for the best mystery set in Europe and the Lambda Literary Award for the Best Lesbian Mystery 1991, it may seem strange to ponder such issues here. And yet, in keeping with a postmodern sensibility within which representation itself has become ever more fragmentary, *Gaudí Afternoon*, in particular, seems only peripherally concerned with what has conventionally been defined as 'crime', and even then only as one strand within an infinite network of textuality incorporating not only novels and films, but also architecture, sexual politics and the border between the cultures of East and West. As it explores such issues, the book blurs the oppositions – fact and fiction, self and other, male and female, mother and father, 'normal' and 'deviant' – upon which most earlier crime fiction and, more widely, Western rationalism has depended.

Attempting to extract the crime segments of *Gaudí Afternoon* is of only limited use in approaching my introductory questions. Initially, it appears that Wilson plans to offer us a fairly standard retelling of the archetypal hard-boiled detective novel. Cassandra Reilly, the narrator-protagonist of both books, is hired by a glamorous American woman (Frankie) to find her ex-husband in Barcelona. In Chandleresque fashion, however, one thing leads to another and Reilly rapidly becomes embroiled in a more complex investigation. Her employer turns out to be a transsexual, and his/her ex-husband, Ben, is in fact a woman, Frankie's ex-*wife*. The often bewildering plot revolves around the repeated kidnapping of their young daughter, Delilah, by both parents (separately) and by a series of other surrogate mothers, and Cassandra is never entirely certain whom she is pursuing. Given the fact that the adults all appear to have what they imagine to be Delilah's best interests at stake, and that no one is murdered or violently assaulted during the course of the investigation, it might be felt that the action fails to live up to its generic promise, especially since readers of the Pam Nilsen mysteries will be aware of Wilson's feminist redeployment of murder and suspense as generic tools in those novels.[2] Even the self-conscious quotation from earlier crime fiction, such as when Cassandra claims to be Brigid O'Shaughnessy,[3] whilst marking out a genealogical heritage for such slippery and possibly depthless constructs of identity, are finally something of a red herring since they are more than matched by a host of allusions to other icons of popular culture. Likewise, the secondary series of crimes – the plethora of threats posed by pickpockets and bag-snatchers, and a spate of thefts carried out by German criminals disguised as participants at a conference of the European Society for Organ Transplantation – fits the same theme of illusion and reality, but scarcely registers as typical subject matter for the genre. Even in *Troubles in Transylvania*, where we are given a murder, the victim is 89 and inseparable from the already dead Ceauşescu regime, and is eased on his way rather than being brutally silenced in his prime.

It might well be argued that Wilson is indeed conforming with the logic of many earlier examples of crime fiction in a number of ways. We need only think back to Poe's 'Murders in the Rue Morgue' (1841) for a text where the detective proves that *no* central crime has been committed, since the brutal killing of two women was perpetrated by an orang-utan rather than a person. As with Wilson's novel, Poe's tale highlights the 'criminality' inherent to a society – xenophobia, imperialism, for example – through the fictional exploration of an improbable set of occurrences. In 'The Purloined Letter' (1845) Poe goes further still, unsettling the distinctions between detective and criminal within a narrative that could well be read as 'postmodern'.[4] Similarly, the above-mentioned incorporation of a quotation from *The Maltese Falcon* not only hints at the disparity between appearance and actuality in persons and objects in both texts, but also reminds us that the notion that there may be nothing beneath surface glitter is not a contemporary invention. Even the theme of cross-dressing was anticipated in the late nineteenth century in Mark Twain's *Pudd'nhead Wilson* and Mary Hatch's *The Strange Disappearance of Eugene Comstocks*.

More recently, Chester Himes' Harlem novels have further problematised the differences between criminal and detective, centre and margin, both through their representation of two law-breaking (and terrifying) yet justice-seeking black cops, and through the tension between the competing needs to expose social injustice and racial inequality on the one hand, and to have morally satisfying textual resolutions based on the re-establishment of a previously existing stable social order on the other. In all the above examples, either through choice or necessity, the detectives are marginal figures: Dupin, the nocturnal scholar and walker; Wilson, the victim of his own half-a-dog joke; Spade, the ambiguous misfit; Coffin Ed and Gravedigger, the black Harlem cops who commute from the suburbs. Finally, it could be proposed that Wilson's intertextual allusions (which, as we shall see, provide the key to an understanding of *Gaudí Afternoon*) mirror other, earlier postmodernist detective fiction. For example, Paul Auster's *New York Trilogy* (1987) also subverts definitions of crime, identity and genre through its own playful deconstruction of persons and their worlds. Auster, too, incorporates a vast array of literary 'voices' within his texts, replacing the distinctive modernist styles of Chandler and Hammett with a polyphonous collage of literary criticism, social comment, plots plagiarised from nineteenth-century American literature, and a wide range of other 'sources'.

And yet, it would, I think, be a mistake to leap to the conclusion that Wilson has merely leaped upon the postmodern bandwagon. Although, like Auster's, her novel is composed of an assemblage of different voices, and features such familiar devices as the novel-within-a-novel, the effortless juxtaposition of 'popular' and 'high' art forms, and the interrogation of the dominant master narratives of both genre and gender, *Gaudí Afternoon* may finally argue that there are underlying certainties, often unapparent from a casual glance at the surface. In the remainder of this chapter, I shall examine a few of Wilson's textual strategies, in an attempt to posit some conclusions on what these 'certainties' might (or might not) be, and how they can be reconciled with the ever-expanding boundaries of crime fiction. To do so, I shall work outward from an analysis of Cassandra Reilly, the narrator-protagonist, in order to reconstruct a wider pattern of textuality and identity in the novel. I shall also draw repeatedly from *Troubles in Transylvania* in order to further illustrate parallels between the two works, though my conclusions will focus on *Gaudí Afternoon*.

Reilly's self-description in the book's opening paragraph immediately alerts us to the blurring of centre and margin:

> My name is Cassandra Reilly and I don't live anywhere. At least that's what I tell people when they ask. I was raised in Kalamazoo, Michigan, but I left when I was sixteen and I can hardly remember when that was. I have an Irish passport and make a sort of living as a translator, chiefly of Spanish, and chiefly of South American novels, at least at the moment. I rent an upstairs room in a tall Georgian house in Hampstead and another room in Oakland, California from an old friend Lucy Hernandez. (*GA*, p. 3)

Wilson both affirms and subverts conventional Western constructions of personal identity. She focuses on those things – name, family, age, occupation, nationality, place of residence – through which most people introduce themselves to others or attempt to categorise new acquaintances, and immediately undermines their importance. Cassandra, we later learn, is Reilly's own choice of Christian name, replacing the more Irish 'Catherine Frances' (*GA*, p. 98), and she only believes that Ireland is her spiritual home when she's not there (*GA*, 3). She has fled her middle-American culture and family for a (typically postmodernist) nomadic existence, and never reveals her exact age, although we learn that she is forty-something. Her current job as a translator confirms her marginal status, stresses the textuality of reality (with Reilly regularly contemplating how best to translate a South American novel written in Spanish into English – by no means a neutral operation), and insists on her refusal to be exhibited as a type. Nevertheless, her apparent lack of home and age in fact hint at an identity beneath the surface, since she qualifies her public utterance, 'I don't live anywhere' with the afterword that this is only what she tells people and might not be true, and also conceals her age beneath the confession that she can '*hardly*' (my emphasis) remember when she left home.

The uncertainty over Reilly's identity is further played out in *Troubles in Transylvania*. Here, we do learn that she is 46,[5] and that she named herself after Jane Austen's sister and a line from *Troilus and Cressida* ('And Cassandra laughed', p. 277), but other details only add to the sense of decentredness. Queuing to request a seat on the Trans-Mongolian Express, she observes:

It's interesting how you adapt to circumstances. If I were standing in a grocery line in New York with six people in front of me and a checker taking his sweet time, I'd be in a state of frenzied indignation like everyone else, muttering loudly, Do I have all day to wait here or what? they oughta fire this guy.

Here I drew into myself, almost physically; my head dropped into my chest, my shoulders slumped forward. (*TT*, p. 26)

Unlike Marlowe, for example, who remains detached from his surroundings, unchanged by what he encounters unless he is actually in disguise, Cassandra is chameleon-like in her adaptability, here blending into the background and appearing to offer no sense of her Americanness.[6] Indeed, shortly after this, she responds to a question about what she does well by suggesting that her skills reside in, 'Crossing borders. Transgressing boundaries. And of course translation' (*TT*, p. 41). Her identity is inseparable from perpetual motion, so that her interest is 'with movement and change' rather than with ever producing a settled self (*TT*, p. 143). Thus, she embodies 'diversity without fragmentation', that powerful combination which Sally R. Munt has identified elsewhere in Emma Victor, Mary Wings' popular lesbian sleuth.[7]

It is clear, too, that for Cassandra the self is primarily linguistic, and she believes that she and others adopt different personalities according to the language they are speaking. Significantly, in a novel largely set in Transylvania, language itself becomes a kind of vampire for Reilly, 'possess[ing] you ... pass[ing] through you ... transform[ing] you' (*TT*, p. 159).[8] It is worth observing here the invasive effects of language on the self and the manner in which the book's construction of selfhood mirrors earlier literary-cultural representations of its setting, since this intertextuality is also highly significant in *Gaudí Afternoon*. Reilly notes:

> When I speak Spanish ... I find my facial muscles set in a different pattern, and new, yet familiar gestures taking over my hands. I find myself shrugging and tossing my head back, pulling down the corners of my mouth and lifting my eyebrows. I touch people all the time and don't mind that they stand so close to me and blow cigarette smoke into my face. I speak more rapidly and fluidly and I use expressions that have no counterpart in English, expressions that for all my experience as a translator, I simply can't turn into direct equivalents. To speak another language is to lead a parallel life; the better you speak another language, the more fully you live in another culture. (*TT*, pp. 159–60)

Clearly, to be a subject in this kind of fictional world involves not only existing in what Deborah Knight has called 'an inter-subjective space, a space mapped out through its relations between subjects',[9] but also in an interlinguistic one, where the subject is transformed by the language she is speaking. The multi-linguistic self, like Cassandra Reilly, is by definition always on the border, always ready to assume a new identity, and is never likely to be constrained by the national or regional selves – American, mid-Western, Spanish, Hungarian, and so on – with which she is constantly contrasted throughout both novels. As such, she is perfectly positioned to play the role of cultural detective, utilising her own border status as a means of revealing the constructedness of behavioural patterns accepted as 'normal' within particular societies. Her nomadic and marginal identity thus proves useful not only in resolving the specific mysteries generated by the 'Americans in Europe' plots of the two novels, but also in addressing the wider 'crimes' of, for example, the oppression of women in Irish-American society or the exploitation of Eastern Europe by Western tourists.

The interest in borders is further underlined in both novels by Reilly's unstable gender identity in the eyes of both herself and others. As her self-description has indicated, she has no inclination to 'settle down', rejecting her Spanish friend Ana's invitation to co-parent a child (*GA*, pp. 34, 52), and telling April, one of the several Americans in Barcelona where most of the novel is set, that 'My life is a series of one-night stands and that's the way I like it' (*GA*, p. 160). Likewise, the whole plot of *Troubles in Transylvania* stems from Cassandra's flight from the offer of a permanent job. Although she does insist on her own status as a gay woman, after cropping her hair she is repeatedly mistaken for a man by representatives of a culture unfamiliar with women with short hair who wear bomber jackets, and observes that she is only seen as a female by a local taxi driver 'because the world thinks in dyads and Ben was more of a man than me' (*GA*, p. 103). Her own adoption of a 'James Dean swagger' (*GA*, p. 69) at this stage confirms the sense that Reilly is herself blurring the distinction between womanhood as a biological given and as a social construct, a point that becomes central in the novel's investigation of transsexuality and motherhood.

This in no way implies a loss of strength or coherence in Reilly's identity. Rather, she appears to exemplify Patricia Waugh's claims about the protagonists of much contemporary feminist fiction in that, in Cassandra, the novel:

> has accommodated humanist beliefs in individual agency and the necessity and possibility of self-reflection and historical continuity as the basis of personal identity. [Such fiction] has modified the traditional forms of such beliefs, however, in order to emphasize the provisionality and positionality of identity, the historical and social construction of gender, and the discursive production of knowledge and power. What many of these texts suggest is that it is possible to experience oneself as a strong and coherent agent in the world, *at the same time* as understanding the extent to which identity and gender are socially constructed and represented.[10]

It is hardly surprising, then, that Reilly views motherhood, for example, in a manner that complicates the opposition between regarding it as a biological function and as an emotional or psychological need. Detective-like, she reads the culturally determined Irish-American approach of her own family, where 'the cult of the baby was diligently practised, birth control was forbidden and motherhood was sacred' (*TT*, p. 255) in such a way as to disclose the oppressive undertones of what is taken superficially as the norm in that community. Going on to ask, 'Does giving birth make a mother?' – a central question in *Gaudí Afternoon* – Cassandra's own immediate answer is to speculate in physiological terms:

> Is a mother merely a gateway through which a new soul passes into the physical universe? Is she a snack bar open twenty-four hours a day but only for nine months? Is a mother a house you can live in through your childhood and longer, a house big enough to hold you both, a house where the rooms connect and the doors are open? Or is a mother

a hotel? Sometimes with a vacancy and sometimes full up. (*TT*, p. 256)

The questions are unresolved in both novels. Cassandra has left home as a teenager and never seen her mother again. Although the maternal presence is occasionally felt, she is certainly not in a 'connecting room' with open doors. And yet, both *Gaudí Afternoon* and *Troubles in Transylvania* – in which the future identity of a Romanian girl adopted by an American family, but being reintroduced to her biological mother, is so uncertain that she refuses to speak either language until the end of the novel – insist on the need to mother and be mothered and depend on Reilly's deductive powers to restore 'order'.

Before making the links between Reilly's challenge to Western constructs of subjectivity and her lesbianism more explicit, it is necessary to provide a contrast to her identity in the very different and insistently 'American' selves of Frankie, Ben, and April.[11] Where Reilly is willing to adopt certain components of Western/American culture in her own self-representation, as we have seen, she also undermines the importance of others such as the nuclear family and national identity. In contrast, both Frankie's and April's transsexuality, and Ben's lesbianism, seek to insist upon reproducing what *they* (but *not* Cassandra) see as essentialist versions of femininity. The first description of Frankie, without revealing that Frankie is a transsexual – a fact that Reilly is unaware of until much later in the novel – teeters on the brink of representing the archetypal drag queen:

A woman in a stretchy bright red tunic, black mini-skirt and black tights came tripping lightly as a gymnast over the stone floor. Her lipstick was a cheerful gash against her pale face and she wore a dozen red and black plastic bangles around her thin white wrists ... Her hair was auburn and chaotically, delightfully curly, corkscrewed like that of a Shirley Temple doll. She was in her late twenties.

She skidded to a stop in front of me; on her feet were silly pointed black shoes. She wrinkled her nose. (*GA*, p. 7)

Clothing, make-up, and the imitation of a child star by an adult replicate popular images of woman as simultaneously sex-object and child, and contrast with the practical 'warm wool jumpsuit' and leather jacket worn by Reilly to keep out the cold English spring weather. The latter immediately observes, 'You could tell she was an American' (*GA*, p. 8), a point confirmed by Frankie's dress, mannerisms and values throughout the novel. Frankie, however, whilst recognising the perfomative nature of his/her identity, also insists on an essentialist version of womanhood, talking of her 'Feminine intuition' (*GA*, p. 10), and later of what he/she calls the universal womanly desire to be a 'perfect mother' (*GA*, p. 84), or 'fucking trying to usurp my biological role!' as Ben puts it (*GA*, p. 64).

April, too, appears (even to Frankie) to be *essentially* female, being the object of Reilly's desire for much of the book, and only being revealed as transsexual at its end. Unlike Frankie's case, there is no apparent confusion of gendered personal pronouns, and it is only Delilah who 'sees through' April's role as a woman. Nevertheless, April has no desire to be a mother – or indeed a parent of any kind – a fact that further complicates her relationship with Ben (who is also oblivious to April's sex-change)! Whereas Frankie was a gay man who has become a straight woman, April's change transforms her into a lesbian. Her half-brother, Hamilton, is a gay man, but likes to 'crossdress sometimes' (*GA*, p. 151). Finally, Ben is first assumed to be a man by Cassandra (because of her name), then mistaken for a boy by her (because of her muscles [*GA*, p. 41]), though Ben also stresses her own identity as woman and mother.

Yet the confusing plurality of gender identities provided here remains insistently American. When Reilly comments that she 'hated to see a woman [Ben] go to pieces like that, especially one who looked like Arnold Schwarzenegger' (*GA*, p. 158), the unintentional irony lies in the fact that, in *Junior* (1994), Arnie subsequently also plays the role of mother on screen. Whereas Cassandra is able to blend into most situations (at least, when her hair is long or concealed) thanks to a decentred selfhood constructed out of a range of cultures and languages, the other Americans are defined entirely by their conformity to and deviance from *American* norms, and the selves they construct both confirm and strengthen the binary logic of those norms. As such, the transsexuals in the novel only *appear* to blur the opposition between men and women, since they argue that, as Frankie puts it, his/her being born into a male body was '*accidental*' (*GA*, p. 84, Wilson's italics), and reinvent themselves as 'perfect' examples of kinds of American womanhood. At the end of the novel, Ben and Frankie are reunited, in an attempt to salvage their nuclear family and 'to be good parents' (*GA*, p. 167), and Hamilton has agreed to what Cassandra rejected – that is, to co-parent a child with Ana. At this level, as in the search for the mother in the South American novel being translated by Reilly, *Gaudí Afternoon* seems to celebrate the virtues of the family in traditional Hollywood fashion, and to endorse the essentialist model of parenthood.

When we return to Cassandra Reilly, however, and to the formal strategies of the novel, such certainty in parenthood, the family and the monocultural values often propagated by Hollywood is immediately undermined. I have already stressed Reilly's decentred, nomadic construction of the self; now, I wish to briefly link this to her own lesbianism. Jonathan Dollimore has argued that:

> For homosexuals, more than most, the search for sexual freedom in the realm of the foreign has been inseparable from a repudiation of the 'Western' culture responsible for their repression and oppression. For some, ... this entailed not just the rejection of a repressive social order, but a disidentification from it requiring nothing less than the relinquishing of the self as hitherto constituted and inhabited by that order. In other words, precisely because of the Western integration of subjectivity and sexuality, deviant desire becomes also a refusal of certain kinds of subjectivity.[12]

For the modernist figures Dollimore discusses, the search for sexual liberation tends to focus on the exotic as the Western self attempts to inhabit the other and extinguish its own cultural origins. In contrast, as both translator and nomad, Reilly's selfhood is a bricolage of allusions to global cultures, in which American popular culture still figures prominently but never overwhelms. It is hardly surprising that such a historical shift is apparent in the novel, given the *non*-repressive social order of San Francisco, the American base of Frankie, Ben and April, who all seem content to live within American constructs of selfhood. Yet Reilly feels the need to go beyond a model that, while allowing for a plethora of sexual orientations still appears to insist on clearly demarcated gender roles. What we might call (following Dollimore) her 'transgressive aesthetic' encodes desire in 'a discourse of liberation inseparable from [a] ... displacement of dominant categories of subjective depth'.[13]

In *Gaudí Afternoon*, in particular, it is finally the tension between the (Western/American) desire expressed by Frankie, Ben, Hamilton and Ana (to establish nuclear families fulfilling their 'essentialist' need to parent) and that of Cassandra to be free from such social and subjective ties, that constructs a kind of textual irresolution. On the one hand, the novel seems to endorse the family unit through the tidy closure in which the couples are united or (reunited) in order to raise children. At this level, all the mysteries have been resolved and Cassandra is free to move on to another strand of her life, or Wilson to another 'detective' novel. On the other, however, the whole logic of the book cautions against such certainty, counterpointing the popular conservative culture of this closure with a structure that deliberately resists it. To conclude, I will outline the manner in which this structure functions, in order to offer some *in*conclusive remarks on what Wilson is doing to the detective genre.

The clue to the form of the book lies in its title – *Gaudí Afternoon* – and in the subsequent repeated allusions both to Antoni Gaudí, the modernist Catalan architect, and to his works, whose 'typical traits', as we are informed by a display board quoted as part of the novel, are 'a variety of forms and a wealth of ornamentation' (*GA*, p. 26). When a guide tells some American tourists of Gaudí's 'encyclopedic taste', and points out how he 'loved to show quite openly the process of construction and assembly' (*GA*, p. 85), the relation between architecture and novel becomes clear. Not only do the book's key dramatic moments take place within or overlooked by Gaudí's works: in addition, the novel itself can be seen as an example of the Gaudí-esque. We have already witnessed the 'variety of forms' in Wilson's book, and Reilly's role as a translator makes explicit the textuality of the work, in an echo of Gaudí's own pointers to 'construction and assembly'. Likewise, her function as detective appears, finally, to restore a pre-existing order whilst simultaneously demonstrating the constructed history of that order. Unlike most American hard-boiled detective fiction, which is set in cities constructed on the grid system and in which vernacular street-talk 'emerges as the privileged voice in contestation with other modes of expression',[14] Wilson's novels subvert the narrative quest for discursive authority.

The decentring of perspective in the novel thus establishes links both with the modernist's rejection of that part of Barcelona constructed on a bourgeois nineteenth-century plan of regulated 'enormous boulevards' (*GA*, p. 21) and with the fragmented sensibilities of the late twentieth century. This is, to adapt what Iain Chambers has said of Derek Jarman's film *Caravaggio* (1986), 'hardly parody or pastiche but rather an intelligent seizure of the traces of the past that flare up in the present'. According to this reading, the novel offers a representation that is 'complex and fragmentary and not the solid referent of a traditional art discourse, [or] a Hollywood film'.[15] In other words, it provides a model that undermines the apparent certainty of its own closure at the very moment that it generates it. It is finally impossible to side with one version of 'reality' above the other, since both are encoded within the text, and yet neither is compatible with the other. *Gaudí Afternoon* stretches the genre of crime fiction to such an extent that it eventually implodes: the novel incorporates American popular culture, and arrives at a form of closure satisfactory to its American parent-protagonists, but refuses to privilege these values over the encyclopedic allusions to global cultures which, like Gaudí's architecture, constitute the novel.

Notes

1. Barbara Wilson, *Murder in the Collective* (1984), *Sisters of the Road* (1986), and *The Dog Collar Murders* (1989), all published in the US by the Seal Press. All three have been published in the UK as part of the Virago Crime series.

2. Think, for example, of *Murder in the Collective*, in which the murder of Jeremy, a member of a Seattle print collective, not only launches a traditional (though ultimately subverted) hunt for the killer, but also provides the conditions for an exploration of the effects of US military-economic imperialism on women in the Phillipines and for the narrator's discovery of her lesbian sexuality.

3. Barbara Wilson, *Gaudí Afternoon* (London: Virago Crime, 1991), p. 55. Subsequent page numbers from this edition are cited parenthetically in the text. Of course, the novel's title situates it as a kind of literary descendant of Dorothy L. Sayers' *Gaudy Night* (1936).

4. See, for example, John P. Muller and William J. Richardson (eds), *The Purloined Poe: Lacan, Derrida and Psychoanalytic Reading* (Baltimore: Johns Hopkins University Press, 1988).

5. Barbara Wilson, *Troubles in Transylvania* (London: Virago Crime, 1993), p. 27. Subsequent page numbers from this edition are cited parenthetically in the text.

6. Cassandra does adopt disguises (or roles that she does not consider to be aspects of herself) as opposed to different selves when necessary. For example, in *Troubles in Transylvania*, she describes herself as a widow as part of her investigation of the murder (*TT*, p. 92).

7. Sally R. Munt, *Murder by the Book? Feminism and the Crime Novel* (London: Routledge, 1994), p. 142.

8. Although the allusion is not developed much beyond the title and a few passing comments, vampires exemplify Wilson's interest in borderlines. As Catherine Belsey has commented, to the extent that:

> they blur the oppositions on which clear rational thinking and empiricist observation depend, vampires come in due course to represent everything that the Enlightenment cannot recognise. Life is the opposite of death: medical science depends on the ability to define the distinction. But vampires are the un-dead; they do not belong with the living; they spend their days in their coffins and inhabit the night; they have no *proper* place. Vampires have a material existence

and they bring about material effects, but at the same time they cast no shadow and are not reflected in mirrors: they exceed the alternatives of presence and absence.

In another clear parallel with *Gaudí Afternoon*, vampire sexuality 'deconstructs' the Western anatomological definition of men and women as *opposite* sexes (established in the eighteenth century): 'both male and female vampires penetrate their victims, but only after they have been penetrated by another vampire; meanwhile, it is the passive victim who provides the vital fluid'. See Catherine Belsey, 'Postmodern Love: Questioning the Metaphysics of Desire', *New Literary History*, vol. 25, no. 3 (Summer, 1994), pp. 683–705, p. 697.

9. Deborah Knight, 'Women, Subjectivity, and the Rhetoric of Anti-Humanism in Feminist Film Theory', *New Literary History*, vol. 26, no. 1 (Winter, 1995), pp. 39–56, 51.

10. Patricia Waugh, *Feminine Fictions: Revisiting the Postmodern*, quoted in Knight, 'Women, Subjectivity, and the Rhetoric of Anti-Humanism', p. 54. Waugh's point would seem to offer a marked contrast to the above-mentioned *New York Trilogy*, where Paul Auster's protagonists become disempowered and decentred precisely because they come to realise the 'provisionality and positionality of identity ... and the discursive production of knowledge and power'.

11. The encounter between American visitors and European cultures is replayed in *Troubles in Transylvania*. In addition to the oppositions highlighted above, this novel, set shortly after the overthrow of Ceauşescu, examines the effects of the collapse of the Iron Curtain, and tensions between ethnic groups in Romania.

12. Jonathan Dollimore, *Sexual Dissidence: Augustine to Wilde, Freud to Foucault* (Oxford: Clarendon Press, 1991), p. 339.

13. Ibid., p. 309. Of course, this 'discourse of liberation' has its limits. As Dollimore continues, 'we go to the exotic other to lose everything, including ourselves – everything that is but the privilege which enabled us to go in the first place' (p. 342). Although Wilson employs diverse forms of otherness in order to deconstruct the 'norms' of

Western/American culture, even Cassandra Reilly is unable to totally separate herself from the fact that she is an American, with all the privileges that entails.

14. Ralph Willett, *The Naked City: Urban Crime Fiction in the USA* (Manchester: Manchester University Press, 1996), p. 8. For example, the 'smooth, devious, clubman's rhetoric of Casper Gutman in Dashiell Hammett's *The Maltese Falcon*' (p. 8).

15. Iain Chambers, *Border Dialogues: Journeys in Postmodernity* (London: Routledge, 1990), p. 1.

6

Reading the Signs: Detection and Anthropology in the Work of Tony Hillerman

David Murray

The depiction of American Indians has been one of the most enduring aspects of American popular culture, but one beset with problems. While recent film portrayals tend to stress the noble, ecologically responsible and spiritually uplifting aspects of Indian life, in contrast to the savage, taciturn figure of earlier Westerns, what they still mostly share with earlier representations is the idea of the Indian as Other, as different, together with a confidence that this difference can be unproblematically represented by whites. Indians have, in fact, largely been used in film and literature not as people in their own right but as vehicles of contrast, expressions of what whites were not, as part of white self-exploration. To do this it has been necessary to fix Indians in ahistoric and stereotyped roles, whether negative or positive, and ignore the present complex reality. Interviewed after *Dances With Wolves* about a sequel bringing the story up to date, Kevin Costner said that 'a sequel couldn't be a very fun picture at all, because we know what happens. Those people that are just left are crushed.'[1] Even a film set on a modern reservation with clear political themes like *Thunderheart* felt the need to link up, through vision sequences, with some sort of essentialised Indian past. The increasing awareness of the issues of power and ethnocentricity involved in any representation of one group by another may have been more explicitly discussed by anthropologists and cultural critics than by popular novelists or film-makers, but I want to show how the work of Tony Hillerman raises many of the same issues, and deals with them in intriguing ways. A white writer representing Navajo Indians, he has been operating in what in many ways could be a cultural and political minefield, but his refusal to see or present his characters as exotic, while at the same time being fascinated by cultural difference has allowed him to produce sympathetic and textured explorations within the conventions of crime fiction. In what follows I hope to explore the concerns and the limits of his writing, and the ways in which his concerns and difficulties overlap with other discursive practices, such as ethnography.

Since 1970, Hillerman has been producing a series of novels set mainly on the Navajo reservation, which occupies some 28,000 square miles across the states of Arizona, New Mexico and Utah. The Navajos are the largest single Indian group in the US (230,000 people, two thirds of whom live on the reservation). The reservation has, as well as its own Navajo-language radio stations, newspapers and schools, its own Navajo Tribal Police force, to which Hillerman's main characters belong. Enclosed entirely within the area of the reservation lies the separate Hopi reservation, and nearby are a number of other small Pueblo Indian communities. As a result there is a crosshatching of Anglo and various Indian cultures which Navajo police officers Joe Leaphorn and Jim Chee have to cope with, together with problems of jurisdiction between tribal, state and federal authorities. Hillerman is at pains to present not only the sense of scale of the landscape, and its capacity to dwarf its scattered inhabitants, but the richness and cultural diversity of these inhabitants – an important thing to stress if he is to avoid making his characters seem too easily to blend into the static and unchanging natural world, and thereby fall into the familiar stereotype of the natural and ahistoric Indian. Certainly the sense of place is often crucial to the success of his detectives, whose forensic skills are as likely to be employed in following tracks as in tracing fingerprints or ballistics, and it is crucial, too, to that spiritual dimension which partly distinguishes his main characters from their Anglo counterparts.

His two main figures, Leaphorn and Chee, have significant differences, though they are similar enough for one critic to claim that Hillerman is evoking echoes of the monster-slaying Hero Twins of Navajo mythology.[2] Having begun his series with three novels featuring the sceptical and pragmatic Joe Leaphorn, Hillerman turned to the younger, more religiously inclined Jim Chee, and now uses them both, but almost always acting separately. They remain wary of each other, even though Leaphorn has made use of Chee as a ceremonial healer. With Leaphorn, part of the interest for the reader is seeing how the normal search for a solution to the particular crime which drives the plot of the book forward is subtly different from that in other crime fiction. Leaphorn has to be aware of cultural patterns or prohibitions, particularly associated with death. It is not permissible, for instance, to say the name of the dead person. Or he has to cope with the pervasive suspicion about witches, and their malign power – something he personally regards as a destructive and irritating superstition. We watch him as his local knowledge enables him to read the cultural signs, and we are given an insight in the process into some sorts of cultural difference. Though Leaphorn's scepticism is often to the fore, his logical approach, his desire to sort out a mystery, is presented as closely related to his Navajo world-view, which stresses the ultimate harmony underlying the universe. As part of a passage in *Dance Hall of the Dead*, in which Hillerman carefully places Leaphorn and his clan in the wider sweep of Navajo history, we are given a little of his grandfather's teachings:

> That had always been the point of the lesson. Interdependency of nature. Every cause has its effect. Every action its reaction. A reason for everything. In all things a pattern, and in this pattern, the beauty of harmony. Thus one learned to live with evil, by understanding it, by reading its cause. And thus one learned, gradually and methodically, if one was lucky, to always 'go in beauty', to always look for the pattern, and to find it.[3]

This principle of harmony, referred to as *hozho* or *hozro*, runs through all of the books as an aesthetic/moral force, and sections from some of the huge range of Navajo chants or 'ways' are quoted within the novels.[4] For Leaphorn the spirit of *hozho* is a vital force in his life not just in ceremonies but in his professional work, as he sees his detective work as partaking in the same process:

> He saw no tire-tracks and he expected to see none. That would have been luck. Leaphorn never counted on luck. Instead he expected order – the natural sequence of behaviour, the cause producing the natural effect, the human behaving in the way it was natural for him to behave. He counted on that and upon his own ability to sort out the chaos of observed facts and find in them this natural order.[5]

Interesting here is the way that Hillerman invokes the cool ratiocination associated with the oldest models of the detective, going back to Dupin or Holmes, but then puts it in a different cultural context, so that we are able to see that this approach is not the only one, and is itself culturally determined. Because, for instance, death – a dead body – is so often just the starting point in crime fiction, the body is ruthlessly dehumanised, demystified. Once the experts get going it is just a collection of evidence, and one might say there is almost a relish in this, in the way science sweeps aside the sacred, or superstitious. For the traditional Navajo, though, death was the ultimate evil:

> That which was natural in him, and therefore good, simply ceased. That which was unnatural, and therefore evil, wandered through the darkness as a ghost, disturbing nature and causing sickness. The Navajo didn't share the concept of his Hopi-Zuni-Pueblo neighbours that the human spirit transcended death in the fulfilment of an eternal kachina, nor the Plains Indian belief in joining with a personal God. In the old tradition, death was unrelieved horror.[6]

Evil, as the antithesis of natural order and beauty, is figured as the force of witchcraft. As Hillerman says, following Leaphorn's train of thought, 'Witchcraft was a reversal of the Navajo Way'(*LW*, p. 363). The belief in witchcraft amongst the Navajo has been widely documented,[7] and in the novels the abiding suspicion of witches, and the refusal to talk openly, often makes investigation difficult, as does the abhorrence of death in general. It is believed that after death the ghost is dangerous and roams abroad, and the place where the death occurred is completely avoided. Hillerman sometimes uses this to add an extra tone of menace to events, as in *The Blessing Way*, where Hillerman has the figure of a Navajo Wolf or witch seemingly on the loose, which tests Leaphorn's rationality and ours. In general Leaphorn is irritated by the gossip and suspicion which accompanies witchcraft belief, but Hillerman's narratives often confront us, and Leaphorn or Chee, with inexplicable things in disturbing and threatening locations, so that the possibility of the power of the supernatural is always floated, creating an additional frisson. Partly by placing us in a world where our normal ways of explaining things are being frustrated, and partly by allowing us to see the consistency of another way of looking at the world, Hillerman allows us to entertain, through our closeness to Leaphorn and Chee, a view of a world ruled by spiritual principles, thereby presenting a challenge to our rationality. Nevertheless, the final explanation is entirely rational and naturalistic, and it is significant, I think, that even though one of the most delicately achieved and impressive aspects of his books is the ability to present the world from a different perspective, Hillerman does always return to the detective formula at the end, rather than flirt with more open or occult possibilities. The furthest he goes is to have a resolution of the plot which satisfies both rational and witchcraft beliefs, so that, for instance, the villain is destroyed by his own weapon – or, in different terms, the witchery is turned back on the witch. The idea of reversing that perversion of values which is witchcraft, of eliminating the witch by turning his own forces back on itself, has an attractive symmetry which Hillerman several times evokes, as when, in *The Ghostway*, Margaret Sosi kills the villain with his own gun, after being cleansed by having a Ghostway held for her.

The question of how far the narrative stance of crime fiction can allow for the genuinely inexplicable, the supernatural and occult, and how far the style of realism it depends on is itself wedded to a particular secular and scientific view which is seamlessly presented as the real, would lead us to a consideration of the ideological underpinnings of realism and the constitution of the subject-position of the reader within it.[8] It might also lead us back to that fateful division adopted from Edgar Allan Poe between tales of ratiocination and of the irrational. More interesting for my purpose, though, is the way in which we can find a directly equivalent discussion over styles of ethnographic description, and the case of witchcraft is particularly relevant. One of the great contributions of anthropology to our understanding of culture has been its demonstration of the logic and sufficiency of other ways of conceptualising the world than our own, and classic ethnographic accounts of witchcraft belief have demonstrated how, in a society which believes in it, witchcraft 'works', in the sense of explaining the world according to a set of self-sustaining criteria. To this extent such ethnographies may serve to relativise our own beliefs, but it is important to note that the form and style of the ethnography ultimately retains a rationalist and scientific stance of objectivity which rests on the same assumptions about the world as realism in fiction. Witchcraft beliefs are taken seriously, but still encompassed within a larger objective view of the world, in which cause and effect is conceptualised in the forms of Western science. Things may go bump in the night, but there must be an explanation in rational terms. Only in a few later ethnographies has the narrative stance allowed for a non-realist mode in which, as Nathaniel Hawthorne much earlier said of his own style of the romance, 'ghosts may safely enter'.[9] Recent debates in anthropology have focused precisely on the ways in which the authority of the ethnographer is established in the style of the text, which presents knowledge as objective, rather than as constructed through a dialogical encounter. In this way the world-view of the ethnographer is not part of the dialogue but outside it, already established, and implicit in the apparently neutral style of realism. Alternative, more dialogical or even occult, forms of ethnography have been considered, raising questions about the adequacy of realism as a style in which to present or represent other world-views,[10] and, while it may at first seem rather perverse to equate this controversy with Hillerman's novels, we do have the same structural situation, with white author presenting and explaining Indians, without himself being explicitly present. I will return later to the particular stylistic means which Hillerman employs, but I want here to remain with witchcraft, and to compare Hillerman's treatment of it with a novel by the Laguna Indian writer, Leslie Silko.

In *People of Darkness*, Hillerman develops a set of interlocking images which relate to the Navajo view of witchcraft. First of all, the phrase 'people of darkness' is a descriptive Navajo term for moles, small stone images of which are important to the plot, but it also suggests the figures of witches, working in the dark. The story revolves around mining and prospecting, and the discovery of uranium. Unexplained deaths are attributed to witchcraft, but are finally explained by the fact that the mole amulets, which have been worn next to the skin, have been carved from pitchblende, and the deaths were from cancer. They were given by the villain of the plot, who has concealed his find and has had to eliminate any threats to his secret. This is the rational explanation, but Hillerman has Jim Chee explain it in different terms. The geologist Lebeck has to fake his own death and come back with a new identity. For Chee this unnatural behaviour connects him to witchcraft via the story of how First Man became a witch: 'because he was first he didn't have any relatives to destroy. So he figured out a magic way to violate the strongest taboo of all. He destroyed himself and recreated himself, and that's the way he got the powers of evil.' Like the First Man, 'Lebeck decided to become a witch. He destroyed himself. And he came back.'[11] Note here that for Chee the unnatural act of destroying all your human connections, your real place in society and family, is a transgression of the same order as murder or incest. This puts him outside the range of normal behaviour, and makes him a witch, and Chee describes him as such, even while detailing his more mundane motives and actions. It is this balancing of two alternative, but for him not mutually exclusive, frameworks which makes Chee so intriguing, and which brings out all Hillerman's delicacy of touch.

The idea of radioactivity as a mysterious, invisible and deadly force corresponds well with witchery, and is used for similar purposes in Leslie Silko's novel *Ceremony* (1977), but the differences in approach are instructive. Silko uses the fact that the location of her novel had been used as an atomic test site, and links it with the bombing of Hiroshima and Nagasaki. Her protagonist Tayo has fought against the Japanese and has been traumatised by his experiences, so that he cannot separate them from the present. He is given a traditional healing ceremony, but the actions of the novel allow him and us to see the connections between a widespread evil or witchery that affects both Indians and Japanese, of which radioactivity is not just a metaphor but a concrete example. As Shamoon Zamir has shown, Silko is writing in a context of a massive despoliation of Indian land for purposes of energy production, nuclear and otherwise, such that the area has been written off as a place worth protecting or preserving for human habitation, and designated a National Sacrifice Area.[12]

As well as drawing larger political parallels, though, Silko also uses the different cultures more contrastively. Where Hillerman incorporates the idea of witchcraft into a realist narrative, Silko deliberately questions the capacity of realist narrative to encompass all the dimensions of what happens. She begins with a mythic figure, Thought Woman, and the events of the novel are already circumscribed within her storytelling:

> She is sitting in her room
> thinking of a story now
> I'm telling you the story
> she is thinking.

At the end of the novel the grandmother of the protagonist echoes this mythic circumscription of the linear narrative of the novel: 'It seems like I heard these stories before ... only thing is, the names sound different.'[13] Silko is useful here in demonstrating what Hillerman does not do, and the ways his realist and linear narrative ultimately frames all others. Nevertheless, given the easy recourse to the mythic and timeless, by lesser writers than Silko, and the ahistoric Indian exotics that result, a reasonable defence of Hillerman would be that he thereby avoids the risk of mystifying and 'othering' Indians, and suggesting absolute differences.

Leaphorn himself has worked out a synthesis, a way of describing witchcraft belief in acceptably objective terms, which yet holds on to the psychological truth of it. In *The Blessing Way* we are told of his dispute with a white anthropologist friend, which recalls 'Leaphorn insisting that there was a basis of truth in the Navajo Origin Myth, that some people did deliberately turn antisocial, away from the golden mean of nature, deliberately choose the unnatural, and therefore, in Navajo belief, the evil way' (*BW*, p. 17). For Chee, though, the pull of the traditional view is stronger, and a reconciliation is less easy, as seen in his attempt to be both policeman and traditional healer. In *The Ghostway*, Hillerman presents us with Chee quite literally at the point of division between two cultural systems. He has to enter a *hogan* where someone has died, but according to traditional Navajo practice, a place of death should be avoided. The duties of a policeman require him to cross the threshold, and Hillerman deliberately uses the symbolism of liminality (literally, the limen or theshold) to focus on the larger tensions within Jim Chee:

> He would either walk back to his pickup, go home and write off this idea as a waste of time or he would search the one place he hadn't searched. That meant taking out his flashlight and stepping through the hole into darkness. At one level of his intellect it seemed a trivial thing ... To the Jim Chee who was an alumnus of the University of New Mexico, a subscriber to Esquire and Newsweek, ... student of anthropology and sociology ..., holder of Social Security card 441–28–7272, it was a logical step to take.
>
> But 'Jim Chee' was only what his uncle would call his 'white man name'. His real name, his secret name, his war name, was Long Thinker, given him by Hosteen Frank Sam Nakai, the elder brother of his mother, and one of the most respected singers among Four Corners Navajos.[14]

It is one of the achievements of Hillerman's work that this double sense of identity – defined either as a separate modern individual guaranteed and authorised by the social security number, or as what unites a group through a network of relations and kinship – is constantly probed, without turning the Navajo characters into mysterious 'others' or versions of noble savage or Vanishing American. Having outlined these divisions in Chee, Hillerman is able to present his delayed step across the threshold as symbolic of his larger dilemma. Chee's white girlfriend, Mary Landon, is encouraging him to go for promotion to the FBI, which would exacerbate the tensions he is already experiencing between the traditional Navajo ways he espouses in his desire to be a singer/healer and his police duties and training: 'He had avoided the hogan, and the decision, all afternoon. Suddenly he understood why. It had something to do, a great deal to do, with Mary Landon – with remaining one of the Dinee or with stepping through into the white man's world' (pp. 42–3).

In the course of the novel Chee does confront the evil, and to some extent steps through into the white world in doing his police duty, but at the end of the book he is planning not only to undertake a Ghostway cure for himself, but to see if he can be taught to perform it for others. Mary Landon's way and his are not to converge. What is interesting in this text is the way that Hillerman draws the villain of the book, Vaggan, in such a way that he mirrors Chee's concerns. This is something Hillerman also does elsewhere, in presenting certain sorts of crime as aberrant and inhuman, in terms which are consonant with the Navajo ideas of evil and witchcraft as a reverse of the good and harmonious. Convinced of the imminent end of civilisation, seeing the lights of Los Angeles as 'the phosphorescence of decay', Vaggan waits for the apocalypse of nuclear war. He listens to *Gotterdämmerung* and remembers his father's dictum: '"Nietzsche for thought, Wagner for music," his father would say. "Most of the rest is for niggers".' We learn that his disciplinarian monster of a father, referred to usually as the Commander, has disowned him, and that he has never known his mother, who is referred to by his father merely as 'the woman'. Hillerman carefully describes how part of Vaggan's survivalist nonsense is a desire for purity, and shows how it can turn into a grotesque parody of Navajo beliefs, in a crazy form of primitivism. He is reading a book on the Navajo, and is attracted to them:

They too were survivors. It was because, he was sure, of their philosophy of staying in harmony with conditions, being in tune with whatever was coming down. That made sense.

He did it himself. The people who refused to believe the missiles were coming and tried to turn it off by denying it, they would die. He'd gotten in harmony with that inevitable truth, accepted it, prepared for it. He would survive. (p. 83)

Hillerman is at pains to present the obsessive and ruthless efficiency of such men as Vaggan in *The Ghostway*, and Colton Wolf in *People of Darkness,* as grotesque versions of the modern rational world, a terrifying expression of expertise, professionalism without feeling. These men have lost their way, their route, but this is closely connected to the fact that they have lost their root too. When we look at the disaster area which constitutes their families, we are reminded of Leaphorn's use of a Navajo expression:

'He acted like he had no relatives', Leaphorn thought and grinned wryly at the old-fashioned expression. When he was a boy, it was the worst thing his mother could say about anyone. But then the Navajo Way made the relatives totally responsible for anything one of the family did. (*BW*, p. 63)

Colton Wolf, it emerges, was callously abandoned by his mother, but he spends his spare time in an obsessive and pathetic quest to trace her.[15] Not sure who his father was, he invents a name for himself: 'She'd tell him his real name. She'd tell him about his father and his grandparents. And about the family home ... Until then, he'd pick a last name. Something simple. He picked Wolf' (p. 48). In his profession as killer, though, he is a man whose survival depends on his anonymity. When he returns from shopping, checking every car and person, Hillerman remarks that 'Colton Wolf had survived another contact with the world' (p. 45). Leroy Fleck, in *Talking God*, is also a loner, cultivating conversations with strangers via the small ads page of the newspaper. He spends his time trying to finance his mother's stay in a nursing home. 'Mama' is disruptive, and hostile to the other patients, but her main characteristic is the guilt and lack of worth she has instilled in Fleck. Her injunction was always to treat everyone as hostile and retaliate ('If you don't even it up they grind you down even more', p. 102) and this acts in the book as a sort of mirror-image of the Navajo principle of reciprocity or balance, so that Fleck functions as a principle of disorder or evil. He has learned to kill efficiently and ruthlessly, and when he kills a policeman in front of his mother, it is almost as if he is acting out her wishes. As he says: 'I got even. Did you see that? I didn't let him step on me. I didn't kiss any boot.' Even then, though, he gets no recognition or approval; 'No words came, and Fleck could read absolutely nothing in her eyes except fear.'[16]

To trace crime back to a broken home, and to social dislocation may be a cliché, something often ascribed to the social-worker-as-apologist, but it also cuts across a spectrum of political positions. The Right may want to stress individual agency and guilt, rather than explanations from social and economic deprivation which it regards as detracting attention from the reality of personal responsibility, but it also stresses family values and the disastrous effects of family breakdown. Hillerman's portrayal of his villains, in stressing their isolation and emotional deprivation contrasted with the Navajo stress on reciprocal and harmonious relations, does create a sense of compassion or understanding – but one which in no sense cancels out how repellent these people are. It is surely significant, though, that this causal part-explanation is at the local and individual level, as the conventions of crime fiction demand, rather than at any larger socio-economic or structural level, and it may be worth following up the ways in which Hillerman adapts the Navajo moral outlook to the codes of crime fiction, as a way of trying to account for his particular and widespread appeal.

One reason for his popularity may be that, as opposed to the existential hero making his own code, or the burnt-out cases of recent, thoroughly nasty individual detectives in James Ellroy, Hillerman offers a really ordered universe, more like that implicit in the chronotope of the English country house than that of Chandler's mean streets. The question then arises whether this is a reactionary appeal or something more fundamental. One could certainly point to a lack of a particular political edge. Even when Indian grievances are mentioned they are never very explicitly developed by Hillerman. This may be meant to imply that these unfairnesses are what the characters regularly live with, but certainly the more radical figures in his fiction, such as the members of the American Indian Movement splinter group who appear in *Listening Woman*, get short shrift. Ward Churchill's characteristically vehement attack on Hillerman's political stance reduces Leaphorn and Chee to quislings and the novels to 'the very quintessence of modern colonialist fiction in the US', but he does make some provocative points about the lack of political dimension in the novels.[17]

Perhaps in the end Hillerman's stress on order is only following the traditional detective story format, which in following up a unique crime is able to show the specific causes in individual terms, as opposed to the sort of epidemiology of crime offered by social analysis and statistics. This latter would show relations between social and economic position and various sorts of criminal behaviour, which are causal, even if not absolutely determining for any individual. It is this larger structure which is usually elided in crime fiction, either by focusing on unique crime totally sundered from any sociological typicality (the country house) or by obscuring the relation between the world of the criminal and the larger society. Franco Moretti, invoking Marx's reading of capitalist society, describes the operation of ideology in obscuring the relation between labour and capital, between cause and effect. Its great achievement is to erase precisely 'the social process which produces those effects – that surface reality – which it places at the centre of the world'.[18] Thus what seems self-evident, natural, at the centre of everything, is precisely that which is the result of a (changeable) social process. The concern to explain something by finding its real cause and origin, to offer an alternative depth to the obvious surface, is in some ways common to a Marxist approach and to the role of the detective, but a crucial difference is that (as Moretti points out) the detective novel in finding the cause never finds it structurally. In this way, it could be said to perform all the operations necessary to explain the crime, but never to transpose this same process to a critique of the larger 'crime'. As one of Bertolt Brecht's gangsters says, robbing a bank is nothing compared to founding one. In concentrating on individual crime, the detective novel is sidetracked from the

larger injustices, which may not even be against the law, and
is trapped in the sphere of circulation rather than production.
As Moretti puts it:

> detective fiction incites people to seek the secret of profit
> in the sphere of circulation, where it cannot be found – but
> in compensation, one finds thefts, con-jobs, frauds, false
> pretenses, and so on. The indignation against what is rotten
> and immoral in the economy must concentrate on these
> phenomena. (p. 139)

In the Navajo case, to remain in the sphere of circulation
rather than production would be to concentrate, as Hillerman
does, on specific crimes of greed or opportunism rather than
on the situation in which rich natural resources are exploited
by government or multinationals while the Navajo remain
largely poor. It could be argued that this is beyond the range
of a tribal policeman, and indeed a fact of life too obvious and
too permanent to be commented on, but it is interesting that,
for all the concern with the land, there is relatively little on
its exploitation, where the natural is affected by the historical.
In *The Blessing Way*, for instance, the use of the land by the
US airforce for testing missiles is a given, and the main concern,
the area of transgression, is the attempt by Mafia-connected
intruders to set up radar tracking equipment on Navajo land
to steal military information.

Similarly the mining of coal and other resources is part
only of the background of *People of Darkness*, and the focus is
on the way an individual corrupt geologist eliminates people
through radioactive contamination to protect his uranium
source, rather than on the wider health risks to a whole
community. Perhaps there is a sign of Chee becoming more
aware, as in the latest novel we are told that he has written to
the *Navajo Times* complaining of the plan to develop a toxic
waste dump on Navajo land as 'symbolic of the contempt felt
for tribal lands',[19] but so far Hillerman's plots have not brought
either of his policeman into direct conflict with outside
corporations or government agencies. More characteristic are
the satisfying small victories over the FBI or government
bureaucracy, in the name of a pragmatic decision about what

is fair or right in a specific instance, rather than in the abstract. In an episode in *Sacred Clowns* which shows Hillerman integrating these concerns in characteristically quiet way into his plot, Jim Chee has to make a decision. He has discovered that the culprit in a hit-and-run accident is an old man who has allowed his grandson, who is mentally handicapped because of foetal alcohol syndrome,[20] to help drive his pickup truck. To arrest him would be legally correct but disastrous to a caring and sustaining relation between the two vulnerable people, a relationship delicately drawn by Hillerman. Chee is with Janet Pete, a lawyer and a Navajo too, though with fewer traditional roots than Chee, and in showing her the situation he is demonstrating why he will avoid arresting the man, even indirectly help him to cover up the evidence: 'The question is belagaana [white] justice, or Navajo justice. Or maybe it's do you try for justice or do you try for hozho'. Traditionally, he explains, if you damage someone, you arrange between the two families to make it good: 'That way you restore hozho. You've got harmony again between families.' But if somebody hurts you 'out of meanness', then 'he's the one out of hozho. You aren't taught he should be punished. He should be cured. Gotten back in balance with what's around him. Made beautiful again' (p. 255).

The question he is posing, then, is how a policeman sworn to enforce the law can also give weight to curing: 'So now what are you going to do if you're this cop?' As the question hangs in the air, Hillerman describes the landscape through which they are travelling: 'They were driving past the Bisti Badlands now, looking into the edge of a wilderness where aeons of time had uncovered alternating layers of grey shale, pink sandstone, yellow caliche and black streaks of coal. Wind and water had played with these varied levels of hardness and carved out a weird tableau of gigantic shapes.' To Janet's 'It's hard to apply normal city street law school solutions where you're looking at this', Chee responds: 'Maybe the landscape is part of the answer ... Maybe it makes the answer a little different' (p. 254). So, a sense of reverence for fundamental principles actually allows or encourages him to be pragmatic about particular laws, and what makes this scene so densely textured is that there is another more personal agenda behind their conversation. Chee, a man with definite traditionalist inclinations is worried that Janet, though her family has lost track of its clan affiliations, might be from a clan forbidden to him to marry into. His question, parallel with the one about his police duties, is how to reconcile laws with his instincts and sense of what is right. In both cases we see his traditional spiritual orientation actually guiding him in a pattern of behaviour which is in keeping with the spirit if not the letter of the law, and it is this subtle shading, the avoidance of the clichéd opposition of traditional and progressive, which Hillerman has been able to develop over his whole series of detective books.

So far I have dealt entirely with Navajo culture, but Hillerman makes great use of the diversity in and around the Navajo reservation. The various traditional Pueblo communities, Hopi, Zuni or Tanoan, which we encounter in the books are in some ways as different from the Navajos as the surrounding Anglo culture. When Chee and Leaphorn confront them they are themselves outsiders, and to some extent the deeply traditional and complex Hopi culture operates as a sort of exotic Other with which the policemen have to cope. Their response, though, is both sympathetic and informed, as they both have anthropology degrees, Leaphorn from Arizona State and Chee from University of New Mexico.[21] Both detectives are able to remember back to their courses for bits of helpful information, which is a useful device for Hillerman to give the reader necessary ethnographic information, and while it sometimes does appear rather contrived, Hillerman makes interesting use of this relation between anthropologist and detective. Chee and Leaphorn are able to 'read' both their own and other cultures in just the way described by Ross Macdonald:

> a good private detective ... likes to move through society both horizontally and vertically, studying people like an anthropologist. And like an anthropologist he tends to fall a little in love with his subjects.[22]

Sacred Clowns is cleverly structured around a set-piece familiar in anthropological accounts of Pueblo cultures: the view from the roofs of the buildings, where strangers can observe the public aspects of some of the ceremonies. Pueblo cultures like the Hopi and Zuni are famous for the strength and pervasiveness of their religion, which involves a large part of their lives in formal observances. They are also noted for the fact that large parts of these observances are deeply secret, and take place literally underground, in *kivas*. The novel begins with the Navajo Chee, with some other strangers, watching the sacred clowns of its title, as they ritually disrupt a Tanoan Kachina ceremony. Chee is there to find a missing boy. An apparently unconnected murder occurs during the ceremony, and we are left with a mystery to be solved. Later in the novel Chee is again an observer of a complex cultural event, but rather more in the know. He and a Cheyenne police colleague, Blizzard, together with Chee's girlfriend, a culturally dislocated part-Navajo, go to a drive-in to watch John Ford's *Cheyenne Autumn*. Hillerman makes full use of the ironies of this scene. When it was made, the film used Navajo actors, speaking Navajo, to play the Cheyenne, and it was filmed on Navajo land, so that the pleasure for this present-day Navajo audience is to spot not only relatives but the occasions on which the Navajos are saying something completely inappropriate unnoticed by the white makers of the film:

> Scenes came in which sombre-locking Cheyenne leaders responded to serious questions in sombre-sounding Navajo. When converted back into English by the translator the answers made sombre sense. But they produced more happy bedlam among the audience and the 'What did he really say?' question from either Janet or Blizzard – and often both. What he really said tended to have something to do with the size of the Colonel's penis, or some other irrelevancy (p. 113).

Hillerman brings out well the way the Navajos have made the film their own. A Western produced in the mould of elegiac pathos about the Vanishing American, about the defeat of the Cheyenne (and often seen within the genre as one of Ford's more positive accounts of Indians) is here subverted: 'Talking about the movie during the movie – celebrating the small victory of The People [the Navajo] over the white man which this John Ford classic represented – was the reason Navajos still came to see it'(p. 111). This complex phenomenon is referred to by one of the other characters as 'Sort of a campy deal, like the Rocky Horror Show' (p. 110). Thus Blizzard, the Cheyenne policeman, is seeing one film, supposedly portraying his ancestral past, while Chee and the other Navajos are seeing something else, and Chee makes explicit the connection with the Tano ceremony which we have seen them viewing from the roof at the beginning of the book:

> I was thinking about you and me and Cowboy sitting on the roof at Tano – watching the Kachina dance. Cowboy's Hopi, and he saw a lot that we missed. But not as much as the Tano People. All of us up there on the roof were outsiders, I mean. Like the Cheyenne watching the Navajos pretending to be Cheyennes. We missed a lot. (p. 122)

What they miss is, of course, the culturally specific material, the signs they do not know how to read because they are not cued in to the semiotic system in which these signs signify. Chee contrasts their position as spectators on the roof ('outsiders') with the participants in the ceremony. Likewise Blizzard, the Cheyenne, was unaware of the full significance of the film, which was just part of a larger cultural performance about subverting the normal relation of film and spectators.

Here Hillerman is drawing our attention to something which is one of the main sources of pleasure in his work, namely that as a rule we are guided, by being party to the thoughts of his protagonist, through different systems of thought. Leaphorn and Chee draw on their insiders' knowledge and Hillerman makes sure that this knowledge is passed on to us through their thoughts, and not as an authorial intrusion. This is at one with his general technique of effacing the authorial presence within the thought processes of the character, in a style which has been called free indirect speech. In this way we move imperceptibly from 'he felt that' or 'he thought that' to a statement that is not marked as such, but still seems to be operating from within the consciousness of the character. This is standard practice in a whole range of contemporary writing, but it is worth pursuing the way it constitutes its reading subject in some detail here, because of the cross-cultural implications. As a non-Navajo, Hillerman's decision not only to tell stories with Navajo characters at their centre but also to efface his own role, so that we are apparently given direct access to Leaphorn and Chee, raises issues very similar to those addressed in recent commentary on the status of ethnographic writing.

The claim to be able to represent another culture has in the past invoked in varying degrees both objectivity and subjectivity, distance and closeness, the detachment of the scientist and the sympathy of the fellow-being, and the exact relation of these elements has been the subject of important contemporary critiques. One particularly relevant line of approach has focused on the ways in which the Western claim to be able to know and to represent (in all senses) the colonised Other is based on these twin aspects of difference and sameness.

Analyses of the varying ways in which native cultures and peoples have been represented in ethnographic writing have demonstrated how the objective stance constitutes the natives as objects of study rather than as subjects in their own right. In addition, even if in accompanying or supplementary material the personal and dialogical aspects of the relation between anthropologist and informants is given, and in fact prized as evidence for the truth of the account, the actual way of presenting the account effaces this dialogical process, so that we are given knowledge as freestanding and unarguable: 'the natives believe that ...' or 'there are six clans'.

In his influential account of a Balinese cockfight, the anthropologist Clifford Geertz attempts to describe the cockfight and its significance to the Balinese who take part, and he uses the metaphor of reading a text. A culture, he says, is 'an ensemble of texts, themselves ensembles, which the anthropologist strains to read over the shoulder of those to whom they properly belong'.[23] This is an intriguing image, which involves a sense of sharing, of intrusion, and perhaps of superior over-seeing. As Vincent Crapanzano points out in a powerful critique of Geertz, 'It represents a sort of asymmetrical we-relationship with the anthropologist behind and above the native, hidden but at the top of the hierarchy of understanding.'[24]

Ethnographic debates may seem far removed from popular detective fiction, but I hope that the structural similarities between the Tano ceremony, the Ford film, and Geertz's metaphor are becoming apparent. Hillerman, through Chee, draws attention to the many levels of cultural interpretation possible for any event, and the similarity of such 'reading' to the activity of detective work, but if we ask who is doing the final 'overseeing' and who is ultimately in the know, it is in fact the reader, given by the invisible author, not more knowledge than Chee, but certainly just as much. The fact that this seems to come from our direct contact with Chee, by means of Hillerman's use of free indirect speech, is an important part of the pleasure. Through our close identification with the viewpoint of Chee or Leaphorn we are guided through the maze, while at the same time we are constituted as comfortably objective subjects. The effect of free indirect speech is that, as Ronald Carter puts it, 'a kind of fusion takes place between authorial and character viewpoint in which the shape and texture of the character's voice can be preserved without any loss of the narrator's objective interpretation of events'.[25]

In aligning this literary technique with the relation between the ethnographer and his or her object of study my intention has been to give a context in which we can appreciate and evaluate Hillerman's particular achievement. For Hillerman, an Anglo writing in conventional and popular forms, has been calmly operating for some time now in what has become a political minefield in the area of social sciences and cultural studies, namely that of cultural difference. In assuming the ability to move in and out of his protagonists' minds, he risks the criticisms levelled at ethnographers, certainly, but his achievement may finally be that he has managed to cut through the self-questionings and reflexivities of postmodern ethnography in creating characters who are different, but with whom we share common and recognisable values.

Notes

1. In a British TV programme, *The Media Show* (presented by Emma Freud), on the reception of his film. For a general and wide-ranging account of the changing representations

of Indians, see Robert Berkhofer, *The White Man's Indian: Images of the American Indian From Columbus to the Present* (New York: Knopf, 1978), and Raymond W. Stedman, *Shadows of the Indian: Stereotypes in American Culture* (Norman: Oklahoma University Press, 1982).

2. William Willard, 'Toward an Anthropology of Anthropology: Culture Heroes, Origin Myths and Mythological Places of Southwestern Anthropology', in Arnold Krupat (ed.), *New Voices in Native American Literary Criticism* (Washington and London: Smithsonian Institution Press, 1993), p. 267.

3. Tony Hillerman, *Dance Hall of the Dead* (New York: Harper and Row, 1973), p. 77.

4. The term is given as *hozro* in *The Ghostway* and *hozho* in *Sacred Clowns*. Hillerman's response, when asked about the different spellings, was a resigned recognition of the diversity not only within Navajo beliefs and practices, but within the expert accounts. His own relaxed approach, which seems to be to get things as right as possible, using written sources and personal enquiry, but not to expect to find or use one authoritative or generalising truth, is more in keeping with the experience of being within a lived tradition rather than outside it, trying to develop a model which would explain it all, as with some earlier anthropological projects. The disclaimers and acknowledgements at the beginning of many of his books mention some of the standard ethnographic works on the Navajo, as well as many personal contacts. On the Hopi, however, Hillerman is more at pains to stress his outsider status, and the book he recommends for further information, Frank Waters' *The Book of the Hopi*, would be regarded with suspicion by many Hopis and scholars.

5. Tony Hillerman, *The Blessing Way* (1970), repr. in *The Leaphorn Mysteries* (Harmondsworth, Middlesex: Penguin Books, 1994), p. 129.

6. Tony Hillerman, *Listening Woman* (1978), repr. in *The Leaphorn Mysteries* (Harmondworth, Middlesex: Penguin, 1994), p. 363.

7. See Clyde Kluckhohn, *Navajo Witchcraft* (Boston: Beacon Press, 1977 [1944]) and Marc Simmons, *Witchcraft in the*

Southwest: Spanish and Indian Supernaturalism of the Rio Grande (Flagstaff: Northland Press, 1974).

8. See for a concise account of the constitution of the subject in realism, Catherine Belsey, *Critical Practice* (London: Routledge, 1980).

9. The genre of romance in nineteenth-century America can be seen as reflecting the same concerns as Poe with different levels of reality, a concern that realism effectively excludes.

10. See, for instance, Stephen A. Tyler, 'Postmodern Ethnography: From Document of the Occult to Ocult Document', in James Clifford and George E. Marcus (eds), *Writing Culture: The Poetics and Politics of Ethnography* (Berkeley and Los Angeles: California University Press, 1986).

11. Tony Hillerman, *People of Darkness* (London: Sphere Books, 1988), pp. 189–90.

12. Shamoon Zamir,'Literature in a "National Sacrifice Area": Leslie Silko's *Ceremony*', in Krupat, *New Voices*.

13. Leslie Marmon Silko, *Ceremony* (New York: Viking/ Penguin, 1977), pp. 1, 260.

14. Tony Hillerman, *The Ghostway* (London: Sphere Books, 1989 [1984]), p. 35.

15. In an interview at the 1995 Bouchercon Conference, Hillerman specifically located his source for this idea. He described covering an execution as a reporter, where the condemned man urged the press to report his execution so that his mother, whom he had never known, would come to claim him, or his body.

16. Tony Hillerman, *Talking God* (New York: Harper and Row, 1989), p. 195.

17. Ward Churchill, *Fantasies of the Master Race: Literature, Cinema and the Colonization of American Indians* (Monroe, Maine: Common Courage Press, 1992), p. 279.

18. Franco Moretti, *Signs Taken for Wonders* (London: Verso, 1983), p. 152.

19. Tony Hillerman, *Sacred Clowns* (London: Michael Joseph, 1993), p. 3.

20. A disease recently and painfully acknowledged as a problem in Indian communities, and caused by alcohol

abuse during pregnancy. See Michael Dorris' powerful personal account in *The Broken Chord* (New York: Harper Perennial, 1991).

21. This may seem improbably convenient, but it is worth bearing in mind that it is anthropology rather than sociology which Indians would be likely to study to find out about themselves and their society. The implications of this, in terms of reinforcing a stress on the static and traditional rather than the modern, are very relevant to any discussion of the determinants of Indian identity but go beyond the terms of this chapter.

22. Quoted in James C. Pierson, 'Mystery Literature and Ethnography: Fictional Detectives as Anthropologists' in P. Dennis and W. Aycock (eds) *Literature and Anthropology* (Lubbock, Texas: Texas Tech University Press, 1989), p. 15. John G. Cawelti, in reviewing the work of the Australian Arthur Upfield, also sees the similarities of anthropologist and detective. The investigation of a puzzling crime, he says, 'casts light on the workings of a society by catching it at a moment of anomaly and disruption'. Nevertheless, he draws attention to the limitations of 'the angle of vision enforced by the conventions of the classic detective story'. See 'Murder in the Outback', in *The New Republic*, 30 July 1977, p. 39. Also quoted in Dennis and Aycock, *Literature and Anthropology*.

23. Clifford Geertz, 'Deep Play: Notes on a Balinese Cockfight', *The Interpretation of Cultures* (New York: Basic Books, 1973) pp. 452–3.

24. Vincent Crapanzano, 'Hermes' Dilemma: The Masking of Subversion in Ethnographic Description', in Marcus and Clifford, *Writing Culture*, p. 74.

25. Ronald Carter (ed.), *Language and Literature: An Introductory Reader in Stylistics* (London and New York: Routledge, 1982), p. 72.

7

The Last Good Place: James Crumley, the West and the Detective Novel

John Harvey

Retrospective

> I have to admit that I'm not even sure where the
> West is any more. Except in my heart.[1]

I know that the first Crumley novel I read was *The Last Good Kiss*, but I can't remember too clearly when this was, nor the exact circumstances which resulted in my possession of a Random House, hardcover first edition. But here it is, a little soiled now and ragged, behind Stan Zagorowski's slightly surreal jacket design – a section of Western town, all brash signs and Hopper colours before a backdrop of towering, featureless mountains and, hanging above Mary's Bar, a pair of full-blooded red lips that seem to have floated off from a Max Ernst canvas in an outsize offer of sexual promise and threat.

I suspect the year was 1978 or 1979. Not long off a brief series of mawkish, London-based, sub-Chandler private-eye novels (James Ellroy was right: follow old Ray down those mean streets and sumptuous sub-clauses at your peril!), and embarked upon a sequence of ten paperback Westerns featuring Hart the Regulator, reading *The Last Good Kiss* affected me in the same way as listening to Philly Jo Jones when I was trying to be a drummer. All the things I had wanted to do, plus several I hadn't even thought of, and all with such apparent ease. If I hadn't already signed the contract, my electric typewriter might well have followed the drum kit into the small ads columns of the local newspaper.

150

I instinctively knew this was the best private-eye novel I'd read since Robert B. Parker's *The Godwulf Manuscript*, some five years before. I think I knew that Crumley's book had elements over and above the verve and freshness of Parker's debut, and that these were to do with the Western setting and something else I had still to identify. Whatever the case, having read it once, I immediately set to read it again and have enjoyed re-reading it every few years ever since. And even if I still don't quite understand the power it works – or the final playing out of the plot – if there's a more singular and compelling PI novel to have been written in the past, almost, twenty years, I don't know what it is.

Of course, I read all of the other Crumley I could lay my hands on; not that, in terms of publications, this amounted to a great deal. Years spent writing and doctoring movie scripts in Hollywood, as well as Crumley's fastidious dissatisfaction with his own work – there are numerous novels begun and set aside as wanting, or, perhaps, wanting their moment – means there are only four other novels so far. *One to Count Cadence*, based on Crumley's experiences in Vietnam, was his first, published in 1969; *The Wrong Case*, featuring private eye Milo Milodragovitch, followed in 1975; *The Last Good Kiss*, featuring C.W. Sughrue, came out in 1978, and the second Milodragovitch book, *Dancing Bear*, was published in 1983. After that there was a ten-year wait for Sughrue to return in *The Mexican Tree Duck* in 1993.

Before ever I met Crumley himself, I encountered Martha Elizabeth, the artist and poet who is now his wife. Participants in a Poetry Conference at Squaw Valley in the High Sierras, I introduced myself to one of the writers I was to share a house with and received an, 'Oh, my husband, Jim, writes mysteries too.' The following year, I met Crumley in London, edgily prowling the book tables in the Camden Town branch of Waterstone's before he gave a fine and fiercely funny reading from *The Mexican Tree Duck*, and a few days later, we met again at *Shots in the Dark*, the Nottingham-based Mystery and Thriller Festival, and I enjoyed, with Jim and Martha, a long and talkative late breakfast which somehow encompassed lunch before shading into high tea. The following year, Crumley and I were both in Seattle, at Bouchercon, the World Mystery

Convention, and this was where – in a hotel room on the twenty-third floor overlooking the Puget Sound and with the help of a brace of Absolut vodkas and some room service hors d'oeuvres – I taped the interview with Crumley that forms the backbone of this chapter.

I began by asking about literary influences and style, and where he saw himself in the American crime-writing tradition – a Chandler man or a Hammett man?

CRUMLEY: If there is a legacy, it seems to me I belong more to the Chandler side of things; what I do is different from what Hammett meant to do. Maybe I could explain it this way – Warren Zevon, he's a friend of mine, he's an American rock 'n' roll singer, and also a tremendous musician, and I was with him at a party one night and somebody was telling him what a great songwriter he was and he sort of brushed it off and said, the words are just something to hang the music on. And so, for me, the mystery novel, the detective novel, is just something to hang the words on. I don't much care about the mystery itself, I don't like puzzle mysteries, don't write them, and in that way I'm more like Chandler, owe more to Chandler, although what Hammett did was a good thing in taking the mystery away from the bloodstained tea cosies. I mean Hammett was an actual working Pinkerton and so he saw the gritty side of life and I think that sort of neo-realism or super-realism, that's important, that's where real life takes place. Whereas Sherlock Holmes and that ilk, it's kind of a lie. You know, in that what they're saying is civilisation works, and what I'm saying and what I think Hammett was saying is that civilisation doesn't work. Whether it's the end of the British Empire or the death of the American Dream or the failure of the Soviet Union, whatever it is we're trying to do doesn't work. And I think it doesn't work because societies and civilisations tend to reflect human failings and we are, unfortunately, all too human. And the other notion that there's a rational universe out there that you can figure out is, as far as I'm concerned, as nonsensical as believing in the risen Jesus Christ, like the Rosicrucians ...

HARVEY: Or the risen Elvis Presley.

CRUMLEY: Well, I'm more likely to believe that Elvis is alive than I am in any of these idiot religions.

HARVEY: But it's interesting, isn't it, that you believe in a view of society that's close to Hammett's, yet feel as a writer you're closer to Chandler. And I wonder if there's some sense in which what Chandler is writing, and so by implication what you're writing, is a romanticised version of Hammett's work?

CRUMLEY: Well, certainly Chandler was a hopeless romantic; hopelessly, helplessly romantic. And for myself, I'm certainly more romantic than Hammett, just in that I really believe that the words are what make up a novel. Every word choice you make is going to make the novel different. So that because I like to write big flowery sentences, I like to play with language and I like to embed jokes in the text, and I like to have a lot of things going on at one time, I think, inevitably, that's going to cause romanticism to creep into your work even if you don't mean for it to. Even if you write about the ugliest thing you can think of, if you write about it in pretty language, it's going to be romantic, it's going to be romanticised.

Of course, nobody ever achieves realism, but if you're going to try and do it you'd need to be able to write something like Dutch Leonard, those good, hard, flat, clean little sentences. You couldn't do it like I do it.

HARVEY: What was it, then, about your influences, that led you toward that more baroque style that Chandler favours?

CRUMLEY: Well, aside from Chandler, the two most important writers in my early life were Lawrence Durrell and Malcolm Lowry. In fact, I didn't even read any Chandler till I was in the middle of my first novel.

HARVEY: How did that come about, Lowry and Durrell?

CRUMLEY: I was in the army before I ever read a serious novel. I ran into what they used to call a beatnik and we got to be pals and he said, you've got to read this book and it was the *The Picture of Dorian Gray*. And so through my three and a half years in the army I met more and more educated people and got turned onto better and better reading lists. Or more sophisticated reading lists, I guess I should say. And then finally when I was in college, after I got out of the army, I was majoring in lots of different things, but I was essentially taking what I wanted to. One of the things I learned in the army was how to manipulate a bureaucracy and so I took what courses I wanted to, I didn't take what the college wanted me to, which is probably the way to get an education. I became my own advisor. And I just stumbled into this course and discovered Lowry and Durrell in the same spring semester and I was just taken away. I still am. I still love *Under the Volcano* and re-read it periodically and I still love *The Alexandrian Quartet*. I used to read that every spring; I did that for about twenty years. Now I only read it about every five years. It's just the sound of the language.

HARVEY: So what was the gap in time between discovering Durrell and beginning the first fiction thing you started writing?

CRUMLEY: Oh, about twenty-five minutes. No, really, it was pretty close to that. I took a creative writing class the next fall semester. And you know I meant to be a poet at one time, but my writing teacher suggested I try fiction after several failed attempts at poetry. So I seriously sat down and tried to write for the first time in my life. I was out of the army and married, I must have been 23. And the first story, which eventually became my first novel, my teacher didn't like very much, but the second story, he said how would you like to go to Iowa? I didn't know what Iowa was or what was there, and he said well it's a place where you can go and read and write for a couple of years and then they'll give you a degree and you can get a teaching job and I said okay and threw all of my other plans aside. I was on my way up here to the University of Washington to get a PhD in Soviet Studies and then probably go to work for the CIA, but I went to Iowa instead and tended bar and cleaned toilets for two years and wrote the first hundred and twenty pages of *One to Count Cadence* and sold it immediately.

HARVEY: Who were your teachers in Iowa?

CRUMLEY: Probably R.V. Cassill had the most influence on me. He was the best teacher. He had great theories about literature and he stuck by them. And then the other kinds of things that you learn, I learned from Dick Yates, like Dick Yates taught me how to drink martinis, and how to have writer's troubles, and how to be sad about your children growing up in someone else's house. And then Kurt Vonnegut taught me the odd thing – he's far and away the most humane human being I've ever run into. Plus I was at Iowa with John Irving and Andre Dubus, these were my classmates. It was great. I went from South Texas where I had one friend who I could talk to about books, to Iowa City where people would phone you up at three in the morning to talk about books, and I just had a grand time. The winter before I started my first novel for the last time, I read *The Brothers Karamazov*, and *Anna Karenin* and *The Rebel*, and, I don't know, the book *did* something that it hadn't done before and took off and it never looked back.

HARVEY: But then, after *Cadence*, after a degree of personal to-ing and fro-ing, why do you up and write a mystery?

CRUMLEY: I discovered Chandler, in Mexico. And I said, Jesus, this is wonderful! I want to try this someday.

The Great American West, the Family, Vietnam

Logan
'Can I have a kiss?'
Jane
'No. I don't know. Yeah. And then after that we can talk about the wild west and how to get out of it.'[2]

The summer I turned sixteen I ran away with the first man who promised to take me as far away from the damned endless horizon as I could get.[3]

Crumley tried it first in *The Wrong Case*, and one of the things that becomes immediately apparent is both the degree to which he is sticking close to the Chandler model at the same time as veering away from it. Here, as in *Dancing Bear*, the other Milo Milodragovitch mystery, our hero is hired by a woman client who, despite appearances to the contrary, lies to him hand over fist, and draws him into a clammy and dangerous web which proves almost fatal. It's private-eye plot A, or at least B, and the similarities between the naive Miss Duffy in *The Wrong Case* and Orfamy Quest in Chandler's *The Little Sister* are noticeable. Not only are they both seeking out a missing brother, both are representatives of another, more innocent world.

> 'Look,' I said. 'You come from Manhattan, Kansas. The last time I memorized the *World Almanac* that was a little town not far from Topeka. Population around twelve thousand. You work for Dr. Alfred Zugsmith and you're looking for somebody named Orin. Manhattan is a small town. It has to be. Only half a dozen places in Kansas are anything else. I already have enough information about you to find out your whole family history.'[4]

> She seemed like a woman from a simpler, better time, a small-town time when sprinklers graced neat lawns and screen doors smelled like rain or dust instead of plastic, when the seasons changed as gracefully as scenes on greeting cards, when snow was never dirty, when fall leaves were never soggy and damp, and when children never cried, except for brief moments, and then were so gently comforted that they didn't mind crying at all. She did that to me, made me homesick for a childhood I'd never really had, the one I sometimes constructed in odd drunken moments to make me forget the real one. And she made me hope, something I hadn't done in years, made me believe in a better, cleaner world where a man and a woman could raise a family in peace. I decided then that she deserved better than my tired version of comfort; she deserved my help, such as it was.[5]

Similarly, when Milo is escorted to the solarium to meet his elderly female client in *Dancing Bear*, we are consciously reminded of Philip Marlowe being taken into the hothouse to talk with General Sternwood in *The Big Sleep*. And perhaps, at first glance, there is not a great difference between Chandler's Los Angeles knight errant, bestriding the mean and dirty streets of the city in the cause of justice, and Crumley's heroes, unwilling and unable to step aside from their task of finding the missing woman (there usually *is* a missing woman) despite self-evident and mortal danger:

> I didn't know much, didn't much care. I knew I had to find out who wanted my ass, and negotiate, accommodate as much as I could and still live with myself. I had to find Sarah, if they had her, and Gail, and when I found the old woman, I had my own peace to make. That old lady and I would get happily stoned and talk about my father. And if I didn't find her, or if I found her dead, I intended to wreak havoc across the land until the guilty were punished under my hand. Even if it cost my life.[6]

Crumley, I'm sure, wants us to notice these similarities, these generic conventions which operate as a shorthand between writer and reader, a way of signalling okay, we both know what's at stake here, now just relax and trust me. Because if we can accept *that*, if we can settle back inside the form, we can enjoy and be stimulated by what else he has to offer.

Initially, of course, there is the language, with the pleasures of its rolling sentences, its cumulative clauses, the gestures towards sentimentality which are held in check by an abundant raw-edged humour and an eye which looks at the world without flinching. And the world, Crumley wants us to know, has changed, continues to change and none of it (almost none) for the better. Remember what he said about Hammett and civilisation.

Crumley's detectives are untrammelled by the almost pious morality which dogs Marlowe. Where Chandler wanted his hero to be neither tarnished nor afraid, Milo and Sughrue are frequently frightened and to call them tarnished is to underestimate the degree to which they have embraced most of the good bad things life has to offer. Not only do they lust (with slightly surprising success) after the women of all ages who wind up in their path, not only do they spend most of their narratives poised between half-drunk and barely conscious, they do drugs with a relish and impunity which would have given Philip Marlowe a coronary. In short, they are creatures of their time. And place.

'This is the Great American West', Milo tells Helen Duffy. 'Where men come to get away from laws.'[7] And one of the things that is played out in these novels is the tension between, on one hand, the urge to keep that freedom and its concomitant distrust of outside (especially, government) interference, and, on the other, the need to act responsibly – and in concert with others – to prevent the last good place from falling further into dissolution and terminal decay:

> Of course, the West always has been a place that puts a high premium on individual freedom and the almost feudal rights of the landowner. Along with a number of other western writers, I sometimes think we have paid too high a price for those myths, that those myths have done as much harm as all the ravenous corporate lions. Individual freedom is anarchy without an individual sense of responsibility, particularly where the land is concerned, and the responsibility of ownership is not just of the land but also to the land.[8]

> The myth of the West must be about hope, the hope that one good man can save a town that neither desires nor deserves salvation ... [9]

The West and the family: these are the two great themes to which Crumley returns again and again, teasing out the shifting ambivalences, trapped in part by an idealised version of each, which seduces even as it is shown as false, impossible to achieve.

There is a distinction in these books between the West of burgeoning crime and industrial mutilation, and that of still unsullied landscape and light; between that which breeds hope and which cannot, once experienced, be denied. At the end of *Dancing Bear*, Milo heads south to California, intent upon staying there, beginning a new life, but Montana claims him back. A Montana winter at that. As Crumley says of himself, 'When I'm gone, something is missing. Coming back, running fast and free, it is as Thoreau said: "Eastward I go only by force; but westward I go free." Nobody ever said it much better.'[10]

Crumley says it in *The Mexican Tree Duck*, not necessarily better, but certainly more romantically:

> The drive wasn't a long one, just long enough for me to ease into the scenery, an old Montana addiction. Under all that baby-blue sky it could have been July, the early snows simply bad dreams. But the cottonwoods and creek willows were seared with borders of yellow, and the western larch on the mountain slope yearned to shed their needles one more time.
>
> Young men find spring the time of renewal, but those of us with a few beers under our belts and even more miles on our butts find spring to be simply a false promise of greenery destined to wither, a flowered, frenzied promise never meant to be kept.
>
> In the clear, hot sunshine of autumn, the promise of winter waits just inside the shade of the pines, a vow always honoured. Whatever winter brings – aching bones, starving elk, frozen children – we've got this moment of blue clarity. Western Montana at its best.[11]

And yet ... and yet ... this is still the state that elsewhere in this piece Crumley describes as a crown colony, a place where outsiders have found ways, and continue to find ways, whether it be mining or lumber, of keeping their hands clean and getting rich at others' expense. Much of Montana has become as tainted by the ugliness of greed and big business as had Chandler's LA in *The Big Sleep*, where the old oil derricks that are the basis of the Sternwood fortune contaminate the landscape, the sump water that has drained from them contains the dead body of a good man, and the corruption of thoughtless avarice has seeped into the Sternwood blood:

When you see places like Butte and the coal strip mines in eastern Montana and the goddamned clear-cuts, try to remember that we may be whores, but it's those pimps playing squash in the Yale Club in New York fucking City who are living fat on their cuts. So shut the fuck up.[12]

And Meriwether, the town where Milo lives and which stands in for Crumley's Missoula, is exhibiting all of the signs of urban lawlessness and blight which had been the property of major cities, with seemingly homeless kids carrying out muggings in broad daylight to support their drug habits, and organised crime closing in for a killing. As well as hope and renewal, winter, it seems, can also bring despair:

Perhaps it was the hard, long winters, months of Canadian fronts falling upon the valley like wolves, howling winds sharp with ice and snow; or maybe the sort of rootless people who drifted into the valley from the urban East or Great Plains, looking for paradise and mad as hell when they didn't find it; or perhaps it was Meriwether's vision of itself as part of the wild and woolly West, the last, lawless frontier. Whatever the cause, Meriwether had divorce, suicide and alcoholism rates that embarrassed the national average. And the dope, which for years had just been another way to get high, had become serious. The kids had moved away from marijuana and had begun to kill themselves with pills and speed.[13]

If there are positive and negative aspects of the West in these novels, the same can he said of the family. The actions of the heroes can often be seen as attempts to hold families together. Indeed, one of the major differences between Crumley's private eyes and Chandler's is that, while the former are prepared to take individual responsibility for their actions, they rarely, if ever, act alone. Like the character played by Clint Eastwood in *The Outlaw Josey Wales*, both Sughrue and Milo draw people to them, forming strange families, not necessarily related by blood, but bound in need and determination.

Often, though, it is an actual family at the centre of the plot. In *The Wrong Case*, Milo is searching for Helen Duffy's brother, a homosexual gun lover and quick-draw artist, who is doing research into the reality and myth of Western gunfighters, and who turns out to be Helen's illegitimate son. In *The Last Good Kiss*, Sughrue is initially searching for the writer, Abraham Trahearne, at the request of his ex-wife. Trahearne located, Sughrue sets off on the trail of Betty Sue Flowers, an unhappy barmaid's daughter, only to find that Betty Sue is one third of the extraordinary family unit – mother, ex-wife, current wife – that Trahearne has assembled round him. In *Dancing Bear*, Milo accepts as a client the now ageing woman who was one of his own dead father's lovers. And in *The Mexican Tree Duck*, Sughrue's journey is triggered by a search for a notorious biker's mother and for much of the journey he is accompanied by Wynona and Baby Lester – an instant family: mother and child. After his mother's death (good women almost all die here, it's more or less a given) the child is returned to Sughrue for him to look after and raise.

Families are often less and more than they seem. They can possess a duplicity which runs counter to the idealised versions which freefloat from time to time through Milo's or Sughrue's heads, versions which are in contrast to the starker realities of their lives. Sughrue's father, an impoverished farmer, an alcoholic, deserted his mother; Milo's father did the same only in a more emphatic way: 'My father had solved his life with whisky and the full-choke barrel of an LC Smith hammerless double.'[14] His mother, likewise: 'Then the chaplain switched to his Dr. Kildare voice and gave me the kicker: she had hanged herself with a silk stocking at a fat farm in Arizona.'[15]

So Trahearne's family in *The Last Good Kiss* – 'We all live together – or nearly together – my mother, my ex-wife, my present wife, and me on a little ranch outside Cauldron Springs. ... One little happy family'[16] – begins by seeming a perfect, neo-hippie compromise, a commune of mutual love and understanding, and is only gradually revealed to be the nest of vipers which Sughrue begins to suspect. 'As I eased back down the sweeping curves of the canyon highway, I told myself that if I didn't watch out, Trahearne's women were either going to break my heart or change my life or be the death of me.'[17] In the end, of course, they nearly do all three.

Aside from the sheer quality of the writing, which is Crumley at his most consistent and assured, it is the sly delineation of maternal and sexual jealousy and power revolving around this trinity of women, and akin to some Western version of Greek tragedy, which gives *The Last Good Kiss* its great force. That, and the character of Abraham Trahearne, to whom Crumley gives a strength and presence equal to Sughrue, so that, instead of the book depending upon Sughrue's vision, it is held in perfect balance between the two.

Trahearne is, I think, one of the most convincing portrayals of a writer in modern fiction, convincing especially in regard to a writer's self-doubt, his weaknesses. He owes a little to Roger Wade in Chandler's *The Long Goodbye*, quite a deal (according to Crumley) to the Southern novelist and poet, James Dickey, but most to Crumley himself. In that sense, it seems not only a truthful picture, but a brave one:

> In *The Last Good Kiss*, the story's subtext is the kind of selfishness it takes some people to be a writer. Because the book is dedicated to my old friend, Dick Hugo, people always want to see him in the Trahearne part, but I don't think so, I think that was a younger me that felt like he had to give up close personal ties in order to retreat into yourself to do this thing and I must say I don't think that any more. I don't feel that way. I don't believe that.[18]

What we are told in retrospect of Trahearne is that he was one of the most alive people the speaker had ever met – 'this huge, beautiful, alive man'[19] – but what we *see* is a man of ragged vitality whose life in some ways stopped when the Second World War ended; who is scared to drag himself out of bars and sober up for fear that he might actually have to settle himself down and write something; and write something better and more honest than the three bestselling novels and six praised volumes of poetry, which he now thinks of as phony and inflated. Trahearne has sufficient self-knowledge to know what he should do, how to live, how to trust and forgive – wants both to do it and to write about it:

'All this time, all these years since the war, I worried about how tough you had to be to live, how I had to live without flinching, but when it came down to it, when it had to do with living instead of dying, I didn't have the guts to forgive the woman I loved. I couldn't cut it, son, not a bit.' He paused long enough to pick up the .45 and shove the stack of pages off his desk. 'So now I'm through with all that. I'm going to write a novel about love and forgiveness. Even if it kills me. And that's why I'm not about to blow my brains out with this.' He tossed the pistol back on the desk. 'It's nothing but a paperweight now.'[20]

But this is not what Trahearne does; finally he lacks both the courage and the moral strength. He does not write the novel about love and forgiveness (though Crumley, of course, does) but he does not die because of this. Because he cannot forgive the woman he loves, he gives his ex-wife the .45 and (as far as we can tell; the narrative is not clear) she exorcises her own jealousy and hate by killing the woman on Trahearne's behalf.

It is the measure of Trahearne's failure. The true sign of strength and integrity for a Crumley hero is that he has – and uses – a capacity to forgive. 'I watched you go after her for a smile and eighty-seven dollars,' Trahearne says of Sughrue, 'and you never judged her, not once, you forgave her without asking anything in return'.[21] And, as Helen Duffy's mother says of Milo in *The Wrong Case*: 'Perhaps you really are that rarest of men, a forgiving man.'[22]

What Crumley himself can neither forgive nor forget is Vietnam: what happened to those Americans who served there and what continues to happen in America in that war's wake. Duplicity, the waste of young lives, the way what he describes as 'the trinity of American power: drugs, cash and automatic weapons'[23] prevailed during that war, as it is prevailing now. By the time of writing *The Mexican Tree Duck*, this has become a major theme, taking its place alongside the West and the family.

Then Willie hooked a boot lace on a trip wire. And froze. Thank Buddha.

I didn't care anymore. I ran everybody out of range of the little bouncing beauty, ran them off at gunpoint, then got on my belly to dig out the mine.

Bellied in the muck, listening to the cool chatter of Willie, smelling the rank bite of hash, watching Willie's knee tremble ever so slightly, I fell in love with life, fell at least as much as was possible for me. And I got him fucking out. About the sweetest moment of my life.

Then the next night in his tent, I pulled an overloaded spike out of his arm, an American-made disposable syringe filled with our heroin. The CIA had bought the opium, flown it to labs on Taiwan, then flown it back to Vietnam just to kill William Curtiss Williams, Jr.

My brief love affair with life ended.[24]

I have to admit to being disappointed by *The Mexican Tree Duck* when I first read it. Well, ten years builds up a lot of expectations, and, anyway, this was a Sughrue novel and I wanted another *Last Good Kiss*. But, of course, there *is* no other last good kiss.

What there is instead is a fast-paced story which draws on the same subject matter as the songs of Crumley's friend, Warren Zevon – lawyers, guns and money. And Vietnam. It is not enough for Vietnam to be present in the underlying structure, the subtext, it has to burst its way through and Crumley invents a cast of larger-than-life grotesques to accompany it. So there are, indeed, enough guns to start another war, but then, as Crumley points out here and elsewhere, 'modern life is warfare without end'.[25] Reading the book again I was happy enough to let myself get carried along for the ride; too much armament, too many serious drugs for my liking, but, as Jim would doubtless point out, that's my problem rather than the book's.

So, I'll bow out with a final question and, with my thanks, leave James Crumley to close.

HARVEY: If I could come back to what you were saying about Vietnam and *The Mexican Tree Duck* and the extent to which the Vietnam experience still affects America and in particular the America that your books are about, I wonder if you'd like to talk a little more about that?

CRUMLEY: Well, one of the things that I think Vietnam did is that it made outsiders of a lot of people. A lot of people who went to the war, a lot of people who protested the war. It put them outside the mainstream, which I think is probably the best place to be. I've also got serious anti-middle class prejudices, left over from my days as a radical and a Trotskyite and I don't trust the middle class. I think the middlebrow of American literature is shameful and I'm not going to apologise for not belonging to it. I still have political leanings and literary leanings that I'm not supposed to have as a redneck writer of hippie life. I mean, I still believe in all that stuff; I think the Sixties were right. I still believe it's possible to change the country, but it would take a revolution now. And we're fixing to get a revolution because, if the polls are right, we're going to get a Republican Congress the next time round. And I find these Republicans to be – well, they're not conservatives, in any kind of sense at all, all they are about's economic things, all they care about's their money. You can see it left over from the Reagan years, if you go somewhere like Sun Valley, Idaho. In the Reagan years all of that tax money went to build three-million-dollar vacation homes in places like Sun Valley. They stripped the government pretty good and I think they're dangerous and stupid and mean-hearted people, and whatever kind of bumbling Mr Clinton does, and he certainly bumbles, he's at least not mean-spirited. George Bush was a mean-spirited son-of-a-bitch and still is, and so, you know, I like to try and write about all of those things in some kind of way without writing about them, if you see what I'm saying. Shake their hand with one hand and pick their pocket with another. I don't want to write a political novel, like *All The King's Men*, but I'd like to maybe make people think about this stuff.

Now there's been a number of novels about the Aryan nation types as the villains, but I don't think approaching it like that is the way to do it. You have to be sneakier than that somehow. So that what I try to do in *The Mexican Tree Duck* is to talk about, as I say, how that war made outsiders of lots of people. For me, the real crimes were committed in Vietnam and that's what's happening to these guys now and this is how they dealt with it and this is what they did. And the last line of the book, when the question is what can I tell the government, is lie to 'em, fuck, they don't mind lying to you.

I don't look at the world the same way as the middle class does, and even though, you know, I live in a house with furniture and I don't have a ponytail any more and I live what looks like a middle-class life, deep in my heart I'm still a hippy and I believe that the DEA [Drugs Enforcement Agency] is more dangerous than the entire South American continent and you're never going to find a good DEA agent in one of my novels and the only cops that you'll find are good are street cops and good working detectives.

I had to put that war to rest finally. You know, I started there and I just had to put it away finally.

HARVEY: And you think that you've done that with *The Mexican Tree Duck*, finally moved through that?

CRUMLEY (Sighs): Yeah.

Notes

1. James Crumley, 'The Great West' in Bryan De Salvatore and Deirdre McNamer (eds), *The Muddy Fork & Other Things* (Livingston, Montana: Clark City Press, 1991), p. 48.
2. Thomas McGuane, *The Missouri Breaks* (New York: Ballantine Books, 1976), p. 48.
3. James Crumley, *Dancing Bear* (New York: Vintage Books, 1984), p. 31.
4. Raymond Chandler, *The Little Sister* (Harmondsworth, Middlesex: Penguin Books, 1955), p. 9.
5. James Crumley, *The Wrong Case* (St. Albans: Granada Publishing, 1976), p. 20.
6. *Dancing Bear*, p. 121.
7. *The Wrong Case*, p. 14.
8. 'The Great West', p. 51.
9. Ibid., p. 53.

10. Ibid., p. 48.
11. James Crumley, *The Mexican Tree Duck* (New York: Mysterious Press, 1993), p. 47.
12. *Dancing Bear*, p. 145.
13. *The Wrong Case*, p. 79.
14. Ibid., p. 77.
15. *Dancing Bear*, p. 33.
16. James Crumley, *The Last Good Kiss* (New York: Random House, 1978), p. 37.
17. Ibid., p. 170.
18. James Crumley in conversation with the author.
19. *The Last Good Kiss*, p. 119.
20. Ibid., p. 226.
21. Ibid.
22. *The Wrong Case*, p. 302.
23. James Crumley, in Charles L.P. Silet, 'Drugs, Cash and Automatic Weapons: an interview with James Crumley', *The Armchair Detective*, vol. 27, no. 1 (Winter, 1994), p. 14.
24. *The Mexican Tree Duck*, p. 225.
25. *Dancing Bear*, p. 228.

Further Reading

Gregory L. Morris, *Talking Up a Storm: Voices of the New West* (Lincoln: University of Nebraska Press, 1994), pp. 47–64.
John Williams, *Into the Badlands: A Journey through the American Dream* (London: Paladin, 1991), pp. 132–52.

8

James Ellroy, Los Angeles and the Spectacular Crisis of Masculinity

Josh Cohen

James Ellroy's four-volume chronicle of the postwar period in Los Angeles subjects the city's baroque criminal history and developmental geography to relentless interrogation.[1] Urban history emerges from this confrontation as startlingly overdetermined, marked by the interpenetration of corrupt political, economic and sexual forces, and generative of violently fractured subjectivities. The *LA Quartet*, spanning some 23 years in the life of the city, intricately maps its postwar boom, playing out Gothic dramas of criminal excess within the context of the reshaping of its built landscape by the convergent forces of land development and mass cultural spectacle.[2] The labyrinthine plots of the novels reveal this process to be underpinned by a confluence of explosive political and economic interests, that functions as a violent inversion of the seamless semiotic facade Los Angeles projects outwards via the media. In the course of this chapter, I intend to show how the crisis-ridden masculine identities of the *Quartet*'s protagonists are intricately bound up with this destabilising experience of urban transformation.

Walter Benjamin's writings on the city provide a number of suggestive points of entry into theorising the logic of Ellroy's Los Angeles. His excavation, primarily from the poetry of Baudelaire, of the figure of the *flaneur*, lone metropolitan wanderer, as a paradigmatic subject of urban modernity, is an initial grid through which Ellroy's protagonists might be viewed. If the Benjaminian *flaneur* is empowered by his capacity to exert a certain perceptual control over the city, by activating a visual mobility that eludes the instrumental imperatives of capitalism, the policemen that dominate Ellroy's novels represent a distorted mutation of *flaneurie,* an urban subjectivity that now operates not with critical autonomy, but in the service of a corrupt informal coalition of urban politicians, racketeers and developers.[3] Indeed, I want to suggest that, just as Benjamin read in the discarded objects of late nineteenth-century Paris the fossilised 'ur-forms' of modernity, Ellroy's reinvention of the emergent landscape of postwar Los Angeles traces the spectacular origins of postmodern urbanity.[4]

As he has explicitly asserted, Ellroy's shift of narrative perspective from the Chandlerian private eye to the waged cop constitutes a critique of the romanticised and historically inaccurate figuration of crime as existential conflict between alienated individual and urban modernity, and consequently marks the progressive cooptation of *flaneurie* by the state.[5] His protagonists' experience of a conspiracy of material forces shaping the urban landscape is felt as a devaluation of status from active subject to victimised object. The hypertrophied masculine anxiety generated by this erosion of agency is persistently articulated by way of a displaced rage against an apparently feminised urban 'object-world'. This anxious projection of the feminine takes a bewildering array of forms, from the murdered prostitute at the centre of *The Black Dahlia,* to the manipulative promiscuity of communist organiser Claire de Haven in *The Big Nowhere,* and the prostitutes surgically transformed to double as movie stars in *LA Confidential.*[6]

Christine Buci-Glucksmann's study of modernism's trope of the 'allegorical feminine' provides an interesting context for thinking about Ellroy's figurations of masculinity.[7] Buci-Glucksmann argues that modernism's representations of women articulate fears about the penetration of an idealised 'organic' femininity by the deceptive logic of the market, a process which engenders a crisis at the heart of masculine identity (her primary example is Baudelaire's prostitute whose body has literally been absorbed into the logic of the commodity). The male protagonists of Ellroy's fictions, I suggest, express their impotence before these 'unreadable' emblems of what Buci-Glucksmann terms the 'destructive principle' of the allegorical feminine (p. 78), in the forms of violent misogyny and racism. It is in the representation of a traumatised (white) masculinity, moreover, that the explosively charged map of the historical and geographical dynamics of postwar Los Angeles can be read. When Ellroy's cops investigate the murders of women, they are in effect tracing the disintegrative narratives of postwar urban space.

Perhaps the most significant, and sinister, feature of Ellroy's projected urban object-world, however, is that it constitutes not only the officially sanctioned mass spectacle that pervades Los Angeles, but equally its 'bastard' progeny. That is, shadowing the commodified images of Hollywood, Disneyland, the Dodgers Stadium, and other emblems of the hegemony of spectacle are their violent inversions. The entranced subject of Benjamin's 'Dreamworld' of mass culture, then, once that world is revealed as the product of specific historical and spatial processes, is 'awakened' less to conscious political engagement than to the 'Nightmare' double that looms beneath its surface. Indeed, in the most startling realisation of this awakening, the murder case that dominates *LA Confidential* is finally tied to the grotesque animations that Raymond Dieterling, a barely concealed fictionalisation of Walt Disney, and founder of the tellingly named 'Dream-a-Dream Land', creates for his illegitimate son. These distorted reinventions of Disney's 'official' cartoon aesthetic feed the son's murderous psychosexual rage. Dieterling's buried creative history thus serves as a discomfitingly literal enactment of Benjamin's famous dictum: 'There is no document of civilization which is not at the same time a document of barbarism.'[8] Indeed, this doubled logic of civilisation and barbarism is at the heart of Ellroy's fiction: the official narrative of Los Angeles' development, projected by its power elite, is perpetually haunted by counter-narratives of a secret and disintegrative cultural history. Ellroy's novels, whilst ferociously demystifying the spectacular life-world of Los Angeles, do not appear to make that world any more available to the agency of the individual or collective urban eye; on the contrary, the material terrors of history and geography are, if anything, more destructive of the imperatives of ethics and politics (other than the corrupt variety) than the dazzling signs that conceal them.

The destabilising relation of the *Quartet's* protagonists to the nightmare landscape of postwar Los Angeles is played out largely on the plane of vision. The novels are haunted by a recurring pattern of the mutilation of the eye. Masculine rage and criminal psychosis, frequently directed against women and homosexuals, are fixated on blinding, conflating the power of the Other with his or her visual capacity. A number of protagonists, notably Danny Upshaw in *The Big Nowhere*, attempt to maintain a hold on their perceptual control over the dizzying scenarios they confront by deploying specifically visual strategies. Thus Upshaw, his sexuality thrown into question with his involuntary arousal by a homosexual orgy he is secretly surveilling, attempts to reassert a masculine vision by an anthropomorphic self-mutation into 'Man Camera', a technique of forensic science that involves 'screening details from the perpetrator's viewpoint' (p. 94). For Upshaw, this strategy presents the possibility of abstracting his vision from its spatial confinement in a crisis-ridden male body, and so of deferring the crisis of sexual definition.

Visuality, then, is the conceptual and material ground of both the dynamic of the urban process and the anxieties it generates. It is this dynamic that I wish to explore in a detailed examination of *The Black Dahlia*, perhaps the novel most explicitly concerned with the masculine eye's relation to urban spectacle. The crisis of urban subjectivity dramatised in *The Black Dahlia* is bound up with the postwar phenomenon of Los Angeles' emergent predominance in the realms of mass spectacle and land development. An intricate fictionalisation of an actual case, the novel centres on the brutalisation and murder of a young prostitute and aspiring movie star (the titular 'Black Dahlia'). Revealing both the dark web of connections between the murder and a powerful Hollywood developer and his family, as well as the appropriation of the case as a public spectacle by the press, the novel establishes the complex and highly charged relation between urban politics and spectacle. Indeed, this relation is thematised before the central murder is discovered, in the events that lead to the narrator Dwight 'Bucky' Bleichert's assignation to the case.

Bleichert is a former heavyweight boxer turned cop, his apparently solid masculine identity called into question by a reputation for padding his undefeated fight record with victories over synthetically built-up middleweights, and for shopping Japanese friends to the FBI during the war. In the opening pages of the novel, he is offered the prospect of moving from his routinised work as a uniformed traffic cop to a place on the LAPD's Warrants Squad, in exchange for participation in a match with a fellow former boxer already on Warrants, Sergeant Lee Blanchard. The contest is the proposition of machiavellian District Attorney, Ellis Loew, who sees in it the potential to employ spectacle as a means of drawing back public enthusiasm for a police force whose battered reputation, after revelations of wartime corruption, has rather muddied the prospect of winning the forthcoming vote over Proposition B to allocate greater financial resources to it. As Loew himself puts it, 'We need to build up morale within the Department and we need to impress the voters with the quality of our men. Wholesome white boxers are a big draw ...' (p. 28). The ensuing local media frenzy once the contest is announced, projecting a prototype American showdown between Blanchard, 'Mr Fire', 'the poet of brute strength', and Bleichert, 'Mr Ice', 'the counter poet of speed and guile' (p. 26), effectively displays the interlocking mechanisms of urban political interests and media spectacle. The boxing match organised for popular entertainment serves as a means of augmenting economically the power of the police, in a disturbing realisation of mass spectacle's function as a regulatory social force.

The context for this burgeoning relation between the politics and spectacle of the city is elaborated by Bleichert, shortly before the discovery of Elizabeth Short's corpse. In the hard-boiled, descriptive vocabulary characteristic of Ellroy's acute *noir* pastiche, Bleichert remarks that:

> The district's main drag ... spelled 'postwar boom' like a neon sign. Every block from Jefferson to Leimert was lined with dilapidated, once grand houses being torn down, their facades being replaced by giant billboards advertising department stores, jumbo shopping centres, kiddie parks and movie theatres ... it hit me that by 1950 this part of L.A would be unrecognizable. (p. 77)

Bleichert's figuration of the landscape of the postwar boom as a 'neon sign' aptly designates the peculiarly spectacular character of the new urban dynamic. The drama that follows will be intimately bound up with this process of creative destruction which will bring the new object-world of urban consumer culture (department stores, amusement parks and cinemas), predicated on the deployment of spectacle, into being. Indeed, the centrality of spectacle to this new urban space is prefigured in the use of 'giant billboards' to 'advertise' the alluring consumerist future, the emergent 'kaleidoscopic' city that defines, for Edward Soja, the decentred logic of postmodernity.[9]

A further brief theoretical detour will help bring to bear Benjamin's critical sensibility once more on the landscape of consumer spectacle described by Bleichert. In excavating the residues of nineteenth-century Paris' extinct commodity culture, Benjamin identifies the many forms that culture took, charging each one with the dialectical insight of his own historical present. Susan Buck-Morss organises these forms into four broad categories, the most salient of which, in the context of the present discussion, is that of the 'wish image'. Benjamin points to the revival of the classical tradition in the architectural and ornamental forms of Haussmann's Paris, in the deployment of Pompeiian columns and Greek mythic figures in public buildings and monuments, as articulations of an unconscious social utopian drive in the dream forms of modern urbanity. Urban spectacle, that is – even as it works to mystify, by way of visual enchantment, the material conditions of social struggle that have brought it into being – nevertheless registers, in the form of the wish image, a collective impulse to resolve that struggle through the reassertion of collective values.

The semiotics of the new urbanity come across as Benjaminian 'wish-images' divested of their dialectical charge, their utopian energy absorbed wholesale by the marketing strategies of the entrepreneurial developers. The new spaces, furthermore, are crucially 'feminine', foregrounding the pleasures of domestic consumption, 'family' leisure and, given the explicitly gendered location of the movie theatres, female spectatorship. Their destabilising effect on masculine identity is bound up with their 'Womanly' elusiveness, their dazzling appearance as floating signs 'unmoored', to use Soja's term, from any material foundations.

It is significant that Bleichert registers these seismic shifts in urban form just prior to the unearthing, on 39th Street and Norton Avenue, of the corpse that will haunt the remainder of the novel. Elizabeth Short's murder is a bleak narrative of the insertion of a young woman into this kaleidoscopic new space, graphically enacting the violent inversion of the utopian individualism (with its fantasies of stardom and romance) intrinsic to Hollywood. Caught, as we gradually discover, in the network of destructive mechanisms of urban development and spectacle, and the destabilised forms of familial, gender and sexual identity that they generate, her murder is a terrible emblem of the underside of the new Los Angeles. Bleichert's unsparingly clinical description of the mutilated corpse, cut in half at the waist, palpably communicates this sense of urban shock. He notes that:

> A large triangle had been gouged out of the left thigh ... the flaps of skin behind the gash were pulled back: there were no organs inside ... the breasts were dotted with cigarette burns, the right one hanging loose ... the girl's face ... was one huge purpled bruise, the nose crushed deep into the facial cavity, the mouth cut ear to ear into a smile that leered up at you, somehow mocking the rest of the brutality inflicted. (p. 87)

The excesses of brutalisation documented here take on a particularly disturbing resonance in the context of an allegorical reading of Los Angeles. Elizabeth Short, as we find in the pages that follow, has aspired to the realisation of the full catalogue of 'wish-images' projected by Hollywood. That is, she seeks to become that object of consumer desire and mass veneration, the screen goddess, which most embodies the new logic of urban spectacle. As I have argued, following Buci-Glucksmann, this 'feminine' object-world has been a consistent repository of masculine anxiety and rage in postmodern American fiction. In the above passage can be glimpsed the accumulated force of that rage, concentrated in the image of a single female body.[10] It is perhaps the grotesque leer of the mouth, a taunting distortion of the smiling female object, which most graphically conveys this sense of viciously inverted fantasy. Betty Short's corpse potently enacts the 'graphic fragmentation' of the feminine wrought by postmodernity's allegorical crisis of seeing.

The Short murder's brutality is not, however, incommensurable with its potential for political appropriation. On the contrary, it is just its intimations of unconstrained and unaccountable evil that render it so expedient an urban political spectacle. As Blanchard puts it, attempting to persuade Bleichert of its value in career terms: 'It's a showcase ... to show the voters that passing the bond issue got them a bulldog police force' (p. 92). The consequent politicised packaging of the case as an exemplary display of the dangerous forces at large in the city, and of the imperative to contain them, is predicated on its crude narrative construction via the media. This conscious elision of the case's complex inflections, in favour of a symbolic narrative of good and evil for easy public consumption, is tellingly figured in Bleichert's image of Ellis Loew before the radio microphones. As the latter speaks to his listeners of the 'Vivisection of a lovely young woman', Bleichert notes the American Legion poppy on his lapel, and remarks that it was probably bought from 'the wino legionnaire who slept in the hall of records parking lot – a man he had once vigorously prosecuted for vagrancy' (p. 102). The poppy serves as a potent allegorical image: a 'wish-image' of collective memory and meaning in its outward display, and a counter-image, as Bleichert reveals, of a latent material history of urban power and domination. Indeed, it reads as a historical and geographical mutation of Benjamin's counter-images (the vagrant, for example) of the spectacular facades of Haussmann's Paris. The 'Black Dahlia' is to become another 'flower' charged by this dialectic of collective spectacle. She emerges, that is, as both the 'glamorous siren headed for Hollywood stardom' (p. 147), constructed by the 'official' media narrative of her murder, and the victimised object of urban power (the actual network of material forces – developers, policemen, and pornographers – embroiled in her murder). Loew's function is to efface the doubleness of her image, to refuse any information that might counter its transparency.

Bleichert's investigation takes him through the range of Los Angeles subcultures and institutions that have impacted on Short's life and death, from the lesbian bars of Crenshaw Boulevard and seedy rented rooms of aspiring starlets, to the monied and elite spaces of the Sprague family and the Hughes empire. His inquiries yield an increasingly convoluted map of Short's place in these interlocking urban spaces, one that shatters her abstracted media image as an unwitting and innocent victim of a cruelly indifferent city. Questioning a fellow aspirant actress and former room-mate, Sheryl Saddon, he learns of the significance of the black clothing that has earned Short her popular sobriquet. Saddon tells Bleichert of Betty Short's compulsive lying, which would extend to explanations of her three-day absences, her avowed 'marriages' to war heroes, and her donning of black outfits 'because her father died or because she was mourning the boys who died in the war' (p. 123: her father, we have already learned, is alive). The black clothing is also 'a gimmick to impress casting directors' (p. 123), and so serves in more than one way as a marker of elusiveness and guile.

The image of the 'Black Dahlia' thus emerges with increasing force as a literally and figuratively dark 'shadow' of the luminous spectacle of Los Angeles' 'dreamworld'. Indeed, the gathering storm of revelations about Short's final days renders Ellis Loew's public projection of a 'lovely young girl' frustratingly difficult to sustain. Short emerges rather as an embodiment of Buci-Glucksmann's allegorical feminine, 'seraphic and hell-black by turns' (p. 78). The mass spectacle of the feminine, available to easy consumption in its officially sanctioned form, becomes dangerously destabilising of this hegemonic illusion as its inverted double. As a signifier of promiscuity and deceit, and a repository of masculine desire, anxiety, and rage, 'black' is the violently material negative inscribed into the abstracted spectacle of Hollywood.

The catalogue of atrocities wrought on Short's body by Ramona Sprague and the other members of her family is surely the culminating articulation of the uncontainable rage generated by the projection of crisis-ridden sexual and gender identities onto this inverted image. Part of the novel's profoundly unsettling effect, however, is derived from the way in which the crisis of gender subjectivity that the Black Dahlia's image embodies is replicated in the very policemen investigating her murder. Both Bleichert and Blanchard experience the accumulating evidence surrounding the murder as an assault on their sexual integrity. As they discover the many layers of sordid exploitation that mark Betty Short's last days, she becomes for each of them a tortuously elusive female object, bringing palpably to the surface the latent anxieties at the heart of their relation to urban spectacle itself. Moreover, this conflict between masculine subject and feminine object is once more played out directly on the plane of the visual, most notably during the scene in which the policemen assigned to the case watch a pornographic film in which Short appears. The film is shot in 'grainy black and white', on a pastiche ancient Egyptian film set (which, as I hope to show, will emerge as central to the murder), and reveals her 'wearing only stockings and doing an inept hoochie-koochie dance'. Bleichert goes on to describe how his 'groin clenched', whilst Blanchard, after witnessing simulated and enforced lesbian sex between Short and a younger girl, 'stood in front of the screen, blinking from the hot white light in his eyes. He wheeled round and ripped the obscenity down ...' (pp. 180–1).

The 'hot white light' that discomfitingly obscures Blanchard's field of vision is an apposite figuration of the effect of the film itself. Blanchard's response to the film, it transpires, is an expression less of moral outrage than of his own implication in the misogynistic violence displayed on screen, and in the corrupt formations that produce it. The novel goes on to reveal him as tied to organised crime and more importantly, a suppressor of crucial evidence in the Short case. Blanchard, we learn at the end, knew the identity of her murderer, and of the complex circumstances surrounding her affair with Madeleine Sprague. Madeleine's history is bound up inextricably with Betty Short's, as an occasional lover, seduced in the lesbian bars of Crenshaw Boulevard, and as the provider of the Egyptian film set for her pornographic film. She is also the procurer of Short for the encounter with George Tilden, her father's disfigured and disturbed former business partner, that would lead to Betty's prolonged torture and murder. Madeleine also emerges as Blanchard's murderer, motivated by the imperative to silence the one individual who knows the Sprague family's role in the Short case. Finally, her striking resemblance to Short leads to her compulsive assumption of the latter's identity, in terms of appearance and claimed personal history, around the seedy bars of 8th Street. Madeleine, in her connections to her father's corrupt development interests, in her own dark sexual pathology (including an ongoing affair with Emmett), and in her obsessive transformations into the Black Dahlia, comes to represent Short in distorted form, foregrounding the destructive urban forces that would conspire in her murder. Madeleine, that is, becomes the Black Dahlia divested of the utopian individualism that had characterised Betty Short's naive hankering for stardom, and so reduced to an emblem of the destabilising new urbanity brought into being by the likes of Emmett Sprague.

Drawn into an affair with Madeleine, as a means, for the latter, of ensuring his silence in the face of revelations of her family's involvement, Bleichert's relation to her is increasingly haunted by the Black Dahlia's shadowy sexual presence. This experience of Madeleine as Betty is registered at the specifically visual level, when he describes how, in the midst of a sexual clinch: 'I made Madeleine Betty – made her eyes blue instead of hazel, made her body Betty's body from the stag film, made her silently mouth, "No, please"' (pp. 210–11).

The transmutations that Bleichert witnesses, enacting the allegorical feminine's destabilising resistance to 'reading', tauntingly elude his perceptual control (his invocation of visual authority in 'I made Madeleine Betty' is surely compensatory given the irresistible force of his obsession). Betty, as an interruptive female object, almost literally invades his field of vision: an object that embodies simultaneously the abstracted fantasies of pornography and the misogynistic force (Betty mouthing 'No, please') that brings those fantasies into being. Madeleine's interchangeability with Betty becomes a further expression of the deceptive, flickering logic of feminised urbanity that threatens the integrity of Bleichert's masculinity. If Madeleine functions as the active, conscious representative of particular material interests and processes (the Sprague family and their development projects), and Betty as the hapless victim of those processes, the two women nevertheless constitute for Bleichert an interlocking, doubled articulation of the urban object-world. This doubled logic is profoundly disorientating for Bleichert as for Blanchard, for the same reason that it displays both the dazzling 'wish-imagery' of urban spectacle, and the destructive material processes that produce it. Once masculine sexual identity is plugged into this logic, confronted by the relentless dynamic of an urbanity that eludes its visual control (as figured, I suggest, by the interchangeable images of Madeleine and Betty), it is predictably traumatised. Bleichert's mounting obsession with the case and the young woman at its centre, and its destructive effects on his marriage, career and mental stability all bear witness to this trauma.

The articulation of violent misogyny via Ellroy's recurrent trope of blinding provides further evidence of the deranged masculinity that drives the events of the novel. The perpetrator of this assault on sight in *The Black Dahlia* is Fritz Vogel, a corrupt cop attached to the Short murder case. Vogel and his son Johnny (also a cop) themselves come under suspicion of the murder when Bleichert traces Johnny as the client of a prostitution job during the 'missing' days prior to Betty's death. Questioning Sally Stinson, Betty's mentor in the business, he learns of the incident that had Vogel transferred from Administrative Vice Squad. Believing he had caught syphilis from a black prostitute, Vogel 'shook down a house in Watts and made all the girls do him before he took the cure. He made them rub his thing in their eyes, and two of the girls went blind' (p. 251). The structure of domination that characterises visual relations between masculine subject and feminine object is here unpalatably realised. There can be no more unequivocal embodiment of masculine authority at the limits of dislocation than a syphilitic policeman, whilst the black prostitutes function as the repository of his projected rage. If, for Benjamin and Buci-Glucksmann, Baudelaire's prostitute constitutes the most potent counter-image of the dazzling dreamworld of the modern metropolis, Ellroy's episode of the prostitute's blinding can be read as a bleak narrative of the fate of that counter-image in the landscape of postwar Los Angeles.

Here, the final degradation of the female object's critical agency takes the form of a viciously enforced eradication of sight, and, implicitly, of the capacity to negotiate the predicament of displacement that the experience of prostitution brings about.

In the crisis-ridden masculinity that plagues the cop protagonists of *The Black Dahlia*, and the *Quartet* in general, can be read the monumental shifts in the visual logic of Los Angeles wrought by the city's postwar boom. The grandiose images of early modern Paris, from the arcades to the World's Fairs, dialectical symbols for Benjamin of both shattering economic power and utopian social hope, have become, in Ellroy's Los Angeles, kaleidoscopic neon abstractions enshrining perpetual consumer desire, and naturalising the urban 'dreamworld' of modern commodity culture. If Benjamin describes the subjective experience of modern Paris as one of 'shock', the subjectivity produced by postwar Los Angeles might be termed a kind of 'hyper-shock', a hypertrophied anxiety before an object-world that seems to resist and destabilise embodied visual agency. This new, traumatised subjectivity is clearly tied to the increasingly pervasive figuration of the landscape of mass spectacle as feminine, as exemplified by Ellroy's protagonists, whose experience of these mutations of urban logic is concentrated in their relations with women. The bodily agency of the city's policemen, supposedly the most controlled and authoritative urban subjects, appears to have been invaded by the forces of mass spectacle that the Black Dahlia and the Sprague family encapsulate.

It is the Sprague family that presides over these violent mutations in the landscape of Los Angeles. Characterised by a kind of Gothic hyper-dysfunctionality that takes in adultery, incest and murder, the Spragues' intricate web of connections to the Short case emerges in a startling procession of revelations during the climactic pages of the novel. Betty Short's torture and murder is discovered by Bleichert to have taken place in one of the shacks in the Hollywood Hills built by Emmett Sprague, and owned in conjunction with Mack Sennett. The links forged by the novel, between Emmett's corrupt development project, the emergent visual dominance of Hollywood spectacle, and the Short murder, converge on a particularly charged flashpoint near the climax. Bleichert is called urgently by Harry Sears, a fellow investigator, to examine the recently stumbled-upon cinderblock hut in which Betty Short spent her last days. His walk through the dense scrubland of the hills is coloured by the image of, quite literally, the birth of Hollywood; that is, by the execution of Mack Sennett's plan to remove the last four letters of the 'Hollywoodland' sign that hovers over his tract, and so to project to the world perhaps the most enduring emblem of the long and dense history of Los Angeles spectacle.

Bleichert is confronted by a doubled image of urban development. On the one hand, he sees the phantasmagoric mass spectacle of the sign, accompanied by a band striking up 'Hooray for Hollywood', and a crowd of gawking 'rubberneckers ... and political types' (p. 338). On the other, he witnesses its secret and blood-drenched underside. The hut is a grotesquely inverted phantasmagoria, with its side walls 'papered with pornographic photographs of crippled and disfigured women ... a mattress on the floor ... caked with layers and layers of blood ... close-up shots of diseased organs oozing blood and pus' (p. 338). Crucially, both the abstracted spectacle of the Hollywood sign and its unpalatably visceral negative looming beneath are tied to the same economic force, namely Emmett Sprague's development interests. The playing of 'There's No Business Like Show Business' that provides the musical score to the disappearance of the fourth and final letter takes on a bitterly doubled charge when counterpointed by the images of butchery lurking beneath the sign. This moment of confrontation with the perverse visual dynamics of Hollywood constitutes for Bleichert a kind of limit-state of Benjaminian shock, in which the most potent global image of the mass cultural urban 'dreamworld' is brought into startling conjunction with its counter-image of the spectacle of bodily mutilation. These parallel images thus encapsulate the postwar period's doubled developmental logic, a logic generative of both the official narrative projected by urban spectacle, and of the counter-narrative articulated by the intensely destabilised gender identity violently figured in the corpse of Elizabeth Short.

The last pages of *The Black Dahlia* are taken up with
Bieichert's interrogations of Madeleine and Emmett and,
finally, Ramona Sprague, and establish the bizarre events,
resentments and desires that result in the identification of the
latter as Short's murderer. These confrontations clarify the
dysfunctional familial relations that underlie the murder of
Elizabeth Short, as well as the private and public phenomena
that help to produce them. The first of these highly fraught
interviews begins after Bleichert walks in on Madeleine and
Emmett tenderly fondling one another, whilst engaged in a
discussion about the latter's mounting legal problems. These
centre on the approaching grand jury probe into his health
and safety violations in building houses with poor materials
and shoddy workmanship. Bleichert has established that Short
has been murdered in one of these houses, apparently by
Emmett's friend, George Tilden. When he confronts Emmett
with the accusation against Tilden, the former is persuaded to
give an account of his relationship with the latter. Tilden, his
former army comrade and business partner, he reveals, is the
natural father of Madeleine, the result of an affair with Ramona
after Emmett had refused to provide her with a child. After
discovering Tilden to be Madeleine's father, Emmett 'played
tic-tac-toe on his face' (p. 345) with a knife, leaving him
permanently disfigured, and went on to show remorse by
finding him work tending his property, and hauling garbage
for the city. He then tells of George's fascination for internal
organs, and of his own obligation to George for his role in
saving his life during the war. Madeleine goes on to confess
how this burden of obligation led to her procuring Betty Short
for Tilden, after the latter has been aroused by watching Betty
in the pornographic film made, with Madeleine's permission,
in one of Emmett's vacant houses (and on Mack Sennett's
Egyptian film set). Both Madeleine and George insist that
they had no suspicion of George's murderous tendencies.
They also account for their own apparently incestuous
relationship on the basis of Madeleine's true paternity.

In these confessions to Bleichert, then, can be excavated the
interlocking crises of gender, sexuality and the family inscribed
into the processes of urban restructuring in which Emmett so
actively participates. His corrupt manoeuvres in property

speculation, executed in conjunction with the power elite of the film industry, give rise to the skewed relations and impulses that culminate in the Black Dahlia murder. George and Emmett begin their (Scottish) immigrant lives as friends, a relationship that turns bitter when the latter is obliged to the former after being hidden by him under a pile of German corpses during the First World War. George's knowledge of Emmett's cowardice acts as a taunting drain on the latter's masculine identity, compounded when he is cuckolded by the same man who saved his life. His masculine identity is destabilised yet further when George and Ramona direct and film Madeleine with her sister Martha, and their friends, in a series of macabre pageants symbolically re-enacting Emmett's various acts of corruption, including the collapse of his shacks in the earthquake of 1933, as well as his desperate crawling beneath German corpses. Emmett's occupation as a contractor and emerging heavyweight in the Los Angeles property market of the 1920s quickly becomes a source of marital estrangement, resulting in Ramona's affair with George. Emmett's consequent relation to George, precariously combining uncontainable rage with guilty obligation, is the articulation of a radically destabilised masculine subjectivity. This subjectivity is registered visibly in George's disfigured face, as well as in Emmett's anxious assumption of the obligation to find the former work on city maintenance projects. George's existence serves as a taunting marker of the new, profoundly unsettled masculinity brought into being by Emmett's role in the shifting urban landscape. His would-be incestuous, if unconsummated, relation to Madeline and increasing neglect of Ramona further mark the penetration of this disrupted masculine identity into the arena of the family, culminating in the calamitous events of January 1947.

The Black Dahlia murder constitutes the final convergence of the crises of sexual and familial identity experienced by Madeleine, George and Ramona, on the body of Elizabeth Short. These crises, to reiterate, are produced by, and played out on, the dislocated terrain of Emmett's corrupt property holdings, and are registered in explicitly visual forms. Thus, Madeleine's narcissistic obsession with her resemblance to Short leads to their affair, and to her eventual provision of her father and Mack Sennett's film set and property for the making of a pornographic film. Her exploitation of the Black Dahlia persona to entrap Bleichert, after the murder, demonstrates her unconscious awareness of its potency as an emblem of the allegorical feminine so unsettling to masculine sexual and epistemological authority. George's covert voyeuristic pleasure in the making of the film, meanwhile, results in his blackmailing of Emmett, demanding sex with Short in exchange for his silence over 'the family's sordid past and present' (p. 369). Emmett's reluctant consent to the terms is overheard by Ramona, whose explosive resentment is finally realised when Betty Short arrives at the Sprague house on 12 January for her liaison with George. George's spurning of Ramona's advances is now bitterly compounded by his lust for a girl who 'looked so much like Madeleine that it felt that the cruelest of jokes was being played on her' (p. 369). Betty's resemblance to her and George's own child, that is, acts as a taunting visual embodiment of her own displacement by the processes of urban change in which Emmett has invested his masculine identity. If Madeleine is the direct product of that displacement, Betty is its haunting shadow and replication (George is fixated on her to the exclusion of Ramona), and as such draws out the incendiary rage accumulated through the years of her husband's corrupt speculations. It is no coincidence, furthermore, that the liaison that eclipses her own sexual function takes place in 'one of his [Emmett's] abandoneds on North Beechwood' (p. 369). It is in this dilapidated residue of Emmett's early ventures into Los Angeles real estate that Ramona determines to reverse her experience as displaced object by violently transposing that status onto Betty Short.

The mutilations to which Ramona subjects Betty, after breaking in on the couple and knocking her unconscious with a baseball bat (as well as persuading George to consent to his partner's torture by promising him her extracted internal organs), become symbolic inscriptions of this rage. When Short's corpse is driven by George and Ramona to 39th and Norton, 'a lot that Georgie used to tend for the city' (p. 370), the collapse of the Benjaminian 'wish-image' that Betty represented in life, into the 'ruin' of consumer culture that her corpse now constitutes, is complete. The fatally mutilated prostitute and aspiring movie star, lying on the city street tended by an accessory to her murder, and presumably developed by the murderess' husband, tears apart, like the prostitutes of Baudelaire's poetry, the harmonising pretensions of the new urbanity embodied in Mack Sennett's 'Hollywood' sign. The corpse palpably underscores the resistance of postwar urban history's counter-images to narrative resolution. Bleichert's 'counter-narrative' inverts the conventional logic of narrative in demonstrating its own failure to render legible the disintegrative history which brings the Short murder into being.

The Black Dahlia, and indeed the *LA Quartet* as a whole, is saturated with demystificatory counter-images of the abstracted object-world of urban spectacle. Despite the relentless identification of the palpably material forces of politics and economics at work in the construction of the dazzling semiotic surface of Los Angeles, however, there is little sense that history and geography can illuminate a path of resistance to urban domination. The implacable dynamics of urban change paralyse any gesture towards political or ethical opposition, toward the activation of agency on the terrain of vision on which the central struggles of the *Quartet* are played out. Embodied agency is reduced by the unremitting processes of urban change to a inarticulably enraged masculine subjectivity, more often directed toward the brutalisation of female objects, who function as repositories of male hysteria, than towards identifiable forces of political and economic power. History and geography, though clearly dramatised as a constitutive interpenetrative logic in this series of novels, are divested of any utopian charge. Ellroy's fiction thus interrogates the crisis of masculine perception produced by the displacement of the detective as master subject, a displacement engendered by Los Angeles' disintegrative logic.

Notes

1. James Ellroy, *LA Quartet* (London: Arrow, 1984–92).
2. For a historical account of this process of reconstruction, see Chapter 9 of David Harvey, *The Urban Experience*

(Oxford: Blackwell, 1989), and Mike Davis, *City of Quartz: Excavating the Future of Los Angeles* (London: Verso, 1990).

3. Benjamin's most explicit theorisation of *flaneurie* is in *Charles Baudelaire: Lyric Poet in an Era of High Capitalism,* trans. Harry Zohn (London: Verso, 1992).

4. For an excellent account of the development of Benjamin's thought on late nineteenth-century Paris, see *The Dialectics of Seeing* (Cambridge, Mass.: MIT, 1993).

5. Ellroy has polemicised against Chandler's romanticism in a number of places, most notably in a Channel 4 TV documentary by Nicola Barker, *White Jazz*, broadcast in May 1995.

6. James Ellroy, *The Black Dahlia* (London: Arrow, 1984); *The Big Nowhere* (London: Arrow, 1988); *LA Confidential* (London: Arrow, 1990).

7. Christine Buci-Glucksmann, *Baroque Reason,* trans. Bryan S. Turner (London: Sage, 1994).

8. Walter Benjamin, 'Theses on the Philosophy of History' (1950), in *Illuminations*, trans. Harry Zohn (London: Fontana, 1992), p. 248.

9. Edward Soja, Chapter 6 in *Postmodern Geographies* (London: Verso, 1989).

10. The murderer, of course, is revealed to be a woman; Ramona Sprague, however, as I shall argue, has been forced by her position within the economy of the family to internalise the crisis of her husband's masculinity.

9

Law Crimes: The Legal Fictions of John Grisham and Scott Turow

Nick Heffernan

Q: What's black and brown and looks good on a lawyer?
A: A Dobermann Pinscher

There is a deeply rooted ambivalence in American culture towards the law and, especially, lawyers. Historically, American political and cultural elites have to a notable degree been dominated by lawyers and those of a legalistic cast of mind. Thomas Jefferson announced the American colonies' rejection of British rule by issuing a 'declaration' – a legal document traditionally lodged with a court to justify self-help – reflecting both his own training as a lawyer and the pervasive legalism of his class. Along with his famous invocation of 'the laws of nature' in the opening paragraph of the Declaration of Independence, this illustrates the extent to which, from its very inception, American nationhood has been bound up with notions of the law and legality. As Jefferson's more forthright revolutionary comrade Tom Paine put it, America had no need of monarchs for 'in America law is king'.[1]

The substitution of the rule of law (and, many Americans would increasingly begin to observe, of lawyers) for the rule of kings gave rise to a culture in which democracy was understood and interpreted in terms of the law and in which the law furnished the popular concepts and vocabulary through which democracy operated. In the 1820s Alexis de Tocqueville was struck by the propensity of even the most lowly Americans to seek legal solutions to all kinds of problem, from the smallest personal dispute to the largest political issue. 'The language of the law', he remarked, had become 'a vulgar tongue' through

187

which the masses pressed their claims and jockeyed for position in a society without traditional forms of entrenched hierarchy.[2] Even the personifications, symbols and secular icons of the Republic were lawyers (Jefferson, Lincoln) or legal documents (the Declaration, the Constitution).

But the American passion and reverence for the law was never unproblematic. The Declaration charged the new nation with the task of embodying the laws of nature in man-made statutes and institutions. These latter, it was feared, might prove more responsive to the material influence of money and power than to the abstract claims of natural justice and the rights of man. The hard facts of Indian slaughter and removal in the West, of chattel slavery followed by racial apartheid in the South, and of the concentration of class power in the industrialising North suggested to some that the rule of law was in fact at variance with natural rights and an impediment to the reign of justice in society.[3] And the adoption by ordinary Americans of the law as a kind *lingua franca* of democracy did not preclude a growing populist hostility toward the legal profession. Lawyers were variously perceived as arrogant demagogues, as overweening and overcharging experts, as puppets of undemocratic vested interests, or as unprincipled hacks willing to argue any case for a fee. Most of all, they came to be viewed as crafty manipulators of language and logic in whose system, at one time or another, persons had been transformed into property (in the case of slaves) and property into persons (in the case of corporations).

Popular culture is the arena in which Americans have articulated and explored this fascinated mixture of attraction and repulsion with which they regard lawyers and the law. Typically, the stock figure of the venal, self-seeking and conniving shyster lawyer has had to compete for popular attention with unimpeachable lawyer-heroes such as Perry Mason and the protagonists of *The Defenders*, stalwart guardians of truth, justice and the rights of the individual. Contemporary representations like *LA Law* have attempted to show lawyers in operation beyond the ready-made adversarial dramatics of the courtroom (the staple of any lawyer narrative) where they embody and act out the contradictions of modern professionalism so resonant in a society whose chief collective goods

– including healthcare, education, science and technology as well as justice – are managed and administered, if not owned, by professionals. Chief among these contradictions is the question about the ends to which specialised knowledge and expertise should be put. Lawyers, to a greater degree perhaps than other modern professionals, find themselves placed between the powerful logic of market forces on the one hand, with its temptations of self-aggrandisement in a comfortable accommodation with power, and an ethical imperative of independent and disinterested service in the name of some higher ideal on the other.[4]

The current surge of popular hostility towards the profession, however, would seem to suggest that most Americans now regard lawyers as incapable of recognising, let alone responding to, such dilemmas of conscience. Books with titles like *Dead Lawyers and Other Pleasant Thoughts* or *What to Do with a Dead Lawyer*, as well as a rash of anti-lawyer jokes, have provoked the American Bar Association to call for an end to 'lawyer bashing' and to seek to have such forms of invective classified as 'hate speech'.[5] Yet such attempts to defend the public image of the profession are undermined by the way in which the line between popular culture and the court system has steadily been erased in the last decade. Court TV and media show trials such as the O.J. Simpson case, while feeding a popular hunger for 'real life' courtroom drama, have only eroded public confidence in judicial processes and caused lawyers (and judges too, in many cases) to be perceived as a class of petulant would-be celebrities. Topics such as 'litigation abuse' are debated on the Oprah Winfrey Show where, it is argued, lawyers hooked on the commission from massive compensation awards are creating a log-jam of speculative corporate liability and medical malpractice suits that is strangling American industrial enterprise and impeding the progress of medical science.

The attacks have also come from within the profession. In a 1982 article in the *American Bar Association Journal*, Chief Justice Warren Burger drew attention to the dangers of what he saw as an unprecedented 'legal explosion', the result of a culture-wide tendency to call on lawyers and the law to resolve questions that were in fact raised by the decline in other, more traditional social and cultural institutions and structures, such as the family, the church and the neighbourhood.[6] Law could not function as a substitute for community, Burger implied. But the massive increase in the number of lawyers and laws since his warning (from 541,000 lawyers in 1980 to about one million in 1995) only testifies to the continuing decline of community and the increasing appeal of the law as a lucrative career choice. Other law professionals have echoed Burger's notions, diagnosing a condition of 'hyperlexis' in which the compulsion to produce new laws and new lawyers has reached the level of 'national disease'.[7] This contention that an impenetrable thicket of overcomplex laws and overpaid lawyers is somehow obscuring and compromising the basic principles of American life is summed up in the title of a recent book, *The Death of Common Sense: How Law is Suffocating America,* with its populist championing of honest, down-to-earth 'common sense' against the self-serving sophistry and manipulations of legal experts and judicial elites.[8]

It is perhaps no accident that this late twentieth-century legal explosion has been accompanied by the rise of a hitherto little-noticed sub-genre of the crime thriller – the lawyer-procedural. While traditional courtroom drama may comprise an element of any lawyer-procedural, the form is actually distinguished by its focus on lawyers *outside* the courtroom, by the way in which it makes lawyers themselves (rather than their clients) the protagonists and bearers of suspense, and by the way in which the narrative draws the reader into the professional and occupational culture of lawyers. In the hands of its principal exponents, Scott Turow (whose *Presumed Innocent* gave the form its breakthrough to bestsellerdom in 1987) and John Grisham (whose formulaic reductions have kept it there ever since), the lawyer-procedural exploits the current fascination with lawyers and the legal apparatus, trades on the historic ambivalence noted above, and offers within the framework of a suspense narrative a set of meditations on American hyperlexis and the status of the lawyer as American hero or hate figure.

The startling publishing success of the lawyer-procedural since the late 1980s (and the relative lack of success of such outstanding forerunners of Turow and Grisham as George V.

Higgins) can be related to massive changes in the historical conditions which underpin the production and consumption of suspense fiction. The collapse of the Soviet Union, the disintegration of the Eastern bloc and the end of the Cold War made the old-style NATO spy thriller obsolete. The lawyer-procedural stepped into this vacant niche in the market, placing the thrills now in a domestic rather than international setting and capturing what commentators identified as a new national mood of introspection brought on by the loss of the ideological certainties associated with the old twin-superpower world system.

The form is also well positioned to register other key economic, cultural and political developments of the last decade and a half, in particular the glorification of wealth and unashamed selfishness in post-Reaganite America. For both Grisham and Turow, the law has been invaded by, and is now a principal vehicle for, this late twentieth-century spirit of aggressive materialism. In their work, law firms are portrayed as the running dogs of capitalist business enterprise; legal expertise as overwhelmingly dedicated to the protection and extension of corporate power; and lawyers themselves as archetypal yuppies, embodiments of contemporary acquisitiveness dedicated to the pursuit of a super-affluent, individualistic lifestyle legitimated by conspicuous workaholism. The lawyer-procedural's focus on the corporate culture of law firms and the lifestyles of well-compensated professionals makes it therefore a key literary reflection of late capitalist, yuppie America. Indeed, Grisham's stock-in-trade is the yuppie-protagonist-in-danger plot (brilliant young lawyer must decide whether to use knowledge/expertise for personal enrichment or public good); while Turow's is the older lawyer responding under duress to the encroachments of the yuppie ethos of competition, ambition and individualistic self-realisation. The pleasure offered to the reader here is one of simultaneous immersion in and implicit criticism of the lifestyles of affluent, upwardly mobile, middle-class professionals.

The post-Reagan Republican years have also created a political context which intensifies the resonance of the lawyer-procedural. The campaign to reinterpret the Constitution according to fundamentalist conservative dogma and to load the federal court system with right-wing judges has made the law into an ideological battlefield where the broadly liberal, redistributionist drift of American society since the 1930s can be arrested and reversed.[9] This overt political manipulation of the law in many ways complements its annexation by powerful economic interests. The law has become a central tool in engineering the historic shift away from American welfare capitalism towards a more volatile, nakedly competitive and socially divisive multinational finance capitalism. The lawyer-procedural dramatises what might be at stake in this contemporary struggle over the meaning and use of the law.[10] Grisham and Turow write about the law as an index of the wider political, cultural and moral health of the nation. The choices and decisions their characters make from within the law stand for the various responses individuals might make to the culture of late capitalist America at large. Their work capitalises on the popular sense that the law is at once the most exalted and compromised of American institutions, the embodiment of founding American ideals and the instrument of their betrayal, and that it is the fulcrum for the economic, cultural and political reshaping of American society. Above all, it cleverly positions the audience at once inside and outside the legal profession, maximising the play of attraction and repulsion that Americans have traditionally felt for lawyers.

Populism, Professionalism, Individualism: John Grisham

In the introduction to his first novel, *A Time to Kill* (1989), Grisham states that in ten years as a lawyer he 'represented people, never banks or insurance companies or big corporations. I was a street lawyer.'[11] This eagerness to present himself to his audience as a man of the people, rather than a hireling of powerful vested interests, illustrates Grisham's sensitivity to populist resentment of the legal profession. Indeed, populist attitudes towards professional elites of all kinds are very deliberately and overtly built into his fiction which, beneath the formulaic crime plotting and one-dimensional legal and political intrigue which are its selling points, can be read as a sustained attempt to balance the antagonistic claims of populism and professionalism in a society dominated by the ideology of possessive individualism.

The Firm (1991), Grisham's second novel and breakthrough bestseller, sets out this agenda very clearly. Brilliant and 'hungry' young Harvard Law School graduate, Mitch McDeere, is lured to work in a Memphis law firm specialising in securities and tax by the $80,000 starting salary, the company car (a BMW), the low-interest mortgage and the pension plan that will make him a millionaire at 45. However, the yuppie fantasy quickly becomes a nightmare as Mitch discovers that the firm is in fact a Mafia-owned money laundering operation and that conscience-stricken lawyers who attempt either to bail out or blow the whistle meet untimely ends. Mitch must seek either to forget his complicity by working the 100-hour weeks, pocketing the salary and enjoying the lifestyle, or honour his responsibilities as a professional and a citizen, a predicament that is sharpened when he is covertly approached by the FBI to testify against the firm and supply evidence that will bring down the Mob's evil Morolto family.

Populist resentment of urban professionals is catered to by the narrative's presentation of yuppie materialism as a Faustian pact with the criminal underworld. Indeed, the firm's senior partner, Nathan Locke, is marked out as none other than Mephistopheles himself by his 'ominous, evil presence', and Mitch knows it is time seriously to review his career choice when, during a particularly heavy week at the office, his secretary tells him that his eyes are beginning to resemble Nathan Locke's.[12] Professionals are referred to as deracinated 'transplants', severed from meaningful ties to local community and even family by selfish dedication to yuppie lifestyles and career development; while the portrayal of lawyers as nothing more than gangsters in brogues and button-downs literalises the populist view of the legal profession as itself a kind of diploma-wielding mafia (*TF*, p. 23).

However, it is important to note that the firm also symbolises the operations of multinational finance capitalism. Through it the Moroltos have created an impenetrable network of corporations and banks that relays illicit money around the globe faster than the authorities can trace it. This equation of the Mafia with the corporate and financial structure of American capitalism links the populist hostility to lawyers with a wider populist distrust of big business or 'the money power'. But it also opens up a debate about the nature of professionalism as seen from within, so to speak, in which a 'bad' version of the professional as pliant servant of unprincipled power (the Mob, the corporations) is played off against a 'good' version of the professional as fiercely independent embodiment of a vocational ideal of selfless commitment to the public good.[13]

The ethical and ideological ambiguities of professionalism are distilled by a colleague, who tells Mitch soon after his arrival at the firm how:

> When you were in law school you had some noble idea of what a lawyer should be. A champion of individual rights; a defender of the Constitution; a guardian of the oppressed; an advocate for your client's principles. Then after you practice for six months you realize we're nothing but hired guns. Mouthpieces for sale to the highest bidder, available to anybody, any crook, any sleazebag with enough money to pay our outrageous fees ... It's supposed to be an honourable profession, but you'll meet so many crooked lawyers you'll want to quit and find an honest job (*TF*, pp. 57–8).

Mitch rejects his colleague's 'bad' professionalism in which the salary compensates for the loss of integrity, a position linked in the narrative to prostitution, the archetype of 'bad' professionalism, through the hooker (the 'pro', as she is called) hired by the firm to seduce Mitch during a business trip. (*TF*, p. 150). He resolves to extract himself from the firm and provide the FBI with evidence for its indictment. Thus while serving as a focus for Grisham's expression of populist hostility towards professionals, Mitch also becomes a figure through whom Grisham can rehabilitate professionalism and restore it to a position of respectability and social responsibility.

Accordingly, Mitch mutates from callow yuppie careerist into a combination of populist hero and principled but hardened professional. His conversion to an ethical, 'good' professionalism is defined in terms of commitment to a cause larger than his own material well-being. 'Committed [is] the word', the Director of the FBI tells Mitch when he signs up to become the agent of the Morolto family's destruction. It is no accident that Mitch's conversion is sealed in the shadow of the Washington Monument and the Vietnam Veterans Memorial as this ethical professionalism is linked to the patriotic and martial ideals of honour, duty and sacrifice. And when the FBI's Director tells Mitch that he has been selected for this task because he is 'self-reliant and independent', it is as though Grisham wants to suggest that the 'good' professional is a blend of the classic Republican virtues with traditional American rugged individualism (*TF*, pp. 204–5). Indeed, Mitch's ability to discharge his civic and professional duty is conditional upon his development of physical and mental courage, cunning and street-smarts. Ethical professionalism is therefore also attached to the qualities of the pragmatic, unsentimental, tough 'pro', a narrative manoeuvre that glosses the image of the white-collar professional with the more appealing codes of the American male action hero.

But Mitch's decision to take on the Mafia from within also makes him into a populist hero, the 'little guy' standing up to the combined might of the criminal and corporate establishments (the firm, as we have seen, stands for both) and, it transpires, of the state to whose service he has just pledged himself. (In one Grisham novel someone observes sagely: 'David pulled it off, but the best bet is always on Goliath.'[14] But Grisham's world is one in which the little guy routinely kicks the giant's ass.) For, Mitch is quick to realise, too close an association with the FBI will arouse suspicion and get him killed: unquestioning service of the state is as dangerous and undesirable as any other kind of unquestioning service – Grisham's moral for all professionals. Thus, in having Mitch go it absolutely alone, Grisham transforms the Ivy League yuppie into an unlikely populist hero who, at the same time, can embody a rehabilitated professionalism based on independence, moral courage and the dedication of expertise to the public good.

Of this uneasy balance of contradictory ideologies that Mitch represents, it is in fact neither populism nor professionalism that Grisham appears ultimately to affirm but, surprisingly, the materialistic individualism that *The Firm* apparently sets out to satirise and critique. Mitch applies his tax lawyer's knowledge of international banking systems not only to the project of incriminating the firm but also to the secret accumulation of eight million of its illegally gained dollars in his own untraceable bank accounts. This, in addition to the three million he extracts from the government in exchange for the provision of evidence, constitutes a personal fortune which enables Mitch and his beautiful young wife to retreat at the end of the novel into a life of luxurious leisure and world travel. Ethical professionalism and populist heroics are therefore not so much positive alternatives to Mitch's original selfish yuppie materialism as they are mere vehicles for its fulfilment. They enable Mitch to achieve his original goal of making a million dollars and retiring early quicker than continuing to work for the firm would.

The Firm's efforts to negotiate a path between populism and professionalism are supervened by a resolution drawn straight out of traditional American success mythology and fables of upward mobility (Grisham makes much of Mitch's childhood poverty and consequent 'hunger' for success). But the novel is also a fantasy of absolute extrication in which the hero's final liberation from every kind of social commitment and connection (save the romantic/erotic one of marriage) and his assumption of a new and completely 'free' identity are as important as his financial reward. In many ways Mitch's story is a curiously prescient allegory of the dramatic change of career path and personal fortune enjoyed by Grisham himself with the success of *The Firm*: disillusioned lawyer 'rats' on profession, makes several million bucks and retires. Subsequent Grisham novels have tended not only to deliver similar fantasies of extrication but also to utilise plots that are virtually identical to *The Firm*'s, while repeating that novel's attempts to do equal justice to the antagonistic claims of populism and professionalism.

In Grisham's next novel, *The Pelican Brief* (1992), a brilliant young law student uncovers a conspiracy including the assassination of two Supreme Court justices that involves a Howard Hughes-type corporate monomaniac, Arab terrorists, and top-level political and legal corruption. For Darby Shaw, as for Mitch in *The Firm*, the exercise of professional expertise and career ambition leads unexpectedly to a terrible and life-threatening knowledge which presents a moral dilemma: should that knowledge be withheld in the name of self-preservation, or communicated at great personal risk in the name of the public interest? Also, as with Mitch before her, Darby's decision to serve the public interest means that she can be a representative of ethical professionalism while also serving as a populist 'little guy', who must stand alone against the corporate, legal and political establishments in order to ensure that justice is done.

Like *The Firm*, *The Pelican Brief* is full of instances of 'bad' professionalism which counterbalance Darby's ethical stance and through which populist resentments can be expressed. The earlier novel's archetype of the 'bad' professional was the prostitute; the latter's is the mercenary, personified by Khamel, the Arab assassin who kills for anyone as long as the price is right and of whose consummate 'professionalism' Grisham constantly reminds us. While Khamel and his fellow mercenaries are always referred to as 'professionals', Darby's integrity and populist credibility are bound up with the fact that, as we are told, 'she's not a pro' (*PB*, pp. 76, 137). And if the connections between the figure of the mercenary, professionals in general, and lawyers in particular were suggested by the description of the latter as 'hired guns' in the passage from *The Firm* quoted earlier, they are cemented by the incident in *The Pelican Brief* in which Khamel assumes the identity of a lawyer in order to attempt to kill Darby.

Despite not being a 'pro' in this particular sense, Darby is nonetheless a vehicle for the rehabilitation of professionalism as a legitimate calling. As with Mitch before her, this requires that she prove herself more of a streetwise, courageous and independently resourceful 'pro' at the art of survival than anyone could reasonably expect of a middle-class, pink-collar heroine. It also requires that, like Mitch, she give voice to Grisham's habitual qualms about the morality of the legal profession. Lawyers might claim to be motivated, Darby remarks, by 'idealism and money', by a desire to 'change the world and get paid for it'. But in fact, she explains, 'It's greed. They want BMWs and gold credit cards.' And despite the self-disgust that sets in, 'they can't leave [the profession] because of the money' (*PB*, pp. 305–6). Conveniently for Darby, she can: her unravelling of the conspiracy has put her in possession of a story that, with the aid of her journalist boyfriend, will make her 'rich and famous' (*PB*, p. 335). Again, the defence of an ethical professionalism in the service of truth and justice becomes a stepping-stone to individual wealth, and the narrative culminates in another fantasy of extrication from all social ties and commitments as Darby abandons law school for an indefinite period of leisured luxury with her lover. The extent of Grisham's ambivalence about his former profession is revealed by the way in which his heroes quit the law the instant they have completed their appointed task of redeeming the integrity of lawyers. Professionalism is rehabilitated and abandoned in the same gesture, while any lingering questions about the possibility of a sustained and socially engaged ethical professionalism are obviated by the escapist endings which lift the protagonists out of social relations altogether.

Grisham's next two novels can be read as attempts to deal with this problem, to produce resolutions that still cater to the antithetical claims of populism and professionalism, but allow greater scope for sustainable social and moral commitment without completely jettisoning the escapist individualism so integral to his two previous blockbusters. This involves making clearer narrative distinctions between populism and professionalism in order to permit them to follow ultimately different trajectories. In *The Firm* and *The Pelican Brief*, populist and professional attributes are uneasily combined in a single lawyer-hero figure. In *The Client* (1993) and *The Chamber* (1994), they are split and attached to two separate characters. For example, 'good' professionalism in *The Client* is represented by Reggie Love, an aptly named and selfless fighter for the rights of the poor and defenceless; while in her client, Mark Sway, Grisham gives us his most literal embodiment of the populist 'little guy' thus far. For Mark is just that – an eleven-year-old working-class kid from a broken home who has become privy to the details of a Mafia political assassination and who is under threat not only from the Mob, but also from the FBI and an aggressively ambitious US District Attorney, both of whom strive to compel Mark to testify with callous disregard for the the little guy's safety.

Reggie's function is to protect Mark from the impersonal and forbidding machinery of the law enforcement agencies and the legal system itself in the name of compassion for, and commitment to, the weak and the vulnerable. Ethical professionalism here is presented as a kind of socialised version of devoted parenting, a notion reinforced by the novel's running theme of maternal suffering and self-sacrifice, as well as by the prominence given to a noble Juvenile Court judge who acts as surrogate legal father to Mark, complementing Reggie's role of legal mother (or mother-in-law). Mark's function, on the other hand, is to provide the streetwise anti-lawyer jibes ('She's a lawyer and she doesn't want money?' he asks incredulously of Reggie) and the obligatory populist heroics by outsmarting the Mob, the cops and the legal establishment using native wit and common sense. Just as important, though, is the way Mark comes to stand for the sense of intimidated mystification any ordinary American at the mercy of the specialised complexities of the legal system might feel. As the various legal authorities argue over Mark's fate, Grisham gives us this passage:

> There was something unfair about a system in which a little kid was brought into a courtroom and surrounded by lawyers sniping at each other under the scornful eye of a judge, the referee, and somehow in the midst of this barrage of laws and code sections and motions and legal talk the kid was supposed to know what was happening to him. It was hopelessly unfair.[15]

Here the populist resentments are not so much directed at lawyers as at a legal system which has grown so complex and labyrinthine that it renders ordinary citizens into helplessly bewildered 'little kids' dependent upon a professional 'parent' to protect them. All the more important, therefore, that the ethical and compassionate lawyer remain within the profession to ensure the provision of such protection. Thus, at the novel's end, as Mark departs for Australia to begin a new life funded by the federal witness protection programme, Reggie returns to her humble office to continue to defend the rights of the underprivileged for a one-dollar retainer. *The Client*'s projection of populism and professionalism onto separate characters therefore allows Grisham to deliver the escapist fantasy ending of extrication from social ties and commitments while at the same time suggesting that an ethical professionalism might possibly be sustainable within the law.

The Chamber employs a similar narrative structure, though perhaps embarrassed at having used the same plot for three novels in succession and finding difficulty in coming up with another, Grisham here offers us not really a thriller at all but what appears to be a novel of psychology and ideas, without much of either. As in *The Client*, populist and professional characteristics are attributed separately to the two main protagonists. Adam Hall is the idealistic young lawyer dissatisfied with his firm's expectation that he be a 'young cutthroat just eager to work eighteen hours a day and bill twenty'. As an embodiment of ethical professionalism, Adam wants 'to do public interest work ... [not] spend my career representing wealthy crooks and wayward corporations'.[16] Sam Cayhall, whom Adam seeks to defend from the gas chamber, is Adam's estranged grandfather, a Mississippi redneck and Klansman awaiting execution on death row for his part in a racist bombing campaign in the 1960s.

Like Mark Sway in *The Client*, Sam is a figure for the ordinary 'little guy' at the mercy of the vast, impersonal machinery of the legal apparatus, though, unlike Mark, he is not an innocent but an unregenerate sinner. Yet he is no less a populist hero, for he has taken on the professionals on their home turf, having taught himself the law and conducted his own appeals procedure for a number of years. He becomes a kind of 'people's lawyer', providing legal expertise to his fellow death row inmates, and is able to voice a critique of lawyers and the law that combines an insider's knowledge with the external perspective of populist 'common sense'. 'I was taught by the same learned souls who provided your instruction', he tells his grandson, 'Dead judges. Honorable justices. Windy lawyers. Tedious professors. I've read the same garbage you've read.'

Sam is thus in a position to demystify the law – previously portrayed by Grisham as mystifying and intimidating for the ordinary American – with this kind of populist relish:

> Why do lawyers practice? Why can't they just work like everyone else? Do plumbers practice? Do truck drivers practice? No, they simply work. But not lawyers ... They're special, and they practice. With all their damned practicing you'd think they'd know what the hell they were doing. You'd think they'd eventually become good at something.[17]

Sam also directs his populist 'common sense' against what he perceives to be the elitist cant of politically correct speech, taunting Adam's liberal convictions and testing his tolerance. That Adam remains loyal to Sam in spite of his bitterness, racism and awful crimes is of course an index of his compassion and commitment to defend the weak and the vulnerable. Though unable to save Sam from the gas chamber, the experience of defending him reveals to Adam the full horror of the death penalty and the pathos of death row prisoners. He quits lucrative private practice to devote himself to their cause and, simultaneously, that of a socially committed, ethical professionalism. Meanwhile, Sam's execution can be understood as a variant of the typical Grisham escapist fantasy of extrication: Sam welcomes death as a release from his guilt and his violent past, as the final liberation from the racist culture of the poor-white South which, it is suggested, is ultimately responsible for his crimes.

That negative overtones are given to populism in *The Chamber* by its association with a racist murderer points to the emergence of a new series of concerns in Grisham's more recent work. It reflects a more cautious and critical attitude towards the populism his books so assiduously court and address, an acknowledgement that the resentment of urban intellectual and professional elites can be based in ignorance and intolerance as much as in a folksy 'traditional Americanism' or a nobly plebeian 'common sense'. Grisham seems to have become particularly preoccupied by the dangers that the manipulation of populism's appeal for reactionary political ends might hold. Since *The Pelican Brief*, his most vilified models of 'bad' professionalism have been opportunistic politicians who exploit a populist rhetoric of prejudice for personal and ideological advantage. There is, for example, that novel's sinister White House chief-of-staff, a yuppie-from-hell, whose manipulation of the President's populist image serves his own ambition and ultra-conservative agenda. There is *The Client*'s overweening District Attorney, whose intimidation of poor Mark Sway is part and parcel of the populist, tough-on-crime posturing he hopes will see him elected to Senator. And there is *The Chamber*'s State Governor whose decision to implement the death penalty is a calculated part of his re-election campaign. These figures represent Grisham's fears about the cynical appropriation of populist impulses by an unprincipled professional political elite.

Here again, Grisham could be accused of biting the hand that once fed him, for during his law-practising days he was elected for a short period to the Mississippi State legislature as a Democrat. Interestingly, however, whilst populist hostility in his novels has shifted decisively from lawyers to politicians, an increasingly explicit party political partisanship has marked his writing. Grisham villains now tend exclusively to be Republicans (they are explicitly labelled as such within his texts) and his recent themes impeccably liberal: corporate despoliation of the environment (*Pelican Brief, Client*); conservative political manipulation of the Supreme Court (*Pelican Brief, Chamber*); the plight of single working mothers (*Client*); the inhumanity of the death penalty and the rise of neo-Nazi groups (*Chamber*). This overtly pro-Democratic inclination is distilled in *The Client*'s mini-portrait of a crusading, paternalistic black judge, significantly called Roosevelt, who defends children – the emblematic 'little guys' – and delights in belittling any 'silk-stocking, blue-blooded Republican mouthpieces' that might enter his court seeking to defend vested interests or the money power.[18]

While it is not surprising, therefore, that Grisham – a self-confessed 'political junkie' – has been befriended by those other baby-boomer Southern Democrat lawyers, Bill and Hillary Clinton, the political turn of his recent work marks more than just the surfacing of his own well-known party loyalties.[19] It can be read as symptomatic of deeper ideological ambiguities that beset not just the Democratic party but liberal politics in the US as a whole. For, despite an historic connection to the idea of standing for the 'little guy' against elites and vested interests, liberalism in the US is increasingly the province of middle-class professionals and intellectuals (like Grisham and the Clintons), who are ever more distanced from the experiences and concerns of ordinary working Americans. Grisham's juggling of the claims of populism and professionalism reflects this social and political contradiction. Indeed, the tactic in recent books of using two central characters – one a populist 'little guy', the other a 'good' professional upon whose expertise and integrity the little guy comes to depend (true even of his most pessimistic book, *The Chamber*) – must be understood as an attempt to arrive at an imaginary resolution of it.[20] That the 'little guy' is typically assigned to a subordinate, client position in the relationship with his or her professional guardian suggests that existing social hierarchies will persist even within this idealised resolution. And the novels' projection of 'bad' professionalism onto Republican politicians who pander to populist attitudes for private advantage betrays perhaps a sense of bad faith on Grisham's part – one that is neatly displaced onto his political opponents. Notwithstanding his anxious parading of populist credentials in prefaces and interviews, then, Grisham's fiction articulates the world-view of a modern, liberal, professional elite whose understanding of itself as a model of responsible social leadership exists in tension with a guilty sense of privileged exclusivity and a healthy regard for the individual social mobility and lifestyle benefits that expertise brings with it.

Unjust Deserts: Scott Turow

If Grisham's novels increasingly strive to rehabilitate professionalism in their depiction of the law, Turow's, by contrast, subtly subvert it. They do so by calling into question not just the dispassionate objectivity of legal professionals, but by interrogating the very notion of rationality upon which codes of professional conduct and the modern understanding of the law itself rest. Max Weber's distinction between the modern, '"rational" interpretation of the law on the basis of strictly formal conceptions' and more traditional, non-rational methods of dispensing justice is one which inhabits Turow's work.[21] His narratives typically revolve around this tension or opposition between reason and unreason: on the one hand, there is the modern democratic view of the law as a rational system based on formal rules which embody the abstract principles of right and wrong; on the other is an atavistic sense of the fundamentally irrational nature of human conduct and motivation, and of the determining role of passion and appetite in public, as well as personal, life. Whereas Grisham more and more tends to present his lawyer protagonists as bulwarks against the seductions of appetite and irrational desire, Turow presents his as battlegrounds for this contest between the rational and the irrational. For Turow, lawyers are representatives of a rational system of abstract justice, embodiments of 'the social world's realm of ultimate restraint', whose daily currency nonetheless is the passion of human conflict.[22] They are therefore placed most suggestively within this contest, and can serve as ideal figures through which Weber's definition of the modern professional as 'the personally detached and strictly objective expert' can be explored and tested.[23]

Rusty Sabich, the protagonist of *Presumed Innocent* (1987), sees himself as 'a person of values', values which he defines in opposition to his father – a fireman who, in his son's eyes, abused his position of civic trust by stealing from the buildings he was supposed to be protecting. As chief assistant to the State Prosecuting Attorney, Sabich feels that he likewise holds a position of civic trust, one in which the subordination of personal interest and ego to the rational administration of justice is paramount. He therefore describes himself as 'a functionary of our only universally recognized system of telling wrong from right, a bureaucrat of good and evil'. His duty is to arrive at the truth through rational processes for, as he habitually asks of his juries: 'If we cannot find the truth, what is our hope of justice?'[24] The narrative, however, strips away these rationalist pretensions. From the moment he lets his professional and ethical restraint slip by embarking on an illicit affair with a colleague, Sabich's assumptions about the law and about himself as a 'person of values' are relentlessly undermined. The colleague is brutally murdered. Sabich is put in charge of the criminal investigation, the success of which is crucial to his boss's re-election as State Prosecuting Attorney. After stumbling across evidence of systematic corruption among his superiors, Sabich, in Kafkaesque fashion, finds himself accused of the murder by a political opponent, abandoned by his erstwhile colleagues and forced to stand trial. By clever manipulation of his knowledge of high-level judicial corruption, he is able not only to secure his acquittal but also to destroy the credibility and careers of his political opponents. He is publicly rehabilitated, rewarded with the post of State Prosecuting Attorney and promised promotion to judge, all the time harbouring the secret knowledge that in fact it was his jealous wife who committed the murder, with the strong possibility that she deliberately set Sabich himself up as fall-guy.

Turow implies, of course, that Sabich's professional code of restraint, detachment and objectivity in the name of truth and public service is after all nothing more than a flimsy fiction glossing over the deeply irrational impulses and desires that inhabit the self and determine public life. Sabich's ability to conspire in and coolly profit from a major perversion of justice reveals to him the existence of another, deeply irrational and instinctual self diametrically opposed to – and far more powerful than – his carefully cultivated 'professional' identity. As he confesses, 'until this happened, I really thought I was Joe College' (*PI*, p. 288). The real lesson, however, is not that this makes him unusual, but rather that it makes him just like everyone else – a slave to jealousy, ambition, greed, lust and the instinct of self-preservation, passions that are revealed to be at the heart of the law, not its antitheses. Indeed, Turow cleverly allows for the possibility that Sabich himself (whose name, we are told, is derived from the Serbian for 'savage') has committed the murder and has constructed the scenario of his wife's guilt as a fail-safe, lest he be unable to manoeuvre his own trial judge into dismissing the case against him. The novel thus concludes in ambiguity and irony with a lawyer who is possibly guilty of murder (his innocence on this charge, as the title suggests, can at best only be 'presumed'), is certainly guilty of perverting the course of justice, and is set to be elevated to judge – the highest embodiment of the law as a rational system of dispassionate adjudication.

Presumed Innocent seems to offer an almost metaphysical argument for the triumph of nature over culture, for the futility of reason (and its social forms such as the law and professionalism) in the face of the 'natural' passions and irrationality that pervade private and public life. The protagonist of Turow's next novel, *The Burden of Proof* (1990), is a fictional mouthpiece for this position. 'In human affairs', observes mandarin Jewish defence lawyer Sandy Stern, 'reason would never fully triumph'; and while he allows that human beings are not innately 'evil', they are through 'self-interest, impulse, anger, lust, or greed ... inclined that way ... [and] know this can never change'.[25] Despite these convictions Stern's calling is to be reason's 'champion' (*BP*, p. 227), to stand for those principles, embodied in the law, that he believes keep us 'decent, civilized' (*BP*, p. 152). And this commitment to reason is what has determined his decision never to act in the capacity of prosecutor, a role that would necessarily demand that he work to 'excite a jury's ugly passions' (*BP*, p. 151). Accordingly, Stern has developed a persona that reflects his commitment to reason and rationality as the benchmarks of civilised life; one that, as his name suggests, is defined above all by unbending propriety and self-restraint. As in *Presumed Innocent*, the thrust of the narrative is to deconstruct this persona and to reveal to Stern the extent to which the irrational determines not so much the life around him (he knew this already) as it does the life *within* him.

The emergence of the impulsive, irrational, passionate Stern is precipitated by his wife's unexpected suicide and is linked to his professional attachment to his brother-in-law and client, the bullish entrepreneur and capitalist Dixon Hartnell. These figures represent the opposing poles of self-restraint and self-gratification respectively, between which Stern himself oscillates. Clara Stern has killed herself out of shame, in part for a single and long-past infidelity (with Dixon Hartnell) which has left her with a recurring genital infection, and in part due to the discovery of her daughter and son-in-law's involvement in illegal and ruinous financial speculations. The novel codes Clara's suicide-from-shame as an extreme instance of that ethos of self-abnegating honour to which Stern himself is committed and which he believes is concomitant with the function of the law in civilised society. Dixon Hartnell, on the other hand, is an embodiment of the lawlessness of impulsive desire, a creature of license and unrestrained appetite, both in his frequently dubious business dealings and his energetic pursuit of sensual gratification. As Stern strives to uncover the circumstances of his wife's death while defending Dixon from federal charges of financial misdemeanour (the two prove to be linked by more than Dixon and Clara's affair), he is drawn into the realm of irrational desire above which he had previously so magisterially floated.

The extent of Stern's 'fall' is marked by the fact that within mere weeks of his wife's death he has had two affairs, bathed naked in a hot-tub with Dixon's (female) prosecutor, and enjoyed an anonymous grope with a perfect stranger in an elevator. This erosion of self-restraint and surrender to the baser instincts is presented as in part a consequence of Stern's increasing closeness to Dixon Hartnell's dubiously acquired fortune (symbolised by Stern's agreeing to 'hide' Dixon's safe from federal investigators in his own office). If the law represents restraint then the free-market represents unbridled appetite, with Dixon the capitalist combining lust and greed in equal measure. As he becomes guardian of Dixon's corporate wealth, Stern's closeness to his client in other, even sexual, matters is emphasised: a dismayed Stern discovers that Dixon has enjoyed relations with every one of his, Stern's, sexual partners (including Clara), even contriving to expire *in flagrante* with the woman who is to become Stern's second wife.

Turow is not concerned here to endorse only one side in this opposition between the rationality of the law and the irrationality of the free market. For while Stern's dalliance with the volatile impulses of the financial and sexual marketplaces embodied in Dixon Hartnell undermines his pose of professional restraint, the new self that emerges is in many ways a more attractive and humane one. Stern discovers that his absolute commitment to the formal and abstract principles of the law has made him cold, judgemental and inaccessible, has excluded him not only from mundane sensual pleasures but also from the turbulent inner life of his own family. Indeed, this family, which Stern had supposed to be the model of restrained bourgeois propriety and rational conduct, is revealed to be a seething hotbed of irrational impulses and transgressions to which Stern had remained oblivious. The lawless Dixon Hartnell, on the other hand, emerges as a curiously honourable figure of noble self-sacrifice, carrying through his promise to Clara Stern to protect her son-in-law and daughter from prosecution for financial crimes even to the extent of taking their guilt on his shoulders. The degree to which Stern has been transformed, humanised, by this new acquaintance with irrational impulse and desire – his own as well as others' – is marked by his willingness not only to accept but to collude in a resolution of affairs in which formal justice is not done. Dixon's example has taught him that other, more visceral attachments – such as a lover's promise – can take precedence over a commitment to the abstract principles of the law. Like Rusty Sabich, who keeps his wife's guilt secret, Stern is prepared to see the dispensation of unjust deserts in the name of non-rational, 'blood' or family ties that prove stronger than professional codes. 'There are no disembodied principles in the practice of law', he muses toward the novel's end. 'There are human beings in every role, every case' (*BP*, p. 559).

While Turow uses the law in these novels to stage a metaphysical contest between reason and unreason portrayed as 'eternally' or 'naturally' opposed forces, there is also a strong current of Darwinism in his writing. This is evident in the way that his protagonists, projected into an environment characterised by relentless struggle, typically shed their civilised veneer of professionalism to reveal the almost savage, instinctual self beneath. This Darwinist current becomes especially pronounced in Turow's third novel, *Pleading Guilty* (1993), where it provides an extra dimension to the 'eternal' contest of reason and unreason, historicising – even politicising – what had heretofore been largely presented as a metaphysical condition.

For Mack Molloy, the novel's narrator, the law is a rational instrument for regulating the Darwinian struggle of modern commercial, urban life:

come into the teeming city, with so many souls screaming, I want, I need, where most social planning amounts to figuring out how to keep them all at bay – come and try to imagine the ways that the vast unruly community can be kept in touch with the deeper aspirations of humankind for the overall improvement of the species, the good of the many and the rights of the few. That I always figured was the task of the law. (*PG*, p. 174)

However, what is disclosed to Mack in the course of the narrative is the fundamental irrationality of rationality. Far from being a force that regulates the competitive anarchy of contemporary capitalism, the law in late twentieth-century America is an extension of it. Mack's law firm is, in effect, no more than a subsidiary of a gigantic multinational corporation, Trans National, whose global drive for profit-by-any-means ('the corporate version of manifest destiny', *PG*, p. 257) exemplifies the modern perversion of rational means for irrational ends. The law, Mack observes, 'is devoted to making the world safe for airlines, banks, and insurance companies' (*PG*, p. 19); legal skills are applied to cases he characterises as 'my robber baron's better than your robber baron' (*PG*, p. 201); and the ultimate inversion of reason and unreason comes when Trans National – among whose major assets is an airline – stands to profit, rather than lose money, by being legally bound to compensate the victims of an air disaster.

Mack's decision to abscond with this money is a further example of the self's 'lower' appetites and impulses shattering the veneer of professional restraint which constitutes the 'higher, better Mack' (*PG*, p. 386). But it is important to note that among these impulses is a kind of class-conscious anger which stirs in Mack a thirst for 'popular', even 'natural' justice, as opposed to the mystifications of the official legal system which can conjure multi-million dollar profits from corporate liability. Mack is from a blue-collar background, an outsider riven by working-class resentment for what he calls 'your corporate types' who, he claims, 'are soon going to be a stateless superclass, people who live for deals and golf dates and care a lot more about where you got your MBA than the country you were raised in' (p. 149). It is this resentment that prompts him not simply to take the money but to 'pass out just deserts' (p. 319) by incriminating the corporate hierarchy and effectively destroying the relationship between his firm and Trans National. Moreover, Mack sees himself as a victim of the competitive system, a loser in the economic and sexual marketplace (his career is on the slide; his wife has left him for another woman), whose last resort is to turn that system's logic against itself. 'Why', he asks, are 'the people the market fucks over ... supposed to let the tea party continue for everyone else'; and he rationalises his behaviour by asserting that 'I showed some initiative, entrepreneurship, self-reliance. I helped myself. Those are free market concepts too' (*PG*, p. 376).

Pleading Guilty therefore suggests that the forces of irrationality are historically incarnated in the structures of multinational capitalism, and that the ostensibly rational principles of the law are entirely annexed to those structures, operating simply to administer the socially unjust and unequal deserts of the market system. There is no ideal space, as there is in Grisham's more recent novels, beyond this institutionalised irrationality in which an ethical professionalism might flourish and serve the cause of reason and social justice. This is the lesson all Turow's protagonists learn. As first- or second-generation immigrants, they embrace the law as their means of assimilation, their ladder of social mobility and Americanisation. But each has ultimately to decide whether being an American consists in unwavering respect for, and service of, the law or the pursuit of happiness in spite of the law. The culture's elevation of self-gratification through the marketplace into a universal principle, and the subordination of the law to the marketplace's corporate imperatives, make any such choice impossible.

That these characters remain sympathetic even as they let their better selves lapse (in Grisham, this would be cause to demonise them as models of 'bad' professionalism) stems from Turow's view of the law and the codes of professionalism alike as rationalist fictions concealing the fundamental irrationality of human life. But the circumstances in which they surrender to impulse and appetite also suggest that the law and codes of professionalism are ideological fictions that legitimate corporate greed and class hegemony and serve social and economic injustice. A metaphysical perspective on the law co-exists here with a political grasp of its social and ideological biases. In this respect, Turow, like Grisham, registers and articulates a populist resentment of the law and of legal professionals. But, unlike Grisham, he does not seek to co-opt or defuse it by rendering it subservient in his narratives to a cleaned-up, ethical professionalism through which the social leadership of a class of affluent, upwardly mobile professionals and managers can be legitimated.

Notes

1. See Kermit L. Hall, *The Magic Mirror: Law in American History* (New York: Oxford University Press, 1989); Robert A. Ferguson, *Law and Letters in American Culture* (Cambridge, Mass.: Harvard University Press, 1984); David Ray Papke, 'Law in American Culture: An Overview', *Journal of American Culture*, vol. 15, no. 1 (Spring 1992), pp. 3–14; and Carl S. Smith, John P. McWilliams and Maxwell Bloomfield, *Law and American Literature: A Collection of Essays* (New York: Knopf, 1983). The Thomas Paine remark is taken from *Common Sense*, quoted in Papke, p. 4.
2. Alexis de Tocqueville, *Democracy in America*, Andrew Hacker (ed.), (New York: Washington Square Press, 1964), p. 106.
3. The tension between natural and social law has been a major theme in classic American literature, as Brook Thomas points out in his *Cross Examinations of Law and Literature: Cooper, Hawthorne, Stowe and Melville* (Cambridge: Cambridge University Press, 1987).
4. Max Weber established this connection between modernity and the rise of the bureaucratic professional: 'The more complicated and specialised modern culture becomes, the more its external supporting apparatus demands the personally detached and strictly "objective" expert.' Max Weber, 'Bureaucracy', in *From Max Weber: Essays in Sociology*, H.H. Gerth and C. Wright Mills (eds), (London: Routledge, 1991), p. 216. On the ethical and ideological contradictions of modern professionalism,

see Bruce Robbins, *Secular Vocations: Intellectuals, Professionalism, Culture* (London: Verso, 1993). Pioneering work on the way in which formula fiction of many kinds (including crime fiction) serves as a vehicle for exploring and interrogating the increasingly important and complex nature of professionalism and the role of professionals in modern societies was done by John G. Cawelti, *Adventure, Mystery and Romance: Formula Stories as Art and Popular Culture* (Chicago: University of Chicago Press, 1976) and Will Wright, *Sixguns and Society: A Structural Study of the Western* (Berkeley: University of California Press, 1975).

5. *The Times*, 7 July, 1993.
6. Quoted in Hall, *The Magic Mirror*, p. 308.
7. Bayless Manning, 'Hyperlexis: Our National Disease', cited in Papke, 'Law in American Culture', p. 13.
8. Philip K. Howard, *The Death of Common Sense: How Law is Suffocating America* (New York: Random House, 1995).
9. See Herman Schwartz, *Packing the Courts: The Conservative Campaign to Rewrite the Constitution* (New York: Scribners, 1988); Ronald Dworkin, 'The Reagan Revolution and the Supreme Court', *New York Review of Books*, 18 July 1991, pp. 23–8; and, on the controversy surrounding President Bush's nomination of Clarence Thomas to the Supreme Court, the volume edited by Toni Morrison, *Race-ing Justice, En-gendering Power: Essays on Anita Hill, Clarence Thomas and the Social Construction of Reality* (London: Chatto and Windus, 1993).
10. On the economic and political restructuring of American capitalism in the 1980s, see Mike Davis, *Prisoners of the American Dream: Politics and Economy in the History of the US Working Class* (London: Verso, 1986). For an illuminating account of the role played by the law in the construction of the modern American corporate political and economic order at the beginning of this century see Martin Sklar, *The Corporate Reconstruction of America 1890–1916: The Market, The Law and Politics* (Cambridge: Cambridge University Press, 1988).
11. John Grisham, *A Time to Kill* (London: Arrow, 1992), p. xi.
12. John Grisham, *The Firm* (London: Arrow, 1991), pp. 61, 100. Henceforth *TF*, page references to follow quotes.

13. On the centrality of notions of independence, occupational autonomy and dispassionate public service to codes of professionalism see Robbins, *Secular Vocations*; Terence J. Johnson, *Professions and Power* (London: Macmillan, 1972); John and Barbara Ehrenreich, 'The Professional-Managerial Class' in Pat Walker (ed.), *Between Labor and Capital* (Boston: South End Press, 1979), pp. 5–45; and Alvin Gouldner, *The Future of Intellectuals and the Rise of the New Class* (New York: Oxford University Press, 1979).

14. John Grisham, *The Pelican Brief* (London: Arrow, 1992), p. 223. Henceforth, *PB*.

15. John Grisham, *The Client* (London: Arrow, 1993), pp. 167, 275.

16. John Grisham, *The Chamber* (London: Arrow, 1994), pp. 38, 39.

17. Ibid., p. 151.

18. Grisham, *The Client*, p. 332.

19. *Guardian*, 30 May 1994.

20. For a theoretical account of the way narratives function to provide symbolic resolutions of real social contradictions, see Fredric Jameson, *The Political Unconscious: Narrative as a Socially Symbolic Act* (London: Methuen, 1980).

21. Weber, 'Bureaucracy', p. 216.

22. Scott Turow, *Pleading Guilty* (Harmondsworth, Middlesex: Viking, 1993), p. 118. Henceforth, *PG*.

23. Weber, 'Bureaucracy', p. 216.

24. Scott Turow, *Presumed Innocent* (Harmondsworth, Middlesex: Penguin, 1988), pp. 378. Henceforth, *PI*.

25. Scott Turow, *The Burden of Proof* (Harmondsworth, Middlesex: Penguin, 1991), pp. 227 and 581. Henceforth, *BP*.

10

Watching the Detectives: Body Images, Sexual Politics and Ideology in Contemporary Crime Film

Brian Jarvis

Preparing to masturbate whilst watching the TV motorcycle cop show *CHiPS*, Frenesi Gates, in Thomas Pynchon's *Vineland* (1990), pauses to consider her amatory attraction to the uniformed body. Could her carnal captivation by images of authority be a genetic inheritance, 'as if some Cosmic Fascist had spliced in a DNA sequence requiring this form of seduction and initiation into the dark joys of social control'?[1] Even as a reformed political radical, Frenesi finds the crude biological determinism underlying this explanation distasteful, but she is unable to arrive at an alternative. Frenesi's inability to solve the mystery of her uniform fetish, however, does not inhibit her when it comes to making sweeping attacks against the culture industry's valorisation of police power:

> Cop shows were in a genre right-wing weekly *T.V. Guide* called Crime Drama ... relentlessly pushing their propaganda message of cops-are-only-human-got-to-do-their job, turning agents of government repression into sympathetic heroes.[2]

Although it is not always accompanied by a concupiscent charge as intense as that experienced by Frenesi Gates, the watching of crime dramas is undoubtedly one of the most prevalent pastimes enjoyed by the consumer of American popular culture. The explosive proliferation of images of lawbreaking and law enforcement within the media has generated a mythic capital around the figures of the Criminal and the Detective. As is suggested by Frenesi Gates' response to Jon and Ponch, the California Highway Patrol's finest, the pleasures and the political imperatives encoded in images of authority and transgression can be complex. Whilst the radical might denounce the crime drama as a reactionary spectacle, designed to consolidate hegemonic power structures, the right-winger can claim that images within the genre actually amplify social disintegration, through desensitising displays of gratuitous violence and criminality.

Bearing in mind that the mechanisms of desire and cultural instrumentality can be extremely intricate, I investigate here some of the most charismatic folk devils and heroes to have appeared in recent years within the crime drama. What functions do such figures perform? What relation, if any, do images of crime and its detection have to the dark joys of social control? Do crime dramas resist or reproduce dominant ideology and its associated gender identities? The films I propose to examine traverse generic boundaries that include science fiction (*Blade Runner*), horror (*The Silence of the Lambs*), Gothic soap-opera (*Twin Peaks*), film *noir* (*Blue Velvet*) and action adventure (*Die Hard*). This formal diversity is a graphic testimony both to the plasticity of the crime drama genre and the value attached to its key players – deviant and detective – within contemporary American culture. Despite the wide range of contexts in which they appear, it is my contention that certain core impulses are in evidence when the cultural practice of watching the detectives is cross-examined. Specifically, the pleasures and the politics of the genre can often be seen to revolve around the body, uniformed or otherwise. The dead body has traditionally been a catalyst for the action in the crime drama. Increasingly, however, the body, dead or alive, is occupying a position centre-stage, as the focal point of mystery, visual pleasure and anxiety.

David Lynch, Intertextualities, Body Images

One of the more intriguing aspects to recent crime drama is the resurgence of the Federal Bureau of Investigation. During a period in which the public image of other branches of American law enforcement was repeatedly tarnished, a batch of charismatic Bureau agents appeared in popular culture: in *Manhunter* (1986), *The Untouchables* (1987), *Twin Peaks* (1989–91), *The Silence of the Lambs* (1990), *The Feds* (1991), *The FBI Files* (1993–) and *The X Files* (1994–).[3] To varying degrees each of these contributions to a burgeoning sub-genre can be read, in line with Frenesi Gates' allegation, as extended commercials or 'infoverts' for an organisation that has a distinguished track record as an agent of government repression.

Despite the ostensible differences in their apocryphal representations of the Bureau, these texts are united by their universal acclaim for the *modus operandi* of Academy graduates. The sympathetic heroes of FBI crime drama are seen to engage in a species of detection requiring a somewhat curious blend of ratiocination and intuition. The inclusion of scenes in this sub-genre that pay homage to the efficacy of forensic medicine, psychological profiling and IT systems, seems compulsory. At the same time, however, the solution to a crime usually hinges upon a moment of illumination that eludes the realm of scientific methodology. Thus, Dale Cooper receives visions that lead him ever closer to the heart of darkness in the Ghostwood forest, Will Graham tracks down the Red Dragon by practising the police equivalent of method acting, Clarice Starling and Fox Mulder rely heavily on hunches to break the case. In this respect the FBI crime drama can be seen to return to the ancestral roots of the detective story. Edgar Allan Poe's work often suggests a sensibility torn between hyper-rationalism (the Dupin triptych, 'The Philosophy of Composition') and anti-rationalism (the tales of the supernatural). The modern FBI fable recuperates this hermeneutic crisis. The agent is confronted by both explicable criminality (Red Dragon, Jame Gumb, Ben Horne) and the Imp of the Perverse (Hannibal Lecter, Bob, the subjects of all those unclosed X files).

The *mise en scène* of David Lynch's cinema is frequently haunted by the ghost of Poe. His spectral presence can be traced not only in the systematic instability informing the Lynch crime drama, but also in his fascination with the bizarre and perverse, his privileging of aesthetic effect over all other considerations, and his predilection for the immaculate stylisation of violence against women. In *Blue Velvet* (1986), an amateur sleuth, Jeffrey Beaumont, investigates the mystery surrounding the brutalisation of a nightclub performer by a vicious criminal. At one point in the case, Jeffrey is challenged by Sandy, his nauseatingly saccharine partner in crime-solving: 'I'm not sure whether you're a detective or a pervert.' Lynch's most commercially and critically successful projects to date encourage the spectator to occupy a similarly equivocal position. *Blue Velvet* received Oscar nominations and won the National Society of Film Critics best film award. *Twin Peaks* collected 14 Emmy nominations in its first season and was one of the most widely watched and talked about murder mysteries in television history. It is unlikely, however, that either was being commended for its disquieting suggestion that the pleasures of watching the detective occupy a grey area between innocent inquisitiveness and lascivious voyeurism.

One of the more innocent pleasures involved in watching a Lynch crime drama is the consumption of its extravagant media intertextuality. Alongside the oblique references to Poe (Laura Palmer's death is the most poetical topic in the world, according to the criteria laid down in 'The Philosophy of Composition'), *Blue Velvet* and *Twin Peaks* continually recycle sets, characters and dialogue from a range of media codes – the detective and mystery genres, film *noir*, horror, soap-opera, the work of specific auteurs and the discourses of advertising.[4]

In *Blue Velvet* the mysterious case begins when the junior private eye discovers a severed ear in a vacant lot. Jeffrey's gradual entanglement in this case transports him from the cosy domesticities of the suburbs to Lumberton's seedy downtown, a nightscape of sexual violence and criminal, subcultural knavery. This opposition between incredulously sanitised, Rockwellian Americana and a Sadeian cityscape of pain reproduces the geography of *noir*, as do the female characters associated with these antithetical zones.[5]

In the film's opening shots, Jeffrey's mother is watching a *noir* crime drama on television, but the family name, Beaumont, also suggests the soap-opera tradition from which Lynch appropriates much of his dialogue.[6] Whilst his surname signifies soap-opera, Jeffrey's forename, and his equivocal voyeuristic tendencies, direct the spectator back to cinematic texts. A reference to Michael Powell's *Peeping Tom* (1959) might be discerned, but a more obvious one is to L.B. *Jeffries* in Hitchcock's wry commentary on the pleasures of watching, *Rear Window* (1954).[7]

Lynch's small-screen crime drama, *Twin Peaks*, encourages the spectator to savour the recognition of predominantly televisual traditions.[8] The *mise en scène* vivaciously pastes together media clichés from cop shows and FBI dramas (particularly *The Untouchables*), daytime soap-operas, teen romances and 1950s advertisements for commodities ranging from coffee to curtain-runners. As in Lumberton, beneath the surface serenity of the Twin Peaks community there lie 'dark' secrets. The archetypal Lynch landscape consists of pockets of criminality that must be patrolled and contained by honest cops, kindly doctors and robust lumberjacks. In this instance the threat to the community is two-fold - terrestrial and supernatural. First, there is the danger posed by white-collar crime in the shape of shady real-estate dealings. This, however, simply becomes backdrop to a Manichean melodrama, a primal struggle between the forces of good and evil embodied in the White and Black Lodges deep in the forest of Douglas firs.

In *Twin Peaks*, Lynch also gestures beyond media mythologies to Greek and Nordic legend. Cooper's quest takes him into the Underworld to rescue Annie, his Eurydice, in a world of giants and dwarves. Other frameworks of reference include Native American and Tibetan folklore, astrology and new-age mysticism. However, as with his cinematic and televisual references, these gestures are largely throwaway. They intimate that no one grand narrative can fix spatial and temporal relations in this strange world. Lynch's crime drama offers a determinedly directionless, intertextual *bricolage* that mocks the very concept of 'significance' as a modernist fetish. Prior to postmodernism, intertextuality in crime drama (as in the novels of Raymond Chandler) was typically functional, a formal device intended to denote deeper meanings and connections. Lynch's references are more playful, and relish their failure to signify further, to lead anywhere. His contributions to crime drama offer the pleasure of *recognition* in place of the possibility of understanding. All myth, all history, is a junkyard for casual reference. The spectator is presented with the media equivalent of Malraux's Imaginary

Museum, an infinite installation of depthless images that exchange exclusively amongst themselves. In classic crime drama, pleasure was largely contingent upon the resolution of the mystery. In *Twin Peaks*, the case is perpetually unresolved, but, in place of the normal curve of the hermeneutic code, one is offered the glazed and mindless ecstasy of *jouissance*. The gratification associated with watching Lynch's sleuths involves a kind of 'primal pleasure, of anthropological joy in images, a kind of brute fascination unencumbered by aesthetic, moral, social or political judgements'.[9]

Alongside this primal pleasure, however, there is considerable anxiety within the Lynch crime drama associated with the body and its image. The iconography of *Blue Velvet* is dominated by sensory organs and orifices – a severed ear, mouths stuffed with fabric or engaged in fellatio, giant tongues, brains oozing out through bullet holes. Similarly, the menu in *Twin Peaks* consists of bruised and battered bodies. Throughout the episodes for which he was responsible, Lynch delights in the visual feast of multiple autopsies and the display of bodies that transgress physical norms, including a giant, a dancing dwarf and a one-armed man. Within the Lynch *œuvre*, representation of the corporeal is characterised by a proliferation of images of disfigurement and decay.

As John Alexander has suggested, body images in Lynch's work are organised around a structural opposition between a 'closed' perfect body and an 'open' abject body.[10] His closed body hero tends to be distinguished by a decidedly conservative sartorial preference – dressed formally in dark suit and tie, and juxtaposed with the degeneracy of the ungroomed open body.[11] This *leitmotif* is particularly apparent in Lynch's use, in *Blue Velvet*, of the clean-cut and boyish actor, Kyle Maclachan. In *Twin Peaks*, too, Agent Dale Cooper, in regulation FBI dark suit and tie, is pitted against Bob, a denim-clad degenerate.[12]

The fear that accompanies this parallelism is two-fold and consists of homophobia – fear that the closed body of the detective hero might be 'open' to a man – and gynophobia – fear of the feminine as the most 'open' of bodies. Lynch's (mis)understanding of gay desire is best described as a species of heterosexual hysteria. Jeffrey Beaumont's violent encounter with the sadist, Ben, is followed by a night ride with Frank which was originally intended to conclude with a literal rape scene, rather than the symbolic performance that takes place at Deer Meadows.[13] Homophobia is less explicit in *Twin Peaks*, but the narrative does follow the exploits of the perverse Bob, hiding inside the smartly-dressed Leland Palmer and fuelling obscene erotic excesses. The horror of being possessed by Bob, of having him *inside you*, represents the climax of the series, when the most closed of closed-body Lynch heroes, Agent Cooper, is penetrated by this libidinal demon.

Anxiety about gay desire and the male body is intermittently evident at both a literal and symbolic level in the Lynch crime drama. However, it is accompanied by a far more pervasive dread – that of the 'dark continent' (in Freud's infamous formulation) that is the open body of a generic Woman. The range of roles permitted to women in Lynch's crime drama is both restricted and reactionary. Their centrality to his plots is as passive figures who function as catalysts to the actions of the detective hero (Jeffrey, Cooper, Truman) battling to rescue them, body and soul. Unless they belong to the cast of extras that includes wholesome secretaries and waitresses, the Lynch actress can expect to play either a predatory *femme fatale*, an innocent small-town all-American Girl, or a confused amalgam of the two. In a flamboyantly self-conscious appropriation of film *noir* archetypes, *Blue Velvet* juxtaposes the dark, foreign spider woman (Dorothy Vallens), with the redemptive, asexual, blonde girl-next-door (Sandy). The absence of psychological depth in such flagrantly one-dimensional figures restricts the possibilities for character development in any conventional sense, but Lynch crime drama is consistently uninterested in such matters from the outset. Instead it explores the female body and the 'mystery' of its desires.

Lynch's gynophobia is most striking in his first film, *Eraserhead*, but persists in his subsequent crime dramas. Frank Booth's sadistic scrutiny of Dorothy Vallens' vagina in *Blue Velvet* is echoed in the multiple autopsies performed on female corpses in *Twin Peaks* and *Fire Walk With Me*. The close-up of the heavily made-up mouth is one of the most conspicuous images in Lynch's framing of his *femmes fatales*. It is an image of desire and dread that signifies other lips that bleed.

In gestures reminiscent of those performed by the narrators in Poe's tales, and especially 'Berenice' and 'The Oval Portrait', gynophobia in Lynch's work manifests itself in a penchant for punishment and photography. The desiring and desirable female is alternately subjected to extremes of physical abuse or confined within the comparative safety of a picture frame. The most disturbing aspect of this representation is its re-inforcement of the notion that women secretly desire (and thus deserve) the pain inflicted on them. In *Blue Velvet*, Dorothy Vallens' masochistic pleasure is foregrounded during the scene with both criminal and budding detective, but there is no psychological prehistory that might explain her response (as, perhaps, an eroticisation of powerlessness). Lynch's own commentary on Dororthy Vallens' victimisation does little to challenge misogynistic mythology: 'There are some women that you want to hit because you're getting a feeling from them that they want it, or they upset you in a certain way.'[14]

Acts of violence towards the female body form the narrative engine of both *Fire Walk With Me* and the *Twin Peaks* series. In his reading of the prequel, Alexander uses Claire Douglas' study of incest trauma (*The Woman in the Mirror*), to suggest that the evil spirit Bob can be understood as an apparition unconsciously devised by Laura Palmer to shield her from the horrific recognition that she has been sexually abused by her father:

> Laura denies the truth, choosing to live in self-manifested illusion. 'Victims of incest ... learn secrecy and subterfuge in order to conceal the extent of their pain even from themselves ... victims of incest need help in calling things by their real names'.[15]

By accommodating Laura's experiences to conventional realist practice, Alexander is also able to make sense of her subsequent turn to prostitution and drug addiction. His reading, however, is problematised by the fact that Bob's evil continues well after Laura's demise. More fundamentally, his explanation of sexual violence in this film is founded upon the notion of a centred subjectivity and the primacy of the real, both of which are continually challenged in Lynch's work. Character is regularly presented in a cartoon and ostentatiously one-dimensional manner. It becomes the space onto which a montage of media and pop psychoanalytical clichés can be projected.

The repeated use of a photographic image of Laura Palmer during the closing credits of each episode of *Twin Peaks* may seem to evoke the presence of absence, the loss of a young woman. But this distracts from the fact that there is a deep epistemological loss at the core of Lynch's work itself. The photographic image does not conceal the true Laura Palmer because there is no 'true' Laura Palmer. The illusion of a coherent, centred subjectivity is shattered. Lynch's depiction of her drifts disorientatingly from innocent prom queen to teenage prostitute, from traumatised incest victim to predatory *femme fatale*, sublimely uninterested in the possibility that there might be an authentic individual beneath the masks. Identity dissolves into the soft-focus *jouissance* of the endlessly reproducible image. In *Blue Velvet*, similarly, *glissante* is visualised as Dorothy slides from one cartooned cliché of femininity to the next: *femme fatale*, willing victim, devoted mom. Dorothy is the 'blue lady', an appellation which signifies her pornographic objectification, but which also anticipates her subsequent redemption as holy mother in the film's closing images (reunited with her child, showered with a kitsch suburban sunshine, as the camera pans to Mary's colour in the cloudless sky).

The foregrounding of artifice in the construction of character in Lynch's films has been applauded as a radical device. Lynda Bundtzen and Tracy Biga, amongst others, have argued that Lynch's work is less an expression of the patriarchal imagination than a deconstruction of it *from the inside*.[16] Dorothy and Sandy conform so completely to the stereotypical figures of the innocent, blonde American Girl and the bad, dark foreign Lady, that it seems to permit the possibility that a self-conscious parody of these ideological constructions is taking place. The Oedipal overdetermination of the relationships in a film like *Blue Velvet*, alongside its Hitchcockian attention to the mechanisms of voyeurism, have led some feminist critics to advance the claim that Lynch's work is about misogyny, rather than being misogynistic. Critics who distance Lynch from the anti-feminist traditions of classical Hollywood cinema rarely detail the precise differences between the two, except by referring to an apparently redemptive self-consciousness. In fact, the play in which Lynch indulges with the archetypes of Madonna and Whore, treads a line between classical sexism and its camp critique so fine as to be practically invisible. Dorothy Vallens wears a black wig during her performances at the Slow Club, but beneath her wig her natural hair colour is also black. Lynch foregrounds patriarchal stereotyping in the ludicrously stark oppositions of Fair Maiden and Dark Lady, but similarly intimates that these myths both conceal and are the essence of female identity. The female body is mapped as a mystery of sliding surfaces, which the closed-body male detective must investigate without hope of solving its enigmas.

Returning to the allegation with which I began this enquiry there are two major findings. The Lynch crime drama does reinforce the fiction of essentially benevolent American law enforcement (Detective Williams, Sheriff Truman, Agent Cooper). Equally significant, however, in terms of their relation to dominant ideology, is Lynch's representation of the female body. His body images both reflect and reproduce the anti-feminism fuelled by the New Right's domination of political and cultural power, apparent throughout American public life at this time.

The Silence of the Lambs

At a glance, Jonathan Demme's film, *The Silence of the Lambs*, might appear to be promising territory in which to find a more progressive representation of the feminine within visual crime drama. Jodie Foster was awarded an Oscar for her portrayal of FBI trainee Clarice Starling. In the film she plays a tough, independent and resourceful career woman, a character type unknown within the Lynch canon. On closer examination, however, it becomes apparent that feminist impulses within Demme's film are undercut in various ways. Agent Starling's autonomy is continually compromised as each of her major decisions are seen to be determined by her relations with male authority figures. Clarice joins the FBI to follow in the footsteps of her dear dead papa. She yearns for the respect of FBI chief

Jack Crawford and receives guidance from her dark father, Hannibal Lecter. Beneath the facade of self-sufficiency the heart of the nineties woman still belongs to daddy. Progressive elements in the narrative, to do with sexual equality and equal opportunities, women's initiative and determination, are contained by Clarice's Electra complex. Consequently, gestural feminism is enmeshed in an Oedipal dragnet, as the FBI detective heroine is caught between the superego of humourless Jack Crawford and the libidinal anarchy of the horrifically charismatic Lecter.

Agent Starling belongs alongside a wave of all-action heroines who have appeared with increasing frequency in Hollywood cinema, as the effects of second-wave feminism, the sexual revolution and changing gender roles spill over into popular culture. These figures have appeared on both sides of the law (in, for example *V.I. Warshawski* and *Thelma and Louise*) and outside the crime drama, especially in science fiction and horror films, most notably in the *Alien*, *Terminator* and *Candyman* sagas. At a symbolic level these texts register aspirations and anxieties associated with the challenge being issued to traditional definitions of gender identity in parts of American society. The usurpation of the role of (crime) fighter by women is clearly related to shifting notions of what constitutes masculine and feminine subjectivity. In this context, *The Silence of the Lambs*, as well as being a glossy, big-budget variant on the B-movie slasher, might also be read as a parable on the horrors and pleasures of *cross-dressing* in a culture experiencing the withering of gender polarities. Whilst Agent Starling assumes the conventionally masculine garb of the law enforcer, Jame (Jane) Gumb spends hours in the domestic sphere sewing himself a 'woman suit'. Hollywood's new breed of action heroine may appear to be successful symbolic transsexuals, but, as is the case with Clarice, they are almost always motivated by relations with male authority figures, or by a near psychotic maternalism – attempting to rescue senators' daughters (*The Silence of the Lambs*), babies (*Candyman*), cute furry creatures (*Alien*), girls (*Aliens*) and boys (*Terminator 2*). Whatever their motivation, however, their mere presence seems to provoke the anxious question of whether men might not be displaced into traditionally feminine activities, such as giving birth (the *Alien* trilogy, *Junior*) and wearing women's suits (*Tootsie, Mrs Mom, Mrs Doubtfire* and the burgeoning sub-genre of 'tranny' films).

An alternative, less gender-specific reading of *The Silence of the Lambs* can be produced by returning to the generic cross-dressing that takes place between the crime drama and body horror. The fetishistic fascination with an abject corporeality in Lynch' and Demme's contributions to crime drama (patches of skin, rotten fingernails, livers eaten with lima beans) might be taken to confirm Julia Kristeva's startling proposal, in *Powers of Horror*, that the inventory of otherness discarded from the body has become a 'substitute for the role formerly played by the sacred'.[17] Without discarding this possibility, I should like to propose that it is more immediately connected to secular concerns associated with the economy of desire within contemporary consumer capitalism.

At root, body horror is a cinematic practice intimately related to the rise of a body culture. Superficially, in consumer society, the body is defined as a private space, but in practice it is increasingly subject to a variety of forms of regulation. Individuals are incessantly bombarded by images of the commercialised means of recreating and idealising themselves. As desire is channelled towards consumerism and the fetishism of commodities, reification intensifies to such a level that the consuming self itself becomes objectified as capitalism's most valuable product. In this process the institutions of advertising perform the crucial function of encouraging self-obsession with the body – its surfaces and its depths, what it absorbs and how it is adorned. Advertising appears to promote affirmative images of the self, but its primary purpose is to produce those feelings of inadequacy and lack which are the essential preconditions for purchase. To this end the body is remorselessly objectified – in televisual images, in magazines and on billboards – with the covert intention of persuading the consumer that they are deficient in some form: wrong size or shape, body odour and greasy hair, mouths carrying germs as repugnant as any death's head moth. A culture of narcissism, to use Lasch's phrase, is a culture of anxiety about the body and its image.[18]

The terrors and pleasures of body horror cannot be dissociated from the terrors and pleasures of a body culture. Wolfgang Haug's evocative description of the commodity as a 'promissory second skin', which the consumer is invited to slip into, is particularly appropriate here: this is the flesh that Jame Gumb covets and Hannibal Lecter consumes.[19] Essentially, their crime is that of taking the hidden persuaders' promises of a new self and of bodies good enough to eat *too* literally. Compelled to satisfy wants and wishes they do not fully comprehend (or in Lecter's case, appear incomprehensible) the serial killer may fascinate because they are a caricature of the psychosis that drives the serial consumer. The Red Dragon's obsession with his 'Becoming', in Michael Mann's chic *Manhunter*, is simply a criminal variant on the psychological condition that the hidden persuaders aim to instil in the consumer.

Mapping the Male Body: the *Die Hard* Sequence

John McClane, the lead character in the *Die Hard* films, has fascinated and excited the consumer of Hollywood action adventure cinema as much as any detective hero in recent years. Although each instalment in this cycle features a different location, a key part of the pleasure associated with them is the phenomenal predictability of narrative development. *Die Hard* (1988) centres on the Nakatomi building in Los Angeles; *Die Hard 2: Die Harder* (1990) is based in Washington at the Dulles International airport; and *Die Hard 3: With a Vengeance* (1995) moves between locations in New York. In each location, however, McClane's dilemma is identical and revolves around his relationship to two sets of villains. The first are evil foreigners from Europe, Latin America and the Middle East, either executing or funding hoax terrorist acts, kidnappings and elaborate bank raids with incredible efficiency. The second comprise a host of inefficient American bureaucrats (from within police, military, airport and government authorities) who aid the bad guys by getting in the way of the lone detective hero. Each adventure involves a revelation with regard to the villains' real intentions or identity, which McClane recognises well in advance of the bureaucrats, and forlornly attempts to communicate. Other compulsory ingredients in the *Die Hard* formula are the befriending of a black American (a cop, a co-opted cop, a chauffeur and an army sergeant), sundry members of the white working class (especially janitors and truck drivers), and the acquisition of a walkie-talkie with which to engage in humorous repartee with the villains.

While the success of the *Die Hard* trilogy can be attributed partly to this proficient recycling of narrative structure, visual pleasure is primarily related to the representation of the detective hero's body. In John McClane the spectator is offered an image of the male body as raw power and indestructibility. In this context the *Die Hard* sequence belongs alongside the extremely popular and lucrative action films produced during the 1980s which paraded a series of sinewy icons such as Sylvester Stallone, Arnold Schwarzenegger and Jean-Claude Van Damme. In these texts, as Susan Jeffords observes, 'the male body – principally the white male body became increasingly a vehicle of display – of musculature, of beauty, of physical feats, and of a gritty toughness'.[20]

In such films the forms of objectifying camera rhetoric that have traditionally dominated representations of the female form in popular culture now frame the male torso.[21] In part this development could be connected to the rise of the body culture – encouraging an obsession with physical self-perfection helps grease the wheels of commodity capitalism, especially its cogs in the burgeoning industries of health, fitness and leisure. However, the dominant readings produced within the field of film studies have tended to focus upon the shock waves sent out by second-wave feminism and to read these images of a hypertrophied masculinity as evidence of a crisis in the symbolic economy of patriarchy. According to such readings, detective John McClane is part of a process of (de)constructing masculinity as a variety of denaturalised performance, as a self-conscious and parodic masquerade. The instantly recognisable formulae of the genre – the ritualised death and destruction, the incessant pyrotechnics and rounds of ammunition – are not the real subjects of the *Die Hard* films. Rather than being violent, sado-masochistic fantasies, they are actually *about* violence, sado-masochism, power and display in a patriarchal culture. Detective McClane is engaged in 'performing the masculine' in an exhibition that borders upon camp critique. He stands alongside a repertory company of comic-book heroes such as Rocky and Rambo, Batman, Superman and Indiana Jones, or more recently in science-fiction crime dramas, *Time Cop* (1995) and *Judge Dredd* (1995), that collectively connote the current crisis in dominant codes of masculinity. Such bodies resemble:

> an anthropomorphised phallus, a phallus with muscles, if you like ... They are simulacra of an exaggerated masculinity, the original completely lost to sight, a casualty of the failure of the paternal signifier and the current crisis in master narratives.[22]

Essentially this reading is a variant on the interpretation by some feminists of the images of women in Lynch's cinema, since it relies upon similar assumptions concerning the redemptive power of self-consciousness. Once again, however, it never adequately explains how the self-reflexive miming of masculine aggression in film differs from its off-screen practice. The images of masculinity produced in Hollywood circulate in fields larger than the cinematic and the discursive practices of film theory. When Ronald Reagan declares, in a public address, that he knows what foreign policy decisions to take in relation to Latin America after watching the exploits of Rambo, it is highly unlikely that his militaristic fervour and big-stick diplomacy was inspired by that film's parodic subtext. The distinctions between a postmodern performing the masculine and old-fashioned macho aggression may be too fine to be recognised outside of the academy.

Other readings are of course possible. For example, the *Die Hard* cycle in part involves a display of the white male body that permits a surreptitious homoeroticism for the male spectator which would otherwise be taboo in a culture which enforces a compulsory and compulsive heterosexuality. To uncover the primary ideological imperative behind the *Die Hard* detective folk hero, however, it is necessary to trace the genre to which it belongs to its specific context in American social history from the late 1960s and the series of vigorous challenges to the hegemony of the patriarchal social order that occurred during this period.

In the 1960s and early 1970s the women's movement and the Civil Rights lobby launched a dual assault upon white male privilege. The concomitant reconfiguration of gender identities was exacerbated by the shattering of a sense of economic self-sufficiency in the wake of the oil crisis-inspired slump. At the same time, in the international political arena, national pride was severely wounded by a spate of hostage crises, Third World revolutions and military failures in Vietnam. Masculinity, accordingly, could no longer be accepted as the given against which the feminine might be defined and displayed. It needed to be *made visible*, to be re-inscribed in the symbolic interstices of an anxious patriarchal order. The dramatic resurgence of the action genre from the mid-1970s onwards, a resurgence greatly consolidated under the Reagan presidency, might then be interpreted as a semiotic salve, a means of sublimating anxieties associated with a series of historical changes understood in terms of an insidious *feminisation* of the nation. For, inevitably, the loss of political, economic and military muscle would be articulated in this way within a culture which symbolically equates the feminine with weakness and with lack.

At the level of ideological symbolism, detective John McClane, and his contemporaries in crime drama/action film crossovers such as the *Lethal Weapon* trilogy, issue a clarion-call for a re-masculinisation of America. This is rather puerilely imagined here and in the wave of comic-book heroes who appeared in Hollywood cinema at this time (*Superman, Batman, Indiana Jones*) as a re-*muscularisation*. In terms of the mapping of the male body in popular culture, this constitutes a recuperation of the most archaic formulation of masculinity as brute physical presence and an ability to withstand and mete out unbelievable excesses of violence. McClane's muscles, as they enable him to elude bullets and explosion and endure dramatic falls, fire and water, are themselves significant signifiers – not as a parodic costume, but as emblems of power and of the traditional forms of manual labour and physical activity which have gone into their production. These signifiers might appear particularly pleasurable both to the disempowered, and to a largely white-collar male labour force sharing space and authority (in some cases, at least) with women, and deprived of its traditional role in the family as the sole source of economic security. As Yvonne Tasker suggests in 'Dumb Movies for Dumb People': 'A reorientation of the relationship between men, masculinity and consumption in the West necessarily affects those definitions of male identity achieved through production.'[23]

Blade Runner

The final detective hero I should like to investigate, as I pursue my thesis that the body has become increasingly central to action, anxiety and visual pleasure in the crime drama, is Deckard in Ridley Scott's *Blade Runner* (1982). Generically, the film is a hybrid which, within the framework of science-fiction fantasy, incorporates horror and romance. It also has an unmistakably *noir* narrative and visual design which echo the Hollywood private investigator thrillers of the 1940s and early 1950s. The plot involves dramatic chase sequences, rooftop confrontations and cryptic clues. Its central character is an isolated, hard-boiled cop, who, in the long overcoat uniform of the PI, makes a habit of hard drinking and getting beaten up, physically and psychologically, by glamorous *femmes fatales* and charismatic bad guys. Los Angeles in the twenty-first century is heavily indebted to the cinematic tradition of *noir* city images. The permanently nocturnal streets of this futuristic LA are partially illuminated by neon signs and a chiaroscuro lighting, whilst its gloomy interiors are drenched in the shadows that fall from drawn blinds and rotating fans.

Watching and detection are entwined from the outset in one of the film's most conspicuous motifs, which revolves around the eye and the subject of its gaze. The opening frames of *Blade Runner* alternate between Leon's eye as it reflects the city and that which seeks to keep it and him under surveillance – the huge panoptican eye of the Tyrell building. Inside Tyrell's headquarters the renegade replicant is subjected to a Voight-Kampf screening which focuses upon reactions in the optic nerve. In the next scene the spectator is introduced to Deckard, the film's private eye, who is regularly involved in the examination of visual clues such as photographs and films, and who scrutinises the eyes of his prey, to determine whether the bodies before him are human or machine.[24]

The criminal replicants' position at the margins of this not-so-futuristic society is signalled in several ways and is continually associated with the transgressive nature of their bodies. This is most apparent in the persistent challenge their presence constitutes to the orthodox romantic opposition between technology and nature. At the same time, Roy's opening lines position him as a romantic and revolutionary culture hero, imbued with the spirit of freedom and rebellion.[25] This spirit is exhibited by each of the replicants as they infiltrate the spaces of authority: the inner sanctum of Tyrell, the Bradbury building, Eyeworld. Both Leon and Pris attempt to enter the corporate body of Tyrell through its waste products: one as a garbage disposal worker, the other as a bedraggled waif. Once inside the various exclusion zones which confront them, these outcasts clash with those who enforce the rigid socio-spatial apartheid characteristic of twenty-first (and, indeed, twentieth) century LA. Thus Leon attempts to kill Holden and Deckard, Pris and Zhora both clash with the blade runner, and Roy destroys both his maker, Tyrell, and J.F. Sebastian.

The replicants' criminality is linked to the fact that their bodies have not been inscribed with the codes of bourgeois patriarchal socialisation. Whilst each of the film's 'human' (this category is placed *sous rature*) characters are known by those impersonal surnames which are the signature of a body's 'normal' entry to the Symbolic, its technological protagonists are identified by their forenames, signalling, in the absence of the name of the father, their anti-Oedipal status. In the apartment of J.F. Sebastian, Roy and Pris are linked with childhood and with toys – unsurprisingly, since they are, after all, only four years of age. Throughout *Blade Runner, les enfants terribles* are associated with the transgression of 'normal' codes of sexuality. There are unmistakable overtones of the homoerotic and sado-masochistic in Roy and Leon's torture and punishment of Deckard. A sado-masochistic element is also conspicuous in the decoration of the replicant body. Pris and Zhora, in their playfully pornographic uniforms (fishnets, stiletto-heeled boots, transparent plastic mac) deliberately flaunt the illicit iconography of sexual fetishism, and both attempt to strangle the detective – one between her thighs; the other with his own tie.

These elements, however, exist solely as a pleasurable and titillating voyeurism for the (implicitly male) spectator, and despite Roy's taunt to Deckard that 'straight doesn't seem to be good enough', they never threaten to coalesce into any distinct challenge to the libidinal economy's heterosexual norms. Indeed, particularly with reference to its representation of the female body, *Blade Runner* might be seen to replicate those norms. During the scenes in which they attempt to kill Deckard, the faces of Zhora and Pris are frozen in a tableau which symbolically equates the sexual female with the 'monstrous mouth' and the patriarchal phobia of the devouring vagina.[26]

The replicants' status as criminalised outsiders is also extended by analogies to the oppressed bodies of racial minorities within white hegemony. As he strips off for battle, smears the blood of his beloved as war paint on his cheeks, howls like a wolf and finally sits down to await his death, Roy is linked to the Native American (or, to be more precise, his equivalent in popular culture). A more overt connection is provided by Deckard's gloss on his superior's use of the term 'skin-job' as slang for a replicant: 'Bryant was the kind of cop who in history books used to call black men "niggers".'[27]

The racial politics of the text are somewhat clouded however by the unmistakable fascist resonances surrounding the 'more human than human' replicants. The body of the Nexus-6 is modelled on distinctly Aryan ideals of beauty and genetic superiority, which confounds any implications of Deckard's statement which might look toward a post-racist culture. They are stronger, more intelligent and charismatic than their makers, and their bodies are adorned with the costume of youth rebellion and punk which incorporates neofascist iconography – their SS boots and black leather overcoats symbolically miming and transgressing authority. 'You're so perfect', exclaims J.F. Sebastian, whose own plight of being stranded on Earth due to genetic imperfections, when taken in conjunction with the racial composition of the city, seems to suggest a very strict master-race migration policy for the Off-World colonies.

In a similar manner, the character of Deckard, the detective, is not without his ambiguities. Indeed, a number of affinities, alongside the obvious differences, exist between the hunter and the hunted in the city of the future. The blade runner, like the private investigator whose mantle he inherits, possesses the status of the ambivalent and compromised agent of authority. Deckard comes out of retirement to 'retire' those who threaten the dominant order by challenging the corporate empire that created them. But the protagonist is both an authority figure and another pawn in the socio-political system; an individual actor in a corporate society which renders all such acts impotent. The labours of the blade runner, as with those of the private investigator, who became an American culture hero during the 1930s and 1940s, seem to provide hope for individual action, courage and spontaneity in a socio-economic order where such attributes are severely restricted.

The body of the detective in *Blade Runner*, in a less explicit, but equally effective manner, also produces anxieties relating to the interface between the organic and the mechanical. In his account of the Off-World 'skin-job' mutiny which has apparently resulted in Deckard's recall, Bryant explains that the group consists of *six* renegade replicants: 'three male, three female'. Deckard tracks down Zhora, Leon, Pris and Roy and one is said to have 'got fried running through an electric fence' at the Tyrell corporation building. This, however, still leaves a missing replicant. Since, in a film which pays such meticulous attention to detail elsewhere, this is not likely to be simply a clumsy error, it might be construed as part of a suggestion that, perhaps metaphorically, if not indeed literally, the sixth replicant may be Deckard himself.[28] Who better, after all, to eliminate the escapees after some reprogramming? Tyrell explains that the new range of Nexus-6 replicants can be equipped with memory implants to shield the details of their origin even from themselves. These implants are the equivalent for technological consciousness of memories and are said to make the 'product' more manageable. Deckard certainly proves to be most amenable to the dictates of authority. During the course of the film he discovers that he is beginning 'to develop emotional responses ... Replicants weren't supposed to have feelings. Neither were blade runners. What the hell was happening to me?!' The audience also discovers that, like Rachel, he has no proof of an authentic past (defined throughout the film as family history) other than a handful of photographs. Rachel's crucial challenge to Deckard is conveniently left unanswered – 'Did you ever take that test yourself?' – and the continuity error whereby Roy identifies Deckard by name without a scene in which this knowledge is made available to him, alongside the almost instant recognition of him by each of the other replicants, is similarly unresolved.

The ambiguities which envelop Deckard's role and corporeal condition contribute to the thematics of authority and transgression within *Blade Runner*. Its critical moment, however, is reached during Roy's confrontation with the corporate executive. The violence perpetrated upon the body of Tyrell by the chief replicant is the major act of resistance within the film against the social injustice and economic inequality which can be seen as endemic to the landscapes of twenty-first/twentieth-century capitalism. Yet, crucially, the scene is carefully structured so as *not* to be recognised as such. Tyrell's fall *ought* to be presented as legitimate and even liberatory vengeance. Instead, it is cast as the narrative's central act of horror. This transformation is achieved primarily through a subtle strategic shift in ideological frames of reference. An alteration in the classification of the bodies of the key players in this scene transforms justifiable socio-political revolt into the transgression of a sacred transhistorical covenant.

During this decisive encounter, the critique of the effects of corporate power upon the city, and the objective class lines which have been so clearly spatially inscribed, become enmeshed in an Oedipal dragnet. The revenge of the representative of alienated slave labour upon the (literal) head of capital is made suitably appalling by cloaking the protagonists in the familiar costume of son and father. Roy identifies Tyrell not as 'master', but as 'fucker'. Moments before his demise Tyrell affectionately strokes the prodigal son's hair to arouse previously unfelt and patently undeserved sympathy. As the subsequent act is translated from valid nemesis to taboo, the object of rebellion is displaced from Capital to the Oedipal Father.

Critical assessment of *Blade Runner* has tended to note both the critique of the capitalist city and the film's Oedipal narrative, with the assumption that they are complementary. However, at its pivotal moment, the latter interferes with the former to suppress the relations between capital and patriarchal authority. The pyramidical Tyrell building loses its hard edges as an architectural metaphor for the spatialisation of class structure in the city and instead becomes home to an Oedipal triangle. As he gouges out Los Angeles' panoptican and Tiresian eye (Tyrell is both father and mother to the replicants), Roy's vengeance is depoliticised. Bodies are defined not by capital, but by the Oedipal complex – the post-industrial city becomes a palimpsest for the timeless stage of psychoanalytical drama. Since the act of militant transgression is traced through an Oedipal stencil, the replicants' bodies are reinserted within the interstices of the Symbolic order which they had previously challenged. Workers may occasionally revolt, but boys (whether or not they are androids) will *always* be boys.

Conclusion

> One of his eyes resembled that of a vulture – a pale blue eye, with a film over it.[29]

The narrator of Poe's 'The Tell-Tale Heart', after conducting nocturnal Voight-Kampf examinations of his own, murders and mutilates an old man. Dismembered body parts are concealed under the floorboards 'so cleverly, so cunningly, that no human eye – not even *his* – could have detected anything wrong'.[30] The denouement to the tale reassures its readers, however, by having officers of the law at hand at the moment that the murderer's monomania explodes into confession. Poe's tales of criminal acts and their detection might be read as a covert valorisation of the police profession that was becoming an increasingly conspicuous presence on the streets of the American city at this time. In this respect the literary father of detective fiction confirms the allegation with which this chapter began: that crime dramas turn agents of government repression into sympathetic heroes. Whilst Frenesi Gates' statement might appear to be a rather crass generalisation, my own findings suggest a considerable degree of synchronicity between contemporary crime drama and dominant ideologies.

The Reagan era witnessed a calculated assault upon those progressive orthodoxies institutionalised in the 1960s concerning the socio-economic and psychological roots of criminal deviance. The rhetoric of the fundamentalists and other branches of the self-proclaimed Moral Majority reinvented evil as an elemental malignity. This resonates distinctly with the trend in recent detective film of focusing upon inexplicable criminality. Jeffrey Beaumont's critical question in *Blue Velvet* remains unanswered: 'why are there people like Frank in the world' (or Bob, Hannibal Lecter and sundry villains in the *Die Hard* films)? Whilst evil is mystified in metaphysical enigma, those designated by the state to eliminate it are lionised.

In its celebration of patriarchal power, reproduction of Oedipal narratives and bursts of blatant misogyny, the anti-feminist crusade initiated by the New Right appears, too, in different guises, within detective cinema. And as I hope to have shown in these readings, the representation of the corporeal in the genre is both a reflection and a reinforcement of that narcissistic introversion encouraged within the body culture that surfaced within a period of right-wing politico-cultural hegemony. Films of this era often ask the question: if not for those brave officers of the law, how many bodies might be hidden under floorboards, brutalised by sociopaths, eaten, turned into clothing, or threatened by evil foreigners? Roy and his replicant renegades confront the brutal conditions of com-modification. They realise that their bodies are programmed and owned by corporate capital. Watching the detectives in *Blade Runner* and elsewhere in contemporary crime film, the spectator can be ensnared in a similarly reactionary and reifying program.

Notes

1. Thomas Pynchon, *Vineland* (London: Secker and Warburg, 1990), p. 83.

2. Ibid., p. 345.
3. For a time during the late 1980s and early 1990s the CIA had to struggle with the legacy of Irangate, whilst local police departments, particularly in metropolitan districts, were discredited by an inability to curb steadily increasing crime rates and by accusations of discrimination and brutality that peaked with the Rodney King incident. It remains to be seen whether the negative publicity from the Waco siege will have any dramatic effect upon the renaissance of the FBI hero in popular culture.
4. The casual and comic appropriation of the *mise en scène* of the commercial, capitalism's official art form, is one of the trademarks of a Lynch production. During the scene at Ben's brothel in *Blue Velvet*, Frank's vehement insistence upon the excellence of Pabst Blue Ribbon beer both sustains the film's central motif and recycles an earlier spectacularly stilted conversation between Jeffrey and Sandy concerning the relative virtues of Heineken and Budweiser. The pastiche of product placement continues in *Twin Peaks* with the detective hero's endless accolades to 'damn fine' cups of coffee and slices of cherry pie.
5. The most obvious similarities are to Fritz Lang's *The Big Heat* (1953) and Jacques Tourneur's *Out of the Past* (1947).
6. Mr Beaumont was one of the stars of a popular 1950s soap-opera set in suburbia called *Leave it to Beaver*.
7. The repeated tracking shot, as the camera spirals into and out of human ears, echoes another Alfred Hitchcock crime drama, *Vertigo* (1958). Jeffrey and Sandy's night-time stroll through Lumberton's leafy boulevards reproduces a scene from an earlier James Stewart role, as George Bailey in *It's A Wonderful Life* (1946). The scene in Frank Capra's Yuletide favourite, in which George and Mary stop in front of a boarded-up house to talk of their dreams for the future, is transformed in *Blue Velvet* into Jeffrey's nostalgic anecdote about the boy with the largest tongue in the world. As well as continuing the sensory organ motif, this might be taken as a hint that Lynch's references to Capra, on the fiftieth anniversary of *Wonderful Life*, are somewhat tongue-in-cheek. This would depend, however, upon there being some position within the film's political and

emotional logic from which to satirise small-town sentimentalism, as Lang does so effectively in *The Big Heat*. Lynch's films do not possess such a position.

8. Although we might add that Lynch's 'Northwest *noir*' is clearly indebted to two films of 1944: Otto Preminger's *Laura* and Gene Tierney's *Twin Peaks*.

9. Jean Baudrillard, *The Evil Demon of Images* (Sydney: Power Institute, 1987), p. 13.

10. See John Alexander, *The Films of David Lynch* (London: Letts, 1993), pp. 24–5. Whilst the closed body tends to remain covered and self-contained, the open body is continually associated with forms of penetration, vice and venality. This can be sexual, spiritual (in terms of possession), or fatal (in terms of gun and knife wounds that reveal sticky interiors).

11. In *The Elephant Man*, the rescue and redemption of John Merrick, from the uniformly vile working-class subjects of London's East End, is accompanied by a change of clothing (to the vestments of a uniformly benign Victorian bourgeoisie). As numerous publicity photographs reveal, the dark suit and tie is Lynch's own preferred attire.

12. A comparable dress code appears to run throughout the FBI crime drama. The smartly turned out Clarice Starling has to track down a scruffy harelipped giant in *The Silence of the Lambs*, and many episodes of *The X Files* pit the immaculately attired Mulder and Scully against mutants and ne'er-do-wells in various degrees of dishevelment. In certain respects this trend recalls the original 'Armani with a badge' in Michael Mann's hugely successful *Miami Vice*.

13. Having been raped by Frank, Jeffrey was to have awoken semi-naked the following morning with 'FUCK YOU' written in lipstick on his buttocks. Even without this denouement, the scene – with Frank alternately singing to, punching and kissing the powerless Jeffrey – manages to convey an equation between homosexual desire and violation of which Hollywood appears especially fond (see, for example, *The Shawshank Redemption*, 1995, and *Pulp Fiction*, 1994).

14. From an interview with Lizzie Borden, '*Blue Velvet*', *Village Voice* (September, 1986), p. 86.

15. Alexander, *The Films of David Lynch*, p. 140.

16. See Lynda Bundtzen, 'Don't Look at Me! Woman's Body, Woman's Voice in *Blue Velvet*', *Western Humanities Review*, vol. 42, no. 3 (1988), pp. 187–203; Tracy Biga, '*Blue Velvet*', *Film Quarterly*, vol. 41, no.1 (1987), pp. 44–9.

17. Julia Kristeva, *Powers of Horror* (New York: Columbia University Press, 1982), p. 26. The modern age has witnessed dramatic changes in cultural attitudes towards the Spirit and the Flesh. Traditionally, one of the functions of a sacred object has been to testify to the primacy of spiritual over physical being. Kristeva appears to be suggesting that modernity has witnessed the eclipse of the totems of organised religion by corporeal *momento mori*. With the collapse of a universal religious infrastructure the abject replaces the sacred object as that which signifies mortality and the interface between the known and the unknowable represented by death.

18. Christopher Lasch, *The Culture of Narcissism: American Life in an Age of Diminishing Expectations* (London: Sphere Books, 1980).

19. Wolfgang Fritz Haug, *Critique of Commodity Aesthetics: Appearance, Sexuality and Advertising in Capitalist Society* (London: Macmillan, 1984), p. 35.

20. Susan Jeffords, 'Can Masculinity be Terminated?', in Steven Cohan and Ina Rae Hark (eds), *Screening the Male: Exploring Masculinities in Hollywood Cinema* (London: Routledge, 1993), p. 245.

21. This is a trend that is increasingly conspicuous in other branches of popular culture, such as advertising and the music video.

22. Barbara Creed, 'From Here to Modernity: Feminism and Postmodernism', *Screen*, vol. 2, no. 28 (1987), p. 65.

23. Yvonne Tasker, 'Dumb Movies for Dumb People: Masculinity, the Body, and the Voice in Contemporary Action Cinema', in Cohan and Hark (eds), *Screening the Male*, p. 232.

24. Like the detective, the deviant leader of the rebellious androids, Roy, is also associated with forms of vision: he

is introduced at the moment of his illegal entry to
Eyeworld; plays with J.F Sebastian's toy eyes; his murder
of Tyrell involves the removal of his creator's bifocal
glasses before a gruesome blinding; and his final words
to Deckard are of the wondrous sights he has beheld, of
scenes beyond the ken of human imagination: 'I've seen
things. Things you people couldn't even dream of.'

25. See Robin Wood, *Hollywood from Vietnam to Reagan* (New
York: Columbia University Press, 1986), p. 185.

26. These gynophobic impulses in the Ridley Scott *œuvre*
have been explored frequently in relation to *Alien* (1979),
his previous exercise in science-fiction fantasy.

27. This remark serves a dual purpose. It brackets the replicants
with an oppressed racial group – they are runaways and
Rachel suggests that she may flee North, a familiar escape
route from oppression in the geography of the African-
American slave narrative. But, at the same time, it seems
to relegate discrimination *amongst humans* to 'the history
books'. This implication is conveniently reinforced by
the puzzling and entirely unexplained disappearance of
Los Angeles' black community. See Stephen Neale, 'Issues
of Difference: *Alien* and *Blade Runner*', in James Donald
(ed.), *Fantasy and the Cinema* (Essex: BFI, 1989), p. 220.

28. This possibility is made even more distinct in the Philip
Dick novel and in the 1992 'simquel', *Blade Runner: The
Director's Cut*. In the closing shot of Scott's recycled version
Deckard discovers an origami unicorn outside the door
of his apartment. His subsequent nod of acknowledgement
suggests two things: that he recognises that Gaff has
decided to allow him to flee the city with Rachel; and that
Gaff may have knowledge of Deckard's 'unicorn' dream
earlier in the film (presumably an out-take from Scott's
Legend). If the latter is true, since the blade runner revealed
this dream image to nobody, the only logical inference
is that Deckard's memories are 'implants' and that he
too is a replicant.

29. Edgar Allan Poe, 'The Tell-Tale Heart', *The Complete Tales
and Poems of Edgar Allan Poe* (London: Penguin, 1982),
p. 303.

30. Ibid., p. 305.

Selected Bibliography

Bailey, Frankie Y., *Out of the Woodpile: Black Characters in Crime and Detective Fiction* (New York: Greenwood Press, 1991)

Bakerman, Jane S. (ed.), *And Then There Were Nine ... More Women of Mystery* (Ohio: Bowling Green State University Popular Press, 1985)

Bell, Ian A. and Daldry, Graham (eds), *Watching the Detectives: Essays on Crime Fiction* (Basingstoke: Macmillan, 1990)

Benstock, Bernard (ed.), *Essays on Detective Fiction* (London and Basingstoke: Macmillan, 1983)

Cawelti, John G., *Adventure, Mystery, and Romance: Formula Stories as Art and Popular Culture* (Chicago: University of Chicago Press, 1976)

Docherty, Brian (ed.), *American Crime Fiction: Studies in the Genre* (Basingstoke: Macmillan, 1988)

Dove, George, *The Police Procedural* (Ohio: Bowling Green State University Popular Press, 1982)

Haut, Woody, *Pulp Culture: Hardboiled Fiction and the Cold War* (London: Serpent's Tail, 1995)

Hilfer, Tony, *The Crime Novel: A Deviant Genre* (Austin: University of Texas Press, 1990)

Klein, Kathleen Gregory, *The Woman Detective: Gender & Genre* (Urbana and Chicago: University of Illinois Press, 1988)

Moretti, Franco, *Signs Taken for Wonders: Essays in the Sociology of Literary Forms* (London: Verso, 1983)

Most, Glenn W. and Stowe, William W. (eds), *The Poetics of Murder: Detective Fiction and Literary Theory* (New York: Harcourt Brace Jovanovich, 1983)

Munt, Sally R., *Murder by the Book? Feminism and the Crime Novel* (London and New York: Routledge, 1994)

Porter, Dennis, *The Pursuit of Crime: Art and Ideology in Detective Fiction* (New Haven: Yale University Press, 1981)

Rader, Barbara A. and Zettler, Howard G. (eds), *The Sleuth and the Scholar: Origins, Evolution and Current Trends in Detective Fiction* (New York: Greenwood Press, 1988)

Reddy, Maureen T., *Sisters in Crime: Feminism and the Crime Novel* (New York: Continuum, 1988)

Roth, Marty, *Foul & Fair Play: Reading Genre in Classic Detective Fiction* (Athens: University of Georgia Press, 1995)

Soitos, Stephen, *The Blues Detective: A Study of African American Detective Fiction* (University of Massachusetts Press, 1996)

Walker, Ronald G. and Frazer, June M., *The Cunning Craft: Original Essays on Detective Fiction and Contemporary Literary Theory* (Macomb, Illinois: Western Illinois University Press, 1990)

Webster, Duncan, *Looka Yonder: The Imaginary America of Populist Culture* (London and New York: Routledge, 1988)

Willett, Ralph, *Hard-Boiled Detective Fiction*, BAAS Pamphlets in American Studies 23 (Halifax: Ryburn, 1992)

——*The Naked City: Urban Crime Fiction in the USA* (Manchester University Press, 1996)

Williams, John, *Into the Badlands: A Journey Through the American Dream* (London: Paladin, 1991)

Winks, Robin W. (ed.), *Detective Fiction: A Collection of Critical Essays* (New Jersey: Prentice-Hall, 1980)

Index

Index by Auriol Griffith-Jones